RACIAL JUSTICE IN THE AGE OF OBAMA

# RACIAL JUSTICE IN THE AGE OF OBAMA

*ROY L. BROOKS*

PRINCETON UNIVERSITY PRESS

PRINCETON AND OXFORD

Copyright © 2009 by Princeton University Press

Published by Princeton University Press, 41 William Street, Princeton, New Jersey 08540

In the United Kingdom: Princeton University Press, 6 Oxford Street, Woodstock, Oxfordshire OX20 1TW

All Rights Reserved

Library of Congress Cataloging-in-Publication Data

Brooks, Roy L. (Roy Lavon), 1950–
   Racial justice in the age of Obama / Roy Brooks.
     p. cm.
   Includes bibliographical references and index.
   ISBN 978-0-691-14198-5 (hardback : alk. paper)   1. United States—Race relations.   2. African Americans—Civil rights.   3. African Americans—Social conditions—1975–   4. Social justice—United States.   I. Title.
   E185.615.B7297 2009
   305.800973—dc22          2009000587

British Library Cataloging-in-Publication Data is available

This book has been composed in Minion

Printed on acid-free paper. ∞

press.princeton.edu

Printed in the United States of America

10  9  8  7  6  5  4  3  2  1

*For Penny Brooks*
*(1950–2006)*

# CONTENTS

## THE AGE OF OBAMA

MANY OF MY WINTRY evenings in the early 1970s were warmed by heated discussions of civil rights theory with my fellow law students at Yale Law School. We met regularly in the law school cafeteria after dinner, usually after Eric Sevaried's commentary on the CBS Evening News with Walter Cronkite. Our civil rights version of the Metaphysical Club—that nineteenth-century conversational club whose membership boasted a young Oliver Wendell Holmes Jr., William James, Charles Sanders, and other Harvard students who helped shape philosophical thought for twentieth-century America—held court at a table near the center window facing the Grove Street side of the law school quadrangle. We often referred to this table as the "Black Table." That label pertained to the topic of discussion—civil rights theory, especially matters regarding racial justice—and to the fact that African American or black (I use the terms interchangeably) students initiated and carried the discussion. The Black Table, unlike the Metaphysical Club, was neither single-race nor single-sex in its membership. White students were welcomed at the table, and, in fact, some (e.g., Bill Clinton and Hillary Rodham) took an occasional seat there. Most white students, including my classmate Sam Alito, simply passed by the table or sometimes looked on with bemused curiosity rather than join in the discussion.

The black students who sat at the table were not monolithic. Clarence Thomas was the contrarian of the group. If someone said it was nighttime, he would argue it was daytime, just for the hell of it. Harry Singleton was persistently conservative and prideful. Lani Guinier was more liberal than either Gil Hardy, Guy Cole, Russ Frisby, or myself. Frank Washington, Tap Taplin III, and Rufus Comier were hard to pin down. But all were extremely bright and very respectful of opposing points of view. All brought considerable food for thought to the table based not only upon a common core of readings (anchored by the works of W.E.B. DuBois) and deep reflection but also upon a personal understanding of the black experience. Each of us had experienced racism and, as a result, knew that the opportunities we were given were precious. Knowing that may have helped fuel the passion with which we addressed the issues. Indeed, a full range of theoretical perspectives were vigorously presented and debated. The Black Table was not a liberal or conservative table; it was a scholar's table, a truth-seeking table. We disagreed routinely, but almost as often conceded opposing arguments. We did not just have opposing opinions; we also had knowledge and integrity, which enabled us to walk away from the table as friends and remain friends to this day.

As black law students, we were not self-removed. Indeed, we were keenly aware of the time and place we occupied. Each of us knew we were living through a transitional moment in American history and that we were among the key participants in this epoch. We could feel the dawn of a new era in race relations in the early 1970s, an era that has come to be known as post–civil rights America. Although we knew that our presence at one of America's elite institutions of higher education in the waning days of the civil rights movement was a harbinger of greater things to come for our race and our nation and ourselves, I doubt that any of us could have foreseen the election of the first black American president of the United States in our lifetime.

## The Obama Phase of Post–Civil Rights America

With 43% of the white vote, Barack Obama was elected the forty-fourth president of the United States of America on November 4, 2008. The "Age of Obama" began on that day, more than three decades into the post–civil rights era. What does the "Age of Obama" mean for racial justice in America? Does it mean that America has now become a postracial society, such that African Americans no longer have to deal with the unspoken or spoken belief that opportunities are limited by race? Is it still about race, or is it now about individual excellence? Does excellence eclipse race in Obama's America? Has the election of a black president brokered new opportunities for black Americans?

The answers to these questions must be contextualized in the black experience. That experience starts with slavery. For two-and-one-quarter centuries, white Americans forced blacks into chattel slavery. Blacks were stolen from the homeland, separated from families, packed like sardines into tiny spaces for the long voyage to America, separated from families again, and forced to work from morning to night for the economic benefit and social comfort of white Americans. None other than the U.S. Supreme Court captured the attitude of the vast majority of white Americans toward blacks when, speaking for the Court, Chief Justice Roger Taney reported in the *Dred Scott* case (1856) that blacks "had for more than a century been regarded as beings of an inferior order, and altogether unfit to associate with the white race, either in social or political relations; and so far inferior, that they had no rights which the white man was bound to respect; and [so] . . . the negro might justly and lawfully be reduced to slavery for his benefit."[1]

Slavery ended de facto in 1865 with the Union victory in the Civil War and de jure thereafter with the ratification of the Thirteenth Amendment to the Constitution. After a brief period of Reconstruction, blacks were forced into approximately one hundred more years of government-sanctioned racial oppression. The Supreme Court in the case of *Plessy v. Ferguson* (1896) constitutionalized this oppression by upholding racial segregation and discrimination under a legal fiction called "separate-but-equal." Justice Harlan issued a magnificent dissent in *Plessy*, insisting that "our Constitution is color-blind, and neither knows nor tolerates classes among citizens. . . . The law regards man as man, and takes no account of his surroundings or his color."[2] But matters are rarely that simple. Justice Harlan did not envision the color-blind principle doing much, if anything, to change the social condition of African Americans relative to whites. As he said, "The white race deems itself to be the dominant race in this country. And so it is, [the dominant race] in prestige, [the dominant race] in achievements, [the dominant race] in education, [the dominant race] in wealth and [the dominant race] in power. So, I doubt not, it will continue to be for all time, if it remains true to its great heritage and holds fast to the principles of constitutional liberty."[3] Thus, Justice Harlan saw the color-blind principle as changing only the *legal* status of blacks rather than their socioeconomic status. As Justice Harlan saw it, a color-blind Constitution would not upset the prevailing racial order—whites would always be on top; they would always be the dominant race. This was more than the soft bigotry of low expectations from one of the Court's most celebrated liberal justices. It was out-and-out white supremacy. Justice Harlan was a man of his times.

Following the Supreme Court's decision in *Plessy*, the South passed so-called Jim Crow laws that touched virtually every form of interaction between blacks and whites. In the South, restaurants, restrooms, public drinking fountains, transportation, housing, schools, and even the storage of school books were segregated by law. Gunner Myrdal, the Swedish social scientist who wrote the landmark work *An American Dilemma* (1944), wondered aloud, "How had the South's certifiable, pathological inhumanity toward the Negroes been allowed to exist for long into the twentieth century? Why didn't anyone outside the South know?"[4] The answer is that the North knew about the South, but it was no paradigm of virtue when it came to racial matters. Jim Crow was based less on law than on custom north of the Mason-Dixon Line, again reaching virtually every aspect of American life. Both regions of the country were drinking the same water. As Gene Roberts and Hank Klibanoff observe in *The Race Beat*, "The segregation of the Negro in America, by law in the South and by neighborhood and social and economic stratification in the North, had engulfed the press as well as America's citizens. The mainstream press wrote about whites but seldom about Negro Americans or discrimination against them; that was left to the Negro press."[5]

Ubiquitous racial discrimination was buttressed by fear—fear of losing one's job at a white employer's whim; fear of being humiliated when going into a department store or restaurant or while simply walking down the street; fear of being arrested under local "vagrancy" laws; fear of being regarded as a "Negro who thinks too much"; fear of being beaten by a group of white males looking to have a little fun; fear of being accused of "eyeball rape" by a white woman; and, worst, fear of being lynched for such "rape" or other purported crimes against whites. The police offered little protection because they typically condoned or even assisted in these and other forms of physical intimidation against blacks. Richard Wright, arguably the most celebrated black writer of the 1940s, insisted that during Jim Crow "the dominant emotion of black Americans was fear."[6] Living under the foot of white America, black Americans had little else to feel.

African Americans, in short, experienced no dearth of privation under slavery and Jim Crow. Slavery created and Jim Crow perpetuated capital deficiencies in black America. These capital deficiencies were not only financial (property and income) but also human (formal education and skills) and social (rank and respect, the ability to get things done). Fear was a constant companion of black Americans. When I think of blacks who had to endure slavery or the worst of Jim Crow, I am amazed at their strength of character and determination. These blacks were the greatest generations.

Jim Crow began a slow death in mid-twentieth-century America. The Supreme Court struck the first significant blow in 1954. A unanimous Court in *Brown v. Board of Education* (1954) overturned school segregation laws in every state of the Union. Congress struck a series of subsequent blows with the passage of civil rights legislation in the 1960s and early 1970s.[7] These laws buried de jure segregation, closed out the civil rights movement, and ushered in the post–civil rights period. The latter brought forth unprecedented racial opportunities for blacks. As a consequence, we now have many wealthy and influential black Americans (such as Oprah Winfrey, Tiger Woods, Michael Jordan, and the black captains of industry) who stand in stark contrast to "Joe six-pack" and "Joe the plumber." First-time racial opportunities have also brought blacks many political successes, including black congresspersons, governors, presidential appointees (e.g., Condoleezza Rice and Colin Powell), and, of course, the presidency itself with the election of Barack Obama. These achievements certainly define the Age of Obama.

In addition to the racial opportunities and successes that have accumulated during the post–civil rights period, the Age of Obama must also be defined by a more ominous racial condition: capital deficiencies created by slavery and perpetuated by Jim Crow have continued throughout the entire post–civil rights period, long after the death of Jim Crow. We hear and read about the racial success stories in the mainstream media, but we hear and read very little about the myriad racial problems black Americans continue to encounter. Here is but a sampling taken from the appendix. In 1974, the percentage of all black families living below the poverty line was about 28%, compared with 6% for all white, non-Hispanic families. In 2005, the black rate decreased by only 7 points to about 21%, whereas the white rate remained unchanged. The median family income for blacks was about $29,000 in 1972 versus about $49,000 for whites, a $20,000 difference. In 2004, the racial differential increased: about $37,000 for black families versus about $63,000 for white families, a difference of $26,000.

Most tellingly, black males with bachelor's or advanced degrees have consistently earned less than their white male counterparts throughout the entire post–civil rights period. For example, black males with an undergraduate degree earned an average of $39,000 in 1975 versus $55,000 for whites, a difference of $16,000. Thirty years later, the racial gap increased by $20,000: $45,000 for blacks versus $65,000 for whites. Young black men are seven times more likely to go to prison than young white men, and less than half as likely to earn a bachelor's degree than young white men.[8] Today, the median net worth (bank accounts, stocks, bonds, real estate, and other assets) of white families is ten time more than that of black families ($67,000 vs. $6,166).[9] The racial gap is unbelievably larger within socioeconomic strata; for example, today "white middle-class families have on average 113 times more financial assets than black middle-class families."[10] Demographics in the appendix regarding housing, high school dropout rates, business ownership, and other areas of American life all show significant racial disparities in resources for the entire post–civil rights period despite scores of black success stories during this time.

Clearly, then, the racial landscape in the Obama phase of post–civil rights America is marked by two contrasting racial dynamics—racial success and racial despair. On the one hand, we have Barack Obama sitting in the White House; on the other hand, we have Berry Osborne sitting in the jailhouse or Lakessha wasting away in a bad public school. Does this duality suggest a continuing race problem, or does it indicate that we are now living in a postracial society? Is the glass half full or half empty?

## THE RACE PROBLEM

The Age of Obama is not, in my view, postracial. It is racial. For that reason I would disagree with the way in which conservatives define the problem blacks face today. Nor would I define the problem the same way that liberals define it. Conservatives typically define what they sometimes term a "black problem" as one of black culture—a class problem rather than a racial problem—while liberals tend to see the problem as a "white problem" defined as white racism. I take issue with both conceptualizations for empirical rather than ideological reasons. It is factually wrong to define the problem facing blacks in the Age of Obama as one of a dysfunctional black culture as conservatives do, because, inter alia, even though college-educated black men have done everything conservatives say they should be doing culturally, they still are paid less than their white counterparts—$20,000 per year today versus $16,000 per year in 1975, as mentioned earlier. Although the problem blacks face is racial, it is wrong to define it as white racism, as do liberals, because, inter alia, white racism has certainly subsided significantly since the end of the civil rights movement (not the least of which is the fact that a significant percentage of whites voted for Obama, and black fear, discussed earlier, has substantially decreased since Jim Crow). Yet, as the appendix shows, significant racial differentials in the distribution of our nation's resources (income, wealth, education, occupation, and so on) have pretty much remained constant since the end of the civil rights movement.

In my view, African Americans face a race problem today, but one that is more accurately described as a paucity of financial, human, and social capital (in other words, capital deficiencies) than as one of white racism. It is, in other words, the maldistribution of America's resources (resource disparity between blacks and whites) that defines the race problem insofar as it relates to black Americans in the Obama phase of post–civil rights America. The race problem is the racial gap in poverty, in net family income, in individual income, in housing, in education—in other words, capital deficiencies in black America that have outpaced slavery and Jim Crow. (I explain in the introduction why I focus on black Americans rather than "people of color.") What I am saying, then, to my liberal and conservative friends is that if racism ended today or if black culture were problem-free, African Americans would still be beset by a collective problem—disparate resources. Neither racism nor culture is coextensive with resource disparity. Neither institutional discrimination nor dysfunctional black behavior (e.g., broken families or black-on-black crime) is coterminous with disparate resources.

This is not to suggest that matters of structure and culture are irrelevant. They in fact play a role in explaining why the race problem continues so long after the end of the civil rights movement. Indeed, I argue that the central question regarding racial justice in the Age of Obama comes to this: What sustains the American race problem, what sustains disparate resources? Is the problem sustained by factors that are beyond the control of African Americans (i.e., *external* factors such as racism or the American culture writ large) or by those that are within the control of African Americans (i.e., *internal* factors such as behaviors and values)? During the civil rights movement, the American race problem was largely sustained by external factors, mainly white racism and racial discrimination. But given the force of expanding racial opportunities during the post–civil rights period (including the election of a black president), fair-minded people should be moved to consider both external and internal coordinates in locating the factors that sustain the problem of race in today's society. In the Age of Obama, Americans must take seriously the possibility that disparate resources may be sustained by a complex array of external and internal factors.

## MODERN CIVIL RIGHTS THEORY

What this means as both a practical and a theoretical matter is that any post–civil rights, Age-of-Obama theory about racial justice (or any other civil rights subject) must deal with external and internal factors. A post–civil rights theory's diagnosis of the American race problem, which is an empirical and backward-looking endeavor, must speak to the external and internal. Likewise, a theory's prescription tendered in response to its diagnosis, which is largely a normative and forward-looking undertaking, must consider external and internal factors. Such evenhanded treatment of civil rights theory is not only conceptually sound but also nonpartisan because it engages the views of both liberal and conservative theorists.

Within this framework, this book collects, organizes, and synthesizes the major civil rights theories articulated during the post–civil rights period that speak to the question of racial justice in the Age of Obama. There is no dearth of important theorists, both academicians and public pundits, with whom to reckon. Among those who appear in the pages of this book are, in no particular order, Thomas Sowell, Cornel West, Stephan and Abigail Thernstrom, Henry Louis Gates Jr., Juan Williams, Gary Orfield, Orlando Patterson, Richard Delgado and Jean Stefancic, Sheryll Cashin, John McWhorter, Joe Feagin, Dinesh D'Souza, Michael Eric Dyson, Jesse Jackson, William Kristol, Clarence Page, Glenn Loury, Bill O' Reilly, Patricia Williams, George Will, Kimberlé Crenshaw, Tommie Shelby, Derrick Bell, Shelby Steele, and myself.

If the Age of Obama consists of conflicting racial dynamics—racial success and racial despair—in search of racial meaning, these theorists offer competing views regarding the proper racial signification that should be given to this new epoch. These positions are harvested and molded into four specific racial justice theories in this book: "traditionalism" (chapter 2); "reformism" (chapter 3); "limited separation" (chapter 4); and "critical race theory" (chapter 5). Hence, I argue that today's national debate on civil rights theory about racial justice is four-sided. In contrast, the debate during the civil rights era was two-sided—racial segregation versus racial desegregation/integration. The civil rights–era discourse no longer speaks to the "felt necessities" of the American people, particularly black Americans, in large part because de jure segregation does not defined the life experiences of African Americans today. Also, many theorists question the effectiveness of racial integration as the sole means of achieving racial justice today. Thus, the old theories are no longer relevant. They cannot in any realistic sense set the parameters of how we think about racial justice in the Age of Obama.

The four major post–civil rights theories presented in this book are constructed around external and internal pillars, reflecting my belief, as discussed earlier, that structural or cultural elements sustain the race problem in the Age of Obama. This is a highly contentious conceptualization of post–civil rights theory because, as Orlando Patterson correctly notes, most theorists are one-sided. They see either structural or behavioral explanations, not both.[11] Part of the nonpartisan approach taken in this book consists of conceptualizing both an external and an internal race problem. Taking this approach, post–civil rights theory can more effectively use the "is" of diagnostic analysis to produce the "ought" of prescriptive measures.

The call for both diagnostic and prescriptive external and internal inquiries suggests a theory about post–civil rights theory—a theory about theory—that I call the "theory of completeness." This theory holds that to be taken seriously in our post–civil rights era, civil rights theory must be complete, meaning it must offer an external and internal diagnosis of and prescription for *any* civil rights problem it addresses, whether that problem be about race, gender, disability, age, or sexual orientation. Hence, a complete post–civil rights theory must be fully descriptive and fully prescriptive. It must offer an external (structural) diagnosis of and prescription for the problem under consideration, and it must provide an internal (behavioral) diagnosis of and prescription for that problem. The absence of any one of these elements indicates theoretical incompleteness. An incomplete post–civil rights theory is insufficiently formed. It is undertheorized and, to that extent, flawed.

As will be seen, some civil rights theorists have championed more than one post–civil rights theory during their professional lives. Changing one's theoretical position in the face of new evidence or better understanding is part of a long tradition of truth-searching in civil rights scholarship. Standing on truth rather than political affiliation is a venerable, nonpartisan practice that traces back to W.E.B. DuBois, our first great civil rights scholar. DuBois, who lived to ninety-three, was an integrationist at the beginning of his long professional life, became a separatist in midlife, and was a Pan-Africanist when he died in 1963. Glenn Loury is a more recent theorist who has changed theoretical horses in midcareer. The desire "to get it right" is a chief characteristic that separates the scholar from the zealot.[12]

My hope is that the public's discussion of the post–civil rights theories presented in this book will not become marred by bitter partisanship. Given the tenor of civil rights discourse since the end of the civil rights movement, I know only too well that it may be fatuous to think that people of contraposed civil rights perspectives could come together for honest, courteous truth-seeking and productive reflection. Vitriolic sermonizing on each side of the debate seems to be the order of the day on radio, TV, and the Internet, and even within the ivory tower, where the pursuit of truth is supposed to be everyone's goal. I have moderated or sat on panels from Cambridge to Berkeley, New York to North Carolina where conservative panelists were treated with disrespect by liberals in the audiences, and where liberal speakers were treated just as rudely by conservatives in the audiences. Today it seems that ad hominem arguments have replaced reasoned thought, and political partisanship has triumphed over the search for truth. But if we were to follow President Obama's demonstrated desire for bipartisanship (he appointed Republicans and political enemies to his Democratic administration) and capture the Black Table's rigorous truth-searching and polite disagreement, we can have productive debates about racial justice in the Age of Obama.

## Chapter Summaries

Chapter 1 of the book sets the table for the book's discussion. It begins by explaining why this book focuses on African Americans rather than on other or all civil rights groups. It then attempts to clarify several important terms used in this book, such as "civil rights" and "race." The chapter ends by elaborating on a disparate-resources definition of the American race problem. The appendix provides the facts and figures that give content to my definition of the American race problem as disparate resources.

Using the theory of completeness as the intellectual framework, the next four chapters attempt to present post–civil rights theory accurately and in a manner that is intellectually accessible to the uninitiated as well as interesting and informative to the civil rights specialist. Some post–civil rights theories are more complete than others. Traditionalism (chapter 2) holds that the American race problem is sustained less by the external factor of race than by the internal factor of culture—bad behaviors and bad values—within the African American community. To the extent that an external factor plays a role, it is affirmative action. Some traditionalists would add the nonracial element of "secularism." Traditionalists define the latter as an American culture damaged not only by the suppression of spirituality but also by a greedy and selfish corporate establishment, a greedy and lazy media, a greedy and morally depraved entertainment industry, and a greedy, incompetent, and sometimes corrupt government.[13] But the solution to the problem, traditionalists maintain, is internal rather than external. Thus, rather than relying on government programs, most traditionalists prescribe a Horatio Alger–type, it-takes-an-individual black self-help program.

Just as traditionalists insist race no longer matters in American society, reformists (chapter 3) are equally sure that race still matters. Racism (both "frontstage" and "backstage" racial antipathy and racial stereotyping) and racial discrimination (individual, institutional, and societal) are the primary external factors that reformists believe sustain the race problem today. Reformists also believe that internal factors sustain disparate resources. To that extent they are in agreement with traditionalists. Yet, unlike traditionalists, they go on to contend that the external factors of racism and racial discrimination condition bad behaviors and bad values (what Cornel West calls "black nihilism") in the black community. This is particularly the case among the black underclass and poverty class. In response to this diagnosis, reformists prescribe a program of external and internal measures. Externally, they prescribe ongoing affirmative action, the strengthening of extant civil rights laws for middle-class and working-class blacks, and job training, child care, and other economic remedies for the lowest black classes. A family-based self-help program, rooted in the black ethos, is their primary internal prescription.

Limited separatists (chapter 4) and critical race theorists (chapter 5) take approaches that are entirely different from those taken by traditionalists and re-formists. Limited separatists (sometimes called "racial solidarists") contend that traditionalists and reformists are not studying the right issue—namely, ra-cial integration. The reason we have the problem of disparate resources so long after the death of Jim Crow, they strongly assert, is because society, including blacks, has placed too much faith in racial integration, a strategy whose success not only depends on the kindness of whites—whites must cede power or oth-erwise disadvantage themselves to help blacks, both going against human na-ture—but also depletes scarce resources from black communities by encourag-ing the exodus of stable families and talented individuals. To resolve the external race problem, limited separatists prescribe the legalization of govern-ment-funded black schools, businesses, and other community institutions in a way that does not exclude or otherwise trammel the interests of whites.

Thus, limited separation is a post–civil rights theory of racial solidarity that does not contain the racial hatred on display in some of the Reverend Jeremiah Wright's civil rights sermons. President Obama repudiated these sermons dur-ing his 2008 presidential campaign on the grounds that they were fixed in the bygone era of the civil rights movement and, hence, did not take account of changes in white attitudes that had taken place in post–civil rights America. Scores of black Americans today believe in a more tolerant form of racial soli-darity—black churches, Historically Black Colleges and Universities, and the like. President Obama preached such racial solidarity as a community orga-nizer in Chicago after he graduated from law school. Hence, a civil rights the-ory of racial solidarity will certainly continue to have a place in the Age of Obama.

Internally, limited separatists adopt the reformist diagnosis of black nihilism but then argue that this sociopsychological problem is conditioned in large part by a number of racial and nonracial external factors, including conformity pressures placed on integrated blacks to be "like whites," society's color-blind rhetoric, and white self-interest, a nonracial factor. Color-blind rhetoric, they aver, is especially damaging to blacks because when society proceeds in a color-blind fashion, it does not see monochrome; it sees white. Whiteness is the de-fault cultural standard, and, thus, it is easy to view even the positive features of black culture as morally questionable. Black children imbibe this message. Cul-tural and economic integration within black society—a robust, it-takes-a-village form of black self-help—is the only proven way to effectively counteract black nihilism, limited separatists argue. The objective is to build strong, nur-turing black communities.

In unique fashion, critical race theorists contend that the other civil rights theorists are merely skimming the surface. Each fails to get at the root of the factors that sustain disparate resources. Each fails to see what is behind the curtain. The problem of race in American society, critical race theorists main-tain, is inextricably linked to the problem of power. When one looks around our society, one sees "outsiders" (people of color, women, and homosexuals) at the bottom and insiders (straight white men) on top. There is something unnatural and unfair about this picture, namely, white hegemony. American society, in other words, is fundamentally slanted in favor of insiders. Society is not objective when it comes to matters of race, gender, and sexual orientation. Society, instead, is "anti-objective"; it favors straight white males by default. That is why, critical race theorists argue, blacks have significantly fewer resources than whites in the Age of Obama.

Somewhat surprisingly, critical race theorists offer little social transformation in their prescriptive analyses. Externally, they do not prescribe a Marxist-Leninist revolution in response to their diagnosis. The problem as they see it, after all, is race, not class. The measures they do prescribe tend to be reformist in nature. Indeed, more rather than less affirmative action is their primary external prescription. Internally, critical race theorists have little to say prescriptively because they have little to say diagnostically. They seem to believe that the American race problem is overwhelmingly an inside (or insider) job. In fact, critical race theorists, or "race crits" as they are sometimes called, are the only civil rights theorists who do not prescribe a self-help program. They lean as much to the external as most traditionalists lean toward the internal. Reformist and limited separatists take a more evenhanded approach.

Collectively, the post–civil rights theories beg an important question, namely, what is the "best" way to understand and resolve the issue of race in the Age of Obama? What is the "best" post–civil rights theory? I address this question in the epilogue. There I argue that the "best" theory should have two qualities. It must be complete (the theory of completeness) and, at the prescriptive end, idealistic yet practical. The latter standard, what I call "practical idealism," means that the prescription, whether external or internal, should be logically connected to an antecedent diagnosis, and it should also be within the reach of morally motivated human beings. In other words, at the initial stage of the national discussion, the "best" prescription must be considered at the normative level rather than at the level of political action. We as a nation need to have a clear understanding of what is morally correct before we begin the process of political compromise. Setting the nation's moral compass is what civil rights theory does at its highest reach. Abolitionism during slavery and racial desegregation and integration during the civil rights movement, although politically untenable theories when initially proposed, were normatively sound, morally correct, and, hence, the "best" civil rights prescriptions during their respective eras.

Within these parameters, I argue that the search for the "best" post–civil rights theory should begin with the post–civil rights theories themselves. The "best" theory can be found, at least initially, in an as-yet-to-be-determined amalgamation of all four post–civil rights theories. One way to make this threshold determination is to look for consensus and confirmation among the theories. Most of the theories come to the conclusion that the disparate re-sources displayed in the appendix are sustained by racialized conditions (mainly racism, racial discrimination, and racial subordination) externally and by despair (a kind of spiritual impoverishment, black victimology, or black ni-hilism), ghettofabulosity (thuggery, misogyny, and instant gratification often glorified in rap music), and defiance (racial sensibility) internally. The latter are conditioned by the former, leading to such social pathologies as teenage preg-nancy, drug use, and black-on-black crime. This diagnosis is complete, con-taining both external and internal diagnoses.

Prescriptively, each post–civil rights theory, with the exception of critical race theory, relies on some form of black self-help to resolve the internal race problem. Each self-help program (traditionalism's it-takes-an-individual, re-formism's it-takes-a-family, and limited separation's it-takes-a-village) is logi-cally connected to the antecedent diagnosis of the internal race problem (de-spair, ghettofabulosity, and defiance), and each program is within the reach of morally motivated individuals and institutions. Even limited separation's it-takes-a-village program is morally acceptable so long as it does not permit the exclusion of whites. African Americans, I argue, should be given a choice of programs based on what will work best for the individual, the family, or the community.

All civil rights theorists, with the exception of core traditionalists, offer an external prescription. There is, however, nothing approaching a consensus here. Nonetheless, I prescribe federal loan guarantees and microlending to re-dress financial capital deficiencies in the black community; expansion of the Harlem Children's Zone (see chapter 4), using big salaries (comparable to what young lawyers make) to flood predominantly black schools with good teachers (a simple but revolutionary prescription), and turning as many of these schools as is possible into KIPP Academies to redress human capital deficiencies; and federal tax credits to induce positive racial images in the entertainment indus-try as a way to alleviate social capital deficiencies. As an alternative to this pre-scription, I suggest something like a GI Bill for African Americans (Plan B), but only if my preferred prescription (Plan A) proves insufficient.

I offer this diagnostic and prescriptive analysis as a way to facilitate a differ-ent type of discussion about the America race problem as it pertains to African Americans. The theories about post–civil rights theory broached in this book— the theory of completeness and practical idealism—can, however, be used by nonblack civil rights groups to analyze their unique civil rights problems in the Age of Obama. In each instance, my argument is the same: the initial stage of prescriptive analysis should take place at the normative level. Considerations of political expediency can come later. We need moral clarity, empirical truth, and logical reasoning before the horse trading or ox goring begins.

# ACKNOWLEDGMENTS

THIS BOOK HAS TAKEN many years to research and write. I had plenty of help along the way. I am deeply indebted to several teams of research assistants who worked on the book at various times. Special recognition goes to John Dana Brown, Steve McGuinness, Alexa S. Zanolli, Kirsten Widner, Brad Johnson, Haley Frasca, Charlotte Hasse, Hillery Stones, Naveen S. Gurudevan, Chaney Hall, and Andrew Stine. Tim Carey, an extraordinarily gifted student, and I had wonderful discussions about Marxism that helped me think through some of the themes in critical race theory. The legendary legal scholar Carl Auerbach has been an inspiration to me for many years. Edmund Ursin, Virginia Nolan, and Virginia Shue have been wonderful colleagues and friends for thirty years. My assistant Daniel Reyes provided excellent service, for which I am truly grateful. Charles T. Myers, Mark Bellis, and Susan Ecklund, my editors at Princeton University Press, were simply superb.

RACIAL JUSTICE IN THE AGE OF OBAMA

## Chapter 1

# INTRODUCTION

IDEOLOGICAL DIVISIONS in civil rights theory too often form along politically partisan lines. Facts are cherry-picked, and formal analyses are shaped to fit preordained political perspectives. Yet, when one steps away from the politics, when one pursues the unvarnished truth, one is humbled by the enormous complexity of the subject matter. Nowhere is this more evident than in the area of race, especially the problems of African Americans. The end of government-sanctioned racial oppression, fading historical memory, the emergence of genuine class stratification within black society—especially the rise of the black upper and middle classes—the concomitant influx of poor immigrants of color, and the inertia of structural barriers that limit opportunities as well as the grudging recognition of dysfunctional behaviors within the black community have converged to make civil rights theory an extremely complex enterprise today. Inclined to provide facile answers to complex problems, political partisanship is very seductive in this climate. But the price of the ticket is quite high: we settle for comfortable positions over painful truths.

This book attempts to provide a nonpartisan approach to civil rights theory. My ambition is to facilitate penetrating and productive discussions about civil rights theory, particularly as it pertains to African Americans. (I shall in due course explain my reasons for limiting my inquiry to blacks.) To achieve this objective, I have created a rhetorical device called the "theory of completeness." This is a theory about modern civil rights theory. It holds that civil rights theory today, in the Age of Obama, must be complete if it is to be taken seriously; that is, it must put forth an external and internal diagnosis of and prescription for the civil rights problem it seeks to address, be it civil rights pertaining to blacks, browns, women, or other groups. To suggest that there is an internal, or cultural, side to the race problem pertaining to blacks may seem like blaming the victim. That certainly is not the case. All I am saying is that given the death of Jim Crow and the concomitant increase in racial opportunities, it is now possible that cultural factors may offer some explanation as to why African Americans continue to face serious racial problems so long after the civil rights movement. Thus, in post–civil rights America—the decades since circa 1972, the end of the civil rights movement and Jim Crow—and most especially with the election of the first black president of the United States, internal factors must be considered along with external, or structural, conditions.

There are several reasons why this book focuses on African Americans. Limiting the focus to a single racial group certainly simplifies the presentation and application of a new theory, the theory of completeness. Also, there is simply more demographic information on African Americans than on any other racial group with the exception of whites. The data on some groups do not even cover the entire post–civil rights period. In contrast, blacks have been studied and recorded since the nation's first census in 1790.[1] Furthermore, even though the number of civil rights groups, or "protected classes," has expanded during the post–civil rights years (now including, inter alia, the disabled and the elderly), the concern for racial justice remains the central preoccupation in civil rights theory. Indeed, most of the major civil rights theorists in the country, academicians as well as public pundits, focus on the question of race and, more particularly, the plight of African Americans, the nation's oldest civil rights group. "If we can address the problems between black and white Americans," former president Bill Clinton insists, "then we will be better equipped to deal with discrimination in other areas."[2] At the other end of the ideological spectrum, conservative James Q. Wilson comes to a similar conclusion: "The main domestic concern of policy-engaged intellectuals, liberal and conservative, ought to be to think hard about how to change these social weaknesses. Lower-class blacks are numerous and fill our prisons, and among all blacks the level of financial assets is lower than it is for whites. Many blacks have made rapid progress, but we are not certain how."[3] Thus, within the civil rights cosmos, concerns about racial disadvantage form the primary galaxy. And within the racial galaxy, black/white relations, which coexist with other racial relations (such as Latino/white, Asian/white, Native American/white, black/Latino, black/Asian, and black/Native American), form the primary constellation. It is foundational, having provided the seed from which theories about other racial relations have developed in the post–civil rights era.

The fact that the civil rights problems of racial groups are sufficiently distinct to warrant separate treatment is yet another reason for limiting my inquiry to blacks. Immigration is a case in point. As I explain at the end of this chapter, immigration has a different effect on the quantum of resources available in Latino and African American communities. The former effect is negative while the latter is largely positive due to the arrival of West Indian blacks. Also, African Americans have an emotional and material connection to slavery and Jim Crow that other racial minorities simply do not and cannot have. Blacks were the main targets of slavery and Jim Crow. It simply cannot be gainsaid that they alone were stolen from their homelands and subsequently persecuted through the Middle Passage. All other racial minorities were either already here or came here willingly. It is factually wrong to say that all racial minorities went through the peculiar institution and Jim Crow together. It is even worse to claim, as some pundits have, that all Americans, including whites, "overcame slavery together." The psychological connection blacks have to slavery and Jim Crow is unique, just as the emotional connection Jews have to the Holocaust is unique, even though other groups, including Africans, were put to death in Nazi concentration camps. Similarly, Latinos have a special relationship to the southwestern portion of the United States not only because the land used to be part of Mexico but also because Latinos were the main targets of racial violence and disadvantage in this territory. Blacks were not. For these reasons, I am not in favor of aggregating all racial minorities under a single conceptual umbrella, whether it is called "people of color" or something else. I am, in fact, a proponent of disaggregation. To me, the black/white binary (which focuses on the relationship between blacks and whites) makes sense, as do other binaries, including the Latino/white and Asian/white binaries. Each civil rights group deserves special attention. Each deserves book-length treatment. This book deals with African Americans, although it certainly provides information that can be used to discuss other civil rights groups.[4]

Focusing on African Americans, this book identifies, synthesizes, and organizes the myriad civil rights theories, half theories, and suppositions articulated during this post–civil rights era. The assembled information is molded into four distinct theories—traditionalism, reformism, limited separation, and critical race theory. Each theory, or, more precisely, post–civil rights theory, is presented along the coordinates of the theory of completeness. Hence, I tease out each theory's external and internal diagnosis of and prescription for the American race problem as it relates to black Americans.

To prepare for this discussion, the remaining sections of this chapter will unpack the book's conceptual tools. Terms like "civil rights" and "race" will be clarified, and the basis for extending civil rights to some groups but not to others will also be discussed. I will end the chapter with a definition of the race problem blacks have encountered since the end of the civil rights movement. The appendix delineates the facts and figures that give content to this definition.

## A. What Is "Civil Rights" or a "Civil Rights Group"?

The term "civil rights" is used in this book in its conventional conceptualization. It refers to the congeries of government-enforced (i.e., legal) freedoms and privileges accorded to a person or group in furtherance of the equality principle enshrined in the Declaration of Independence.[5] This notion of "equality," as has been noted, "does not require that things different in fact be treated in law as though they were the same. But it does require . . . that those who are similarly situated be similarly treated. The measure of the reasonableness of the classification is the degree of its success in treating similarly those similarly situated."[6] In its conventional sense, then, the term "equality" in the context of civil rights means equal treatment or, more precisely, similar treatment for similarly situated individuals or groups.[7] Thus, civil rights are government-enforced freedoms and privileges designed to ensure that our society accords similarly situated groups similar treatment, especially "equal opportunity."

The ideal of equality embedded in this definition—similar treatment for similarly situated groups—reflects a classical liberal view of the world that seems intuitively fair. Although I certainly embrace the liberal notion of similar treatment for similarly situated individuals and groups, I wish to make the logical point that where it can be shown that blacks and whites are *not* similarly situated in society because of historical forces, blacks must be treated differently if they are to be accorded equal opportunity, or similar treatment. My argument—equal opportunity requires different treatment for differently situated groups—is conceptually consistent with the liberal edict of similar treatment for similarly situated folks. I would hope, then, that those proceeding under the liberal view would accept the fairness of different treatment if it could be shown empirically, as the appendix seems to indicate, that blacks and whites are not similarly situated.

In light of this discussion we can remove the "similarly situated" language from the conventional definition of civil rights. That is, we can now say that the goal of civil rights is equal opportunity, and that this goal can be achieved either by treating similarly situated groups similarly or by treating differently situated groups differently. Civil rights, in a word, can be defined as *government-sanctioned freedoms and privileges designed to promote equal opportunity.* So defined, civil rights has several features that should be noted.

Although first enshrined in the Declaration of Independence, civil rights are now codified in federal and state constitutions, statutes, and case law. The U.S. Constitution, for example, delineates several basic freedoms and privileges: " . . . nor shall any State deprive any person of life, liberty, or property, without due process of law; nor deny any person within its jurisdiction the equal protection of the laws."[8] Freedoms and privileges provided by federal statutes include the right to be free from discrimination based on race, color, sex, national origin, age, disability, or religion in education, employment, the electoral process, public places, and other areas of American life.[9] Judges often discover civil rights through their interpretation of constitutional and statutory law, especially the former. *Brown v. Board of Education* (1954),[10] for example, found in the Constitution the right to attend public schools without regard to race or color. The Supreme Court has discovered other civil rights, including affirmative action and the right of alien children to receive a free public education.[11]

Civil rights have certain peculiarities that often seem surprising. For example, citizenship is not a prerequisite for civil rights. Some civil rights extend to any person or group merely physically present within the jurisdictional reach of the United States. The due process and equal protection rights quoted here apply to every "person," meaning citizens and noncitizens alike, and, as just mentioned, alien children have a civil right to receive a free public education. In addition, although civil rights primarily protect the individual or group from governmental transgressions, they also protect against private wrong-doing under certain conditions (such as private parties who burden interstate commerce,[12] receive federal funds,[13] or act under the authority of state law).[14] Finally, civil rights operate both substantively and procedurally. Substantive rights, such as the right to be free from racial discrimination,[15] are what we normally think of when we think about the term "civil rights." Procedural rights, however, are just as important. These rights, such as the right to be heard in a timely fashion before suffering legal action or the right to a trial by jury, prescribe the rules by which substantive freedoms and privileges are initially established and subsequently enforced.[16]

Another peculiarity about civil rights is that not all similarly situated groups receive the same level of opportunities created by civil rights. Citizens have more government-enforced freedoms and privileges than noncitizens, who nonetheless receive some level of protection. Aliens have civil rights, to be sure, as mentioned earlier, but they do not have the same level of civil rights opportunities as do U.S. citizens. Native-born citizens, for instance, have the right to be elected the president of the United States, but foreign-born citizens as well as noncitizens in the country do not. The Constitution expressly states: "No person, except a natural born citizen, . . . shall be eligible to the office of president."[17] Civil rights, then, do not necessarily mean equal treatment, or opportunities, even for similarly situated groups.

Likewise, for most of this country's history, whites received far more opportunities created by civil rights than did blacks. This infamous example of the unequal quality of civil rights occurred under the government's "separate-and-unequal" and "separate-but-equal" civil rights policies. These policies predate the nation's current official civil rights policy of formal equal opportunity.[18] Under the separate-and-unequal civil rights policy, blacks "had no rights which the white man was bound to respect," to quote the Supreme Court.[19] Blacks did not have civil rights until President Lincoln signed the Emancipation Proclamation.[20] Although the Civil War created the political conditions for broadening the scope of civil rights accorded to blacks—most important, the Thirteenth,[21] Fourteenth,[22] and Fifteenth[23] Amendments—white male owners and nonowners of property exercised considerably more civil rights than blacks, including the right to maim and murder blacks almost at will. This state of affairs continued through the postbellum period and well into the next century.

Ira Katznelson brings the story of unequal civil rights into the twentieth century. In *When Affirmative Action Was White*,[24] Katznelson describes how governmental policies during the New Deal and Fair Deal of the 1930s and 1940s created racial preferences for whites. The majority of blacks lived in the seventeen southern states that had enacted Jim Crow laws before the turn of the century. Southern democratic members of Congress, the Dixiecrats, who chaired important congressional committees and subcommittees, used the principle of federalism (states' rights), occupational exclusions, and the absence of antidiscrimination language in the statutory law to protect the Jim Crow racial order of the South from egalitarian federal legislation. Jobs held disproportionately by southern blacks, such as farmworkers and maids, were excluded from Social Security pension laws and denied the right to unionize. Veteran benefits were administered at the local level, which left them vulnerable to local racism that was pervasive in the South. For example, the GI Bill, which provided educational and housing benefits to American soldiers returning home from World War II and, thus, created no small amount of America's postwar prosperity, was implemented in ways that deliberately discriminated against blacks. Government-insured loans were administered in a racially discriminatory manner or not extended at all to blacks who fought in the war. Mississippi illustrates the level of discrimination: "Of the 3,229 GI Bill-guaranteed home, business, and farm loans made in 1947 in Mississippi, . . . only 2 went to black veterans."[25]

Affirmative action for blacks was instituted in 1965. But this form of affirmative action does not, in my view, demonstrate unequal treatment, or unequal opportunities, as did affirmative action for whites under Jim Crow. (This is a bit redundant because Jim Crow means, in part, affirmative action for whites.) Instead, it is a manifestation of equal treatment, or equal opportunities, accorded to a differently situated group. Jim Crow tipped the racial balance in favor whites; affirmative action for blacks was a limited attempt to balance things out. As Katznelson remarks, "The black affirmative action programs instituted . . . were paltry in their scope and scale compared to the massive governmental transfers that disproportionately aided whites in the previous three decades, 1935–1965."[26] They did not deny opportunities to whites en masse. Affirmative action that grew out of the civil rights movement was very different from the Jim Crow version in yet another way: it did not stigmatize nonbeneficiaries as an inferior race, totally undeserving of government-sanctioned freedoms or privileges.

What groups are entitled to civil rights protection today? Why, for example, are blacks, Latinos, and whites among the groups protected by our civil rights laws today while ugly, short, or poor people are not? True, it is difficult to base public policy or law on a factor as subjective as beauty. But height and poverty are measurable qualities. What, then, is the line of demarcation between those who are deemed to be within and those who are deemed to be outside the protected classes? Is there a principled way of explaining such differential treatment? These are recurring civil rights questions, each in search of a good answer.

The conventional answer is that civil rights protection, at least after *Brown v. Board of Education*, is accorded to what the Supreme Court has termed "discrete and insular minorities."[27] These are minorities who have historically been targets of discriminatory treatment in our society and who lack political power to protect themselves. A protected class is a group as to whom "prejudice . . .

may be a special condition, which tends seriously to curtail the operation of those political processes ordinarily to be relied upon to protect minorities."[28] Laws directed toward protected classes, defined in this instance as "discrete and insular minorities," are subject to "more exacting judicial scrutiny" than other types of laws and, hence, are more likely to be overturned.[29]

As the primary victims of slavery and Jim Crow, blacks were the first group to be viewed as a "discrete and insular minority." The meaning of the term, in fact, is virtually synonymous with the sociopolitical status of black Americans during the 1950s and 1960s.[30] Today, other racial minorities—Latinos, Asians, and Native Americans—are also viewed as "discrete and insular" due to their own histories of discrimination. So, too, are religious groups, who have experienced discriminatory treatment in the past, and women, who have a history of political vulnerability and continue to experience sex discrimination.[31]

The disabled and, to a lesser extent, the elderly and homosexuals also receive civil rights protection. Looking back at the historical experience of the disabled at the time it enacted the Americans with Disabilities Act (ADA), Congress found that "individuals with disabilities are a discrete and insular minority who have been faced with restrictions and limitations, subjected to a history of purposeful unequal treatment, and relegated to a position of political powerlessness in our society, based on characteristics that are beyond the control of such individuals and resulting from stereotypic assumptions not truly indicative of the individual ability of such individuals to participate in, and contribute to, society."[32] The civil rights protection Congress has given to the elderly relates primarily to employment matters. Echoing a congressional finding, the Supreme Court has determined that "it is the very essence of age discrimination for an older employee to be fired because the employer believes that productivity and competence decline with old age."[33] Most of the civil rights protections given to homosexuals are at the local rather than federal level. State and municipal governments have passed laws banning discrimination on the basis of sexual orientation. Slowly, however, the Supreme Court, more than Congress, is beginning to view gays and lesbians as "discrete and insular minorities," bringing them within the ambit of full civil rights protection.[34]

But the conventional view as to who is entitled to civil rights protection does not explain why some groups that have been historical targets of discrimination and exercise no political power (such as ugly, short, or poor people) are not protected by federal civil rights laws, and equally important, why other groups that cannot remotely be described as "discrete and insular minorities" (most particularly white males) are extended the full range of government-enforced freedoms and privileges. One might wish to argue that historical discrimination against ugly, short, or poor people is qualitatively different from the type of discrimination racial minorities have faced. But how so? Is it that discrimination against racial minorities involves immutable characteristics? Well, being short is just as immutable as race or color. In some instances, it is more so, as in the case of a black person who is light enough to "pass" for white and chooses to do so.

Some scholars, in their search for a principled explanation for the granting of civil rights opportunities, have suggested that civil rights protection is based on the antidiscrimination principle. Claims that vindicate this principle receive civil rights protection even where the plaintiff, unlike the plaintiff who, for example, experiences employment discrimination, suffers no real harm. For instance, in *Shaw v. Reno*,[35] white plaintiffs were permitted to advance a civil rights claim to invalidate a voting district in North Carolina that the state legislature created to give voting power to blacks. Although the Court recognized blacks as a historically disadvantaged, politically weak minority,[36] the plaintiffs themselves "were not required to . . . show that they were part of a discrete and insular minority. Nearly all the plaintiffs . . . were white voters whose claim was simply that they objected to the reliance on race in the redistricting process." In fact, as one scholar has noted, "The Supreme Court seemed to require no showing of injury at all for plaintiffs to invoke judicial review of a state's redistricting decisions. Several of the plaintiffs did not live in either of the majority-black districts they had challenged."[37]

While the antidiscrimination principle seems to explain *Shaw*, the principle actually does a poor job of determining who is within or without the protected classes. The principle does not work well when, as in the case of legally permissible affirmative action, preventing discrimination against one group (say, African Americans) arguably aids discrimination against another group (say, whites). Not everyone receives protection from discrimination in this instance, albeit the discrimination is rather limited. The antidiscrimination principle, in addition, begs the question of how protected classes are determined in the first place. Again, why do we prohibit discrimination against blacks and whites but not against ugly, short, or poor people? Why is it not a violation of the antidiscrimination principle to treat poor people less favorably than blacks or whites?

My best answer is that civil rights opportunities are granted to those groups that are *not* politically powerless but, instead, are politically influential. In other words, it is just the opposite of the "discrete and insular minorities" theory. Civil rights are extended to groups that are politically powerful, including those who are able to gain political influence from their ability to pose a threat to domestic peace and tranquillity. Blacks, for example, have demonstrated a willingness as well as the wherewithal to rebel against discriminatory treatment; ugly, short, and poor people have not. And while it is true that the elderly enjoy civil rights even though they have not posed a threat to peace and tranquillity, unlike the unprotected classes, the elderly have strong advocacy groups, such as the AARP. So it may be that civil rights protection is, to a large extent, based on which group makes the most noise. This theory—call it "the squeaky-wheel theory"—would certainly explain why civil rights have been extended to white males. This is a group that has no history of discriminatory treatment, but it certainly has political power, as well as power to disturb the peace and tranquillity of our society. Even intuitively reasonable extensions of civil rights protection to whites, as in the case of allowing white employees who suffer employment discrimination the right to sue,[38] can be explained by the squeaky-wheel theory.

The theory that I think ought to be used to determine civil rights protection is called the "perfectionist theory," which holds "the view that legislators and officials may consider what is good and valuable in life and what is ignoble and depraved when drafting the laws and setting the framework for social and personal relationships."[39] Under this theory, ugly, short, or poor people should be given civil rights protection. That fact that they are not demonstrates the theory's limited explanatory power. Our society would, however, be much improved if civil rights protection were based on the perfectionist theory.

## B. What Is a "Race" or "Racial Group"?

The term "race" is another important conceptual tool in civil rights discourse. "Race" or "racial group" is typically defined sociologically in civil rights theory. A sociological definition of race emphasizes phenotypical differences—differences in facial features, skin color, hair, and so on. In contrast, a biological definition of race stresses genetic differences. Because biologically there is only one race, the human race, some scholars would retire the concept of race from civil rights discourse. They would not use the term to refer to any social group. Orlando Patterson would go further. He would jettison the terms "black" and "white" because these "are linguistically loaded terms and emphasize the physical, which is precisely what we want to get away from in inter-ethnic relations."[40] He favors the term "ethnic group" over "racial group." "Ethnic group" is defined as a group that has a distinct heritage or culture. Patterson also favors the term "Afro-American" (which he defines as "persons of African ancestry who identify themselves with this ethnic group").[41] He would use that term instead of "black" or even "African American" to describe slave descendants living in the United States because the latter term's "emphasis on . . . Africanness is both physically inappropriate and culturally misleading."[42] Patterson would use "African American" to describe recent African immigrants who make their home in the United States. As Patterson would abandon the term "black," he would also do away with the term "white." He posits that "it makes no sense to continue to use the term 'white.'" Patterson's arguments are intended to clarify the terms we use in civil rights theory and, to that extent, are similar to the more recent argument that the term "enslave" should replace the word "slave" in our discourse. The former, it is argued, is less derogatory and more accurately describes the condition of human bondage in which blacks were held.

There is much truth to these arguments. I believe, however, that, in the context of civil rights discourse, the sociological concept of race is preferable to the biological concept. I give two reasons. First, the sociological concept is cognizant of the human tendency, as regrettable as it is, to differentiate on the basis of phenotype—in other words, to judge a book by its cover. People see phenotype and not genes. There is, in addition, a tendency for society's phenotypical preferences to change over time (such as from pale white to tan-white to café au lait), to which civil rights theory must respond. Second, the entire regime of civil rights law is founded upon prohibitions based on the sociological concept of race. Legal and social expectations have developed around this concept of race.[43] Civil rights law is committed to a concept of race that is both socially real, albeit constructed, and subject to change over time. For these reasons, I use the sociological concept of race in this book.[44]

Whether sociologically or biologically defined, race remains the primary question within contemporary civil rights theory. But what is the nature of the race problem African Americans encounter today? Is it racism, as liberals contend? Is it an impoverished culture, as conservatives insist? The answer, I contend next, is neither.

## C. What Is the Nature of the Race Problem Facing Blacks Today?

I take issue with both liberal and conservative conceptualizations of the American race problem, at least insofar as it pertains to African Americans. Liberals define the problem as racism. Conservatives define it as a misguided black culture, which is to say they see not a race problem but a class problem as to which the government can do little. I believe it is more accurate to describe the race problem blacks have faced since the end of the civil rights movement as one of *disparate community resources*. Perhaps the following allegory can help us see the problem more clearly:

> Two persons—one white, the other black—are playing a game of poker. The game has been in progress for almost four hundred years. One player—the white one—has been cheating during much of this time, but now announces: "From this day forward, there will be a new game with new players and no more cheating." Hopeful but somewhat suspicious, the black player responds, "That's great. I've been waiting to hear you say that for some four hundred years. Let me ask you, what are you going to do with all those poker chips that you have stacked up on your side of the table all these years?" "Well," says the white player, somewhat bewildered by the question, "I'm going to keep them for the next generation of white players, of course."[45]

The cheating (slavery and Jim Crow) caused the maldistribution of poker chips. The maldistribution of poker chips (disparate resources) is the American race problem in post–civil rights America, particularly as it relates to African

Americans. I am arguing, then, that the problem of race in the Age of Obama is not racism but racial inequality, and that the first step in concretely measuring racial inequality, or the absence of equal opportunity, in a diverse society is to look at the distribution of societal resources among racial groups. A small amount of racial disparity is, of course, to be expected. Hence, my argument is this: *significant maldistributions of societal resources along racial lines, while not conclusive, give strong, rebuttable evidence of the absence of equal opportunity and, hence, the presence of a race problem.* To arrive at this conclusion, one must assume, as I do, that racial groups are equally endowed in their ability and desire to acquire societal resources.

It is important to note that my definition of the American race problem as disparate resources does not refer only to financial resources. This definition also includes human and social resources. That is, the resource disparity that I describe in this book consists not only of financial capital deficiencies (income and property) but also of human (education and skills) and social (public respect, racial stigma, and the ability to get things done in society) capital deficiencies.[46] Thus, I would not agree with those who riff about the wealth gap.[47] The race problem is not just about wealth. Inequality is not simply measured by income and property. A group's level of educational achievement, occupational status, family structure, incarceration rates, racial profiling, political influence, social respect, and other human and social assets also count. A statistical profile of these capital deficiencies, this maldistribution of poker chips, appears in the appendix.

Whether these capital deficiencies require the ministrations of the federal government depends largely on whether they are fixable through governmental action. Capital deficiencies, or disparate resources, are fixable through governmental action if they are sustained by external factors, such as racism or racial discrimination. Disparate resources are far less repairable through governmental action if they are sustained by internal factors, namely, bad behavior or bad values within black society. Thus, my argument is that if we can say that the cheating has ended with the death of Jim Crow in the early 1970s, as I think we can, and if we can acknowledge the availability of racial opportunities (not the least of which is the election of a black president), as I think we must, the critical question facing civil rights theorists today is this: What *sustains* the maldistribution of poker chips, external or internal factors? Post–civil rights theory today can largely be viewed as a vigorous debate over this question. Indeed, each of the post–civil rights theories discussed in this book can be understood as offering a particular response to this important question—what sustains disparate resources?[48]

If resource disparity is the most accurate description of the race problem insofar as it applies to blacks in this post–civil rights era, it may not be the best way to completely define the problem historically. The problem during slavery was mainly human bondage, the absence of freedom. This profound privation, which was accompanied by disparate resources, was rationalized and sustained by the profit motive and various forms of racist rhetoric, including racial antipathy toward blacks and the "white man's burden" to "civilize" Africans.[49] After emancipation, the race problem largely became a problem of second-class legal status and racial violence (punctuated by lynchings) as well as disparate resources.[50] Government-sanctioned racism was both a cause of and a sustaining factor for the resource-disparity problem during Jim Crow. The 1910 edition of the prestigious *Encyclopaedia Britannica* gave evidence of the level of racial antipathy in Jim Crow America when it asserted that "the negro would appear to stand on a lower evolutionary plane than the white man, and to be more closely related to the highest anthropoids."[51]

Defining the American race problem as disparate resources is a materialist way of viewing it.[52] This approach fundamentally rejects the long-held Myrdalian definition of the race problem, taken from Gunnar Myrdal, in which the race problem is largely seen as a sociopsychological or state-of-mind problem, that is, a problem that exists largely in the minds of whites.[53] A disparate-resources approach discounts negative personal opinion as a defining feature of the race problem to the extent that such opinion does not materially harm blacks. It is profoundly unfortunate, but in a free society there will always be racist, sexist, homophobic, anti-Semitic, and other forms of disgusting personal opinion. That is the price we pay for freedom of speech. While certainly an important problem, negative personal opinions alone do not create a level of concern commensurate with disparate resources. The Archie Bunker type, white but powerless, who utters racial slurs at his dinner table every night is nothing compared with the black/white differential in family financial assets (such as bank accounts, stocks, bonds, and real estate): the median net worth of African American families is about ten times less than that of white families: $6,166 versus $67,000.[54] Racist personal opinion becomes a serious concern for government action when it sustains disparate resources—in other words, when racist commentary turns into or otherwise encourages discriminatory or subordinating behavior.[55]

Do disparate resources also define the race problem as it relates to nonblack racial minorities? I will not try to answer this question definitively here. Suffice it to say that the appendix charts resource disparities, or capital deficiencies, for Latinos and Asian as well as blacks. Important differences among these groups can, however, be seen. For example, Asians experience less resource disparity than blacks or Latinos, especially in areas of income and education. Indeed, in these categories Asians are at parity with whites and slightly exceed whites in some instances.[56] This raises an interesting question: If whites earn less than Asians or have lower college participation rates, do we to that extent have a race problem (disparate resources) *for whites* vis-à-vis *Asians*? The assumption has to be that these disparities are quite significant or at least statistically significant. Otherwise there is no race problem.

Assuming the Asian/white disparities are significant, there is an interesting argument that one might want to consider in the future. The argument is that there is no race problem, no problem regarding the absence of equal opportunity, because whites are the numerical majority in our democracy and, as such, they control the institutions that determine who gets paid for what and who gets into the best colleges. If whites exercise their power in ways that ultimately benefit minority groups (e.g., by repealing Prop 209, which ended affirmative action in higher education and public contracting in California), that can hardly be termed a race problem for whites. Whites, the argument continues, should be allowed to cede some of their power or resources to "discrete and insular minorities" without calling that a race problem. This argument is suggested in a position John Hart Ely took in a different context. Speaking about affirmative action as a form of reverse discrimination, Ely posited, "There is no danger that the coalition that makes up the white majority in our society is going to deny to whites generally their right to equal concern and respect [at least on racial grounds]. Whites are not going to discriminate against all whites for reasons of racial prejudice, and neither will they be tempted generally to underestimate the needs and deserts of whites relative to those, say, of blacks."[57] Again, I will not attempt to determine here whether this is a persuasive argument. I simply place it on the table to stimulate our thinking about how best to define the race problem for particular racial groups in the Obama phase of post–civil rights America.

Like Asians, Latinos are beset by disparate resources, some of which track those of blacks.[58] But the post–civil rights forces that sustain resource disparity between whites and Latinos are not necessarily the same as those that sustain the American race problem relative to blacks. For example, immigrant flow and its attendant privations have carried and continue to carry substantial capital deficiencies into many Latino communities.[59] One simply cannot make this factual observation about black communities. Immigration does not sustain the race problem in black communities to the extent that it does in Latino communities. In fact, immigrant flow in black communities has just the opposite effect: "Black immigrants from Africa average the highest educational attainment of any population group in the country, including whites and Asians."[60] This not only points to the dangers of aggregating all racial minorities under one conceptual umbrella but also tells us that taking disparate resources at face value will not give us the complete picture. Whether the focus is on blacks or other racial minorities, we get a truer picture of the American race problem in post–civil rights America when we also consider the factors, external or internal, that sustain capital deficiencies. Focusing on African Americans, we begin to develop that picture through the perspective of the first civil rights theory to arrive in the post–civil right era—traditionalism.

*Chapter 2*

# TRADITIONALISM

## A. Overview

FOR MORE THAN forty years, large numbers of Islamists, mainly from Morocco and Turkey, have immigrated to the Netherlands, perhaps the most liberal of Western European democracies. Rather than encouraging its Islamist population to assimilate, the Dutch government tolerated and even supported the Islamist lifestyle. Islamist children were never required to learn the Dutch language, culturally distinct Islamist schools were funded with public money, and illiberal practices within the Islamist community, such as the subordination of women, were permitted even though they were very much at odds with the mainstream culture. The Dutch attitude of extreme tolerance changed after the murder, in 2004, of the prominent filmmaker Theo van Gogh in Amsterdam by a Dutch-born Islamist named Mohammed Bouyeri. A young Islamist extremist, Bouyeri was enraged by a film van Gogh had made with the Somali-born feminist politician Ayaan Hirsi Ali. The film, titled *Submission*, portrays the subjugation of women under Islam. Ali herself had received numerous threats on her life due to her public criticism of the treatment of women under Islam. In the aftermath of van Gogh's murder, the Dutch have become less tolerant of cultural differences. Before foreigners are allowed to immigrate to the Netherlands, they are now required to view a film produced by the Dutch government that depicts various aspects of the Dutch culture. The film emphasizes the openness of Dutch society and, as if to drive home the point, shows nude swimmers frolicking on public beaches. The message is clear: if you can't tolerate this, then you can't live here. What the government now seeks is less difference and more assimilation, in other words, a society of shared values, a culture that is more homogeneous.[1]

Traditionalists, more than other civil rights theorists, see danger in a society that celebrates or even recognizes racial differences over racial similarities. While acknowledging that the cultural divide between blacks and the white mainstream in America is not as large as it is between the Islamist and Dutch cultures or between minority and majority groups in other countries, traditionalists nonetheless desire racial symmetry over racial conflict in mainstream society. Every group is entitled to "equal treatment." No group is entitled to "special treatment." What this means, then, is that our government must remain neutral as to matters of race. It should not favor some races and disfavor other races.

Although it operates along politically conservative lines today, traditionalism appeared as a liberal civil rights theory during the civil rights movement. During Jim Crow, traditionalism presented a sustained attack against that sociolegal order of racial oppression. It was a dissenting voice in the wilderness, very much looked upon with intense suspicion by most white Americans in the North as well as in the South. Some traditionalists managed to hold powerful public offices as Republicans despite their views on civil rights. As Clarence Page, a black newspaper columnist, reminds us:

> Just about everybody "liked Ike" [President Dwight Eisenhower] in my little Ohio factory town, including the "colored" folks. I recall my childhood's greatest political turning point in 1957, when our little black-and-white TV screen showed Arkansas National Guard troops with bayonets on their rifles keeping black students out of Little Rock's Central High School. The next day, I turned on the news to see those same troops escorting those same black students into the high school, past jeering white mobs.
>
> What happened? "President Eisenhower must have made a phone call," my father explained. After that, I really liked Ike!
>
> We also liked moderate Republicans such as Gov. Nelson Rockefeller of New York, Sen. Jacob K. Javits, also of New York, and Sen. Edward Brooke of Massachusetts, the first black senator since Reconstruction.
>
> And we really liked Illinois Sen. Everett Dirksen, who rallied enough senators from both parties to overcome fierce resistance from Southern Democratic senators like Robert Byrd of Virginia, a former Ku Klux Klansman, and Al Gore Sr., of Tennessee, father of the future vice president.[2]

Today's traditionalists are a mixture of Jim Crow liberals (people who have always believed in equal rights) and Jim Crow conservatives (people who fought to uphold segregation but have subsequently had a change of heart). Some Jim Crow liberals have now turned libertarian or neoconservative. Traditionalist Irving Kristol has described the latter as liberals who have been mugged by reality.[3] Switching theoretical horses in the midstream of one's professional life is not untoward behavior for truth-seekers. As I mentioned in the preface, W.E.B. DuBois, the first great civil rights scholar, switched horses more than once.[4]

While traditionalists acknowledge that African Americans continue to struggle for worldly success and personal happiness decades after the end of the civil rights movement, they contend that capital deficiencies in today's black society are sustained by circumstances for which blacks themselves are responsible. Black-on-black crime, high rates of out-of-wedlock births, low academic performance in the classroom and on standardized tests, low occupational status, low wages, and poor housing (see the appendix) are the products of a dysfunctional cultural orientation in black society. Although a few traditionalists believe greed and corruption in corporate America contribute to the formation of these bad behaviors and bad values, they, like other traditionalists, still see the problem of disparate resources not as a problem of race but as a problem of culture, or class. They argue that the only way a race problem can arise, whether in today's society or during Jim Crow, is when American institutions—such as the government, universities, and corporations—employ race-conscious practices or policies.

If internal factors are what sustain disparate resources today, then the solution to the problem, traditionalists argue, lies within the control of blacks. It is a problem that *only* African Americans themselves can resolve. Cultural miscues cannot be resolved through the ministrations of government. A few traditionalists do, however, concede the usefulness of governmental policies in alleviating some of the internal factors that sustain disparate resources. Government can, for example, spearhead educational reform in K–12 schools, so long as it does not prescribe racial preferences. Notwithstanding such concessions, traditionalists in the main believe that because the most important factor sustaining disparate resources is internal, the only true solution to the problem is internal—cultural or individual transformation. We are all masters of our own destiny.

My ambition in this chapter is to discuss and critique these and other salient features of traditionalism. Along the way, I shall pay particular attention to the diversity of thought among traditionalists. The principal architects of the theory shall be identified, and their theoretical nuances preserved. What the reader shall find in the end is that traditionalism is a fascinating civil rights theory.

## B. External Analysis

### 1. Diagnosis

Contrary to what some civil rights theorists maintain, traditionalists do, in fact, recognize the existence of racism or racial discrimination in contemporary American society. Thomas Sowell, for example, observes that discrimination is "more fierce against some groups than others and more pervasive at some periods of history than in others."[5] Sowell, however, undercuts the import of this recognition by asserting that the effects of discrimination are hard to measure in this post–civil rights era because of the presence of "so many other powerful factors creating disparities in income and wealth."[6] Sowell is not alone among the traditionalists in holding this belief. Commentator Bill O'Reilly, whose writings on racial matters are noticeably more penetrating than his off-the-cuff TV or radio utterances, writes, "While overt racism is not the primary reason inner-city neighborhoods are neglected and overlooked, *stealth* racism is definitely in play in America. That is sneaky bigotry that, sometimes unintentionally, insults and demeans" (emphasis in original).[7] But, like Sowell, O'Reilly makes it clear that he does not see race as a material factor in sustaining disparate resources. He believes there are very few racists in our society today who can hurt blacks: "Racism is death in corporate America, in law enforcement, in the media, in the military, in politics, and in every other powerful institution in the U.S.A."[8] Racial insensitivity can even end a career, O'Reilly asserts, citing Trent Lott's fall from power as exhibit A.[9] Of course, Senator Lott returned to a leadership position in the Senate, chairing the Committee on Rules and Administration, a few years after making the racist remarks that got him in trouble.

Like O'Reilly, other traditionalists, such as Dinesh D'Souza, do not believe "racism today . . . [is] potent enough and widespread enough" to prevent blacks from accumulating sufficient resources.[10] D'Souza, an Asian Indian, is even "surprised by how much I hear racism talked about and how little I actually see of it."[11] If there is a problem of racism today, D'Souza calculates, it is manifested by the fact that "universities, companies, and the government . . . actually discriminate *in favor* of African Americans and other minority groups, and against white males."[12]

Therein lies the traditionalists' central take on the subject of race in America. Traditionalists strongly contend that the government creates a race problem when it fails to faithfully follow the ideal of a color-blind society. It is only through a strict adherence to the ideal of racial neutrality that we avoid the problem of race in our society. Race matters only when the government promulgates race-conscious policies. George Will explicitly argues that "today a—perhaps the—principal discriminator is government, with racial preferences and the rest of the reparations system that flows from the assumption that disparities in social outcomes must be caused by discrimination, and should be remedied by government transfers of wealth."[13] Thus, the argument is that a race problem can arise only if disparate resources are mandated or sanctioned by race-conscious governmental policies. Racial discrimination, in other words, is narrowly defined by traditionalists as "the distribution of [governmental] benefits and burdens on the basis of race."[14] Other traditionalists who subscribe to this view include Thomas Sowell,[15] Shelby Steele,[16] and Stephan and Abigail Thernstrom.[17]

Stephan Thernstrom and Abigail Thernstrom add the point that racial preferences are racially divisive. They maintain that whites become angry by the perception or reality that the government is favoring blacks. This, in turn, causes many angry whites who would otherwise support African American causes to withdraw their support. The adverse effects of racial preferences are quite real and extensive.[18]

Traditionalists contend that when the government enacts race-conscious policies, it not only creates a race problem, angering whites, but also indirectly creates a class problem, hurting blacks. The argument is that race-conscious policies, such as affirmative action, condition bad behavior and bad values in the black community. Supreme Court justice Clarence Thomas has been an eloquent spokesman for this view. He argues that even though intended to be remedial, racial preferences are harmful to African Americans. Whether invidious or remedial, racial classifications are "engine[s] of oppression," because they induce African Americans to imbibe the notion that they are a disadvantaged people.[19] Justice Thomas explains:

> There can be no doubt that racial paternalism and its unintended consequences can be as poisonous and pernicious as any other form of discrimination. So-called "benign" discrimination teaches many that because of chronic and apparently immutable handicaps, minorities cannot compete with them without their patronizing indulgence. Inevitably, such programs engender attitudes of superiority or, alternatively, provoke resentment among those who believe that they have been wronged by the government's use of race. These programs stamp minorities with a badge of inferiority and may cause them to develop dependencies or to adopt an attitude that they are "entitled" to preferences. . . . In my mind, government-sponsored racial discrimination based on benign prejudice is just as noxious as discrimination inspired by malicious prejudice. In each instance, it is racial discrimination, plain and simple.[20]

Other traditionalists agree with Justice Thomas's concern about the negative impact affirmative action has on African American behaviors, values, and attitudes. Stephan and Abigail Thernstrom insist that color-conscious policies, even when remedial, are paternalistic and do not recognize African Americans' inherent dignity. "The drive for racial equality," they argue, "has had the opposite of its intended effect. . . . [S]tandards are lowered [and] tests are attacked because both whites and blacks—for different reasons—fear black failure": whites because they fear being labeled racist, and blacks because they fear being stamped racially inferior.[21] Stephan Thernstrom makes clear what is only implicit in that argument: black students admitted to institutions of higher education with the aid of affirmative action do not enter as prepared as their fellow students who were admitted purely upon the basis of test scores and grades. This, then, creates a "mismatch," which often causes affirmative action beneficiaries to end up at the bottom of the class or drop out. Blacks students are, therefore, less likely to achieve successful careers. Thus, the use of racial preferences only serves to fuel low self-esteem among black students and feelings of superiority among white and Asian students.[22] More recent research by Jesse Rothstein and Albert Yoon involving law schools and by William Bowen and Derek Bok involving colleges conclude that there is no such mismatch. These scholars point to the fact that graduation rates of white and black students at the nation's most prestigious colleges and universities are quite comparable.[23]

The Thernstroms' arguments are based in part on an assertion previously made by Shelby Steele. Racial preferences, Steele insisted, remove the excuse provided by segregation that "buffered" blacks from racial vulnerability. Entitlements based on race engender a kind of disabling dependence. They may appear to be a victory for blacks, but whites see them as paternalism. Affirmative action may result from good intentions, but these good intentions yield bad effects—the "old sin is reaffirmed in a new guise." Preferential treatment leads to doubt, exploits victimization, diminishes incentive to develop, and hence yields no ultimate advantage to blacks or society.[24] Thus, Steele, like other traditionalists, believes that the use of race in any fashion by American institutions creates a class as well as a race problem in today's post–Jim Crow society; consequently, it is in the best interests of all Americans if we simply ignore race.

Steele views affirmative action as an outgrowth of white guilt. "White guilt is the vacuum of moral authority that comes from simply knowing that one's race is associated with racism."[25] In other words, whites who operate out of guilt are fearful of being associated with racism. To avoid such association, they attempt to empathize with blacks, who exploit this feeling to avoid taking responsibility for black failure. Steele believes white guilt transposes white supremacy in that guilt-feeling whites, not unlike whites during slavery and Jim Crow who believed that an inferior race could only be elevated, or civilized, through white benevolence, believe that blacks today can only be elevated through the moral authority of whites.[26]

One prominent traditionalist, commentator Bill O'Reilly, has identified an external factor other than affirmative action that also conditions bad behaviors and bad values within the black community, thereby indirectly sustaining disparate resources. Somewhat reminiscent of Cornel West's critique discussed in the next chapter, O'Reilly asserts that the power elite of our society—specifically our political leaders, big business, and the media—are ultimately looking out for themselves and not for the average citizen, least of all the poor and blacks. O'Reilly points out, for example, that the power elite take exorbitant salaries and bonuses while paying their workers relatively little. (One report notes, "In 1995, the median CEO pay was 94 times median worker pay; by 2005, it was 179 times.")[27] The power elite issues pardons to one another, and, notwithstanding a few high-profile white-collar criminal prosecutions after the stock market crash of 2000, they regularly do not prosecute some forms of corruption. Those in power have no desire to clean up black communities like Englewood on the South Side of Chicago, where crime runs rampant, "because there is little gain in it for them. . . . Cleaning up drug trafficking in poor neighborhoods does not win elections, lead to high lecture fees, or excite public adulation."[28] O'Reilly often cites the Florida scandal involving Rilya Wilson. Rilya was a little black girl who disappeared during a time when a social service worker was supposed to be visiting her home on a regular basis. Instead of doing her duty, the government employee falsified reports and, as a result, the little girl's disappearance was not discovered for four months. O'Reilly notes that no one in the department lost his or her job or was subject to any heightened scrutiny as a result of this case until the governor of Florida came up for reelection. One of the few traditionalists who was very critical of our government prior to the 2008 collapse of our financial markets, O'Reilly argues that even our legal system too often disregards the public's best interest. Information is regularly concealed from or skewed when presented to juries, and judges sometimes render ridiculous sentences.[29] O'Reilly ties this shameful abuse of power not to racism but to greed or incompetency. Given the impact on blacks, some civil rights theorists, most notably critical race theorists, would wonder what the difference is.

O'Reilly argues that the media and the entertainment industry are especially culpable in creating an American culture that disadvantages blacks. Rather than reporting on the good deeds blacks do, newscasters prefer to cover the criminal acts of a few bad apples. This paints a distorted picture of African Americans for all Americans to see. The media are not singling out blacks, O'Reilly insists; they are simply motivated by profit and, as such, spend too much time covering the worst of society. Not enough time is spent covering good news, which promotes good values, because there is no money to be made in doing so. Bad news sells; good news does not.[30] O'Reilly believes the entertainment industry, especially the music industry, has had the greatest impact both in shaping bad behaviors and bad values within the black community and in skewing the public's image of blacks, especially young black men. Referring to rap music, O'Reilly notes that the power elite in the music industry "mak[e] money from lyrics that encourage drug use, destructive sex, gun possession, and a staggering variety of felonies."[31] Similarly, television programs and movies present a "message that bad behavior doesn't matter," and that "all that matters is fame and getting what 'you need.'"[32] *Get Rich or Die Trying* is the title of one movie starring rapper 50 Cent. Again, O'Reilly does not characterize any of this as racism, notwithstanding its negative impact on African American culture; rather, he sees it as a bigger problem that involves the debasing of the American culture writ large.

Unlike other civil rights theorists, most traditionalists do not regard statistical disparity as problematic in itself. Statistical disparity does not necessarily demonstrate racial disparity in the eyes of most traditionalists. Nonracial factors, such as the ones to which O'Reilly points, can explain some statistical disparities. In addition, traditionalist Thomas Sowell argues that each individual in our society brings to the table a different set of personal strengths and weaknesses as well as social advantages and disadvantages. For example, some individuals are tall, others are short; some are mentally disabled, others have highly advanced mental abilities; some live in impoverished areas of the world, others live in resource-rich environments; and some people experience significant losses, others enjoy windfall gains. Because we are all subject to the luck of the draw, we should expect various levels of resource disparity among groups. It would, in fact, be highly unusual to see equal results across the board. To think otherwise would launch us into a foolhardy quest for cosmic justice, Sowell contends.[33] Given this fact of human nature, Sowell argues, we must insist that "everyone plays by the same rules and gets judged by the same standards—*regardless of what the outcome may be*" (emphasis added).[34] As long as the process is race-neutral, Sowell asserts, we can disregard disparate results with the confidence of knowing we have done the fair and just thing.[35] Ward Connerly captures the traditionalists' position most succinctly when he declares, "Some things can't be compromised, and equality under the law is one of them."[36]

Some traditionalists disagree slightly with Sowell and Connerly. They believe there is value in statistical inquiry and that, consequently, this mode of racial analysis should not be jettisoned. "Racial breakdowns of social and economic data are useful to monitor progress," Stephan and Abigail Thernstrom concede. They caution, however, that the "problem is that they are so easily abused. Statistical disparities—a situation, for example, in which only 10 percent of city contracts are awarded to black-owned firms although the city is 30 percent African American—are taken as proof of discrimination."[37] Reformists argue in the next chapter that this is an incorrect reading of both the law and their position. Like the law, reformists only hold that statistical disparity merely creates a rebuttable presumption of discrimination, not absolute proof of discrimination.

## 2. Prescription

Because traditionalists do not believe external factors, save affirmative action, sustain disparate resources, they offer little in the way of an external prescription. What some traditionalists do offer, however, are measures to deal with the external factors that help condition bad culture in black America—incompetent government and greedy corporations, especially the media and entertainment industry. In addition, another small group of traditionalists, called "compassionate conservatives" or "comcons," offer a few prescriptive measures in the form of government assistance. Proceeding from "a moralizing doctrine that the federal government ha[s] a duty to reverse society's moral decline,"[38] the comcons argue that the government should help African Americans make crucial lifestyle adjustments. But the comcons' prescription is based on socioeconomic class, not on race. Core traditionalists, who believe prescriptive measures should be internal, are reluctant to accept any external prescription. I begin with the position held by the core traditionalists.

According to Thomas Sowell, a core traditionalist, the first step in doing anything about the problems facing blacks is to identify these problems as honestly as we possibly can and then set realistic goals aimed not at race but at poverty. He states:

> If we are serious about wanting to enlarge opportunities and advance those who are less fortunate, then we cannot fritter away the limited means at our disposal in quixotic quests. We must decide whether our top priority is to smite the wicked or to ad-

vance the less fortunate, whether we are looking for visions and rhetoric that make us feel good for the moment or whether we are seeking methods with a proven track record of success in advancing whole peoples from poverty to prosperity.[39]

Similarly, Shelby Steele, another core traditionalist, asserts that the external prescription, such as it is, must identify blacks as citizens deserving of complete fairness. What this means, Steele asserts, is that to the extent one feels impelled to support external assistance for blacks, such assistance must not be in the form of an entitlement based on color.[40] At the very least, this amounts to a ban on race-conscious affirmative action. Steele argues that racial preferences reinforce the idea of black inferiority, "America's oldest racial myth," and that this stigma undermines fair treatment of blacks.[41]

Some noncore traditionalists, such as the Thernstroms, explicitly embrace external prescriptions in the nature of color-blind educational reforms. "For those concerned with racial equity, nothing can be more important than reforming K–12 education so as to close the large current racial gap in cognitive skills."[42] Vouchers, charter schools, standardized testing, and merit-based pay are the major K–12 reforms these traditionalists favor. In higher education, they recommend that universities and colleges de-emphasize racial differences and focus more on student commonalities. Very few details are provided to explain how these educational reforms are to be implemented.

Core traditionalists would criticize these educational reforms not because they lack detail but because they give the false impression that an external solution to the resource-deficit problem in black communities is possible. These traditionalists firmly believe no external prescription can compensate for that lack of internal vigilance and diligence. Thomas Sowell, for example, argues that "resources have had little or nothing to do with educational quality."[43] As evidence, Sowell cites the schools in the District of Columbia. When these schools were segregated and their funding was low relative to what white schools received, black students had higher test scores than they have today, even though the schools today are integrated and have one of the highest "per-pupil expenditures" in the nation.[44] George Will notes that "America has tripled inflation-adjusted per-pupil spending in the last four decades, and since 2001 has increased federal spending for grades K through 12 by 37.4 percent. By now, informed Americans know that money is a very limited lever for moving the world of education." Will further asserts that "schools reflect the families from which their pupils come—the amount of reading material in the homes, the amount of homework done, the hours spent watching television, etc." On that basis as well as on grounds of federalism—George W. Bush's education secretary is a "sassy Texan" who "can say 'We're all good federalists' with a straight face"—Will criticizes the No Child Left Behind law, an educational regime established by Bush's administration that sets national educational goals and national testing to measure states' progress in reaching such standards (the so-called national report card).[45] Because of the importance of parental support in a child's educational achievement, Sowell concludes that if blacks do not change their ways, we can expect to see racial differences in educational achievement even if every black child had the same amount of resources at his or her disposal as the wealthiest white child.[46]

Bill O'Reilly does not disagree with the architects of the canon. He, in fact, notes that while expenditures for the Washington, D.C., public schools are high when compared with those for the parochial schools in the area, the latter have much higher test scores.[47] But O'Reilly believes there are external forces at work that cannot be ignored. Greed and incompetency are widespread in the American culture, which has had a deleterious effect on black culture. O'Reilly, however, offers no specific solutions for dealing with this external condition. He simply advises that all Americans should resist what he calls "secularism" or "secular progressives."[48] As an external prescription, this means more church and less state: "If spirituality is encouraged in the public arena, then questions about violent crime, corrupting media products, drug use, abortion, sexual behavior, conspicuous consumption, irresponsible parental conduct, and a myriad of other personal issues will be raised."[49] Without the rise of spirituality in the public arena, O'Reilly continues, cheating, theft, lying, and other forms of immoral behavior will continue to run rampant among high school students, despite their parents' wishes to the contrary.[50] O'Reilly, a devout Catholic, concedes that scandals within the Catholic Church tend to undercut his message and, indeed, contribute to the problem he has identified. He notes, however, that such scandals are far from the norm in this country.[51]

Other noncore traditionalists, the comcons, offer several specific external prescriptions. These prescriptions are nonracial but call for more active governmental involvement than core traditionalists would desire. Specific comcon prescriptions include workfare rather than welfare; restigmatizing illegitimacy and placing welfare mothers and their babies in residential hostels run by private groups, such as churches, that will make sure babies get the nurturing they need and teenage mothers will get an opportunity to learn and excel in school; "activist" policing, which places more officers on the street and thereby makes for safer neighborhoods; tougher tests for teachers and students; and vouchers to place school choice in the hands of parents.[52] Myron Magnet explains the thinking behind these class-based prescriptions:

> [Comcons] offer a new way of thinking about the poor. They know that telling the poor that they are mere passive victims, whether of racism or of vast economic forces, is not only false but also destructive, paralyzing the poor with the thoughts of their own helplessness and inadequacy. The poor need the larger society's moral support; they need to hear the message of personal responsibility and self-reliance. . . . They need to know, too, that they can't blame "the system" for their own wrongdoing.[53]

Core traditionalists are not unsympathetic to this moral message. They simply believe that the construction of such a wide-ranging set of prescriptions falsely suggests that the problem of disparate resources has an external solution and, hence, an external component; that if these prescriptions do not materialize, blacks will, in fact, have reason to "blame 'the system.'" Steele ends his book *White Guilt* with the following admonition: "If I've learned anything in all of this, it is that if you want to be free, you have to make yourself that way and pay whatever price the world exacts."[54]

Thus, core traditionalists (e.g., Sowell, Thomas, Steele, and Will) differ from other traditionalists (e.g., comcons and the Thernstroms) not only in their diagnostic analyses of the race problem but also in their prescriptive analyses. Unlike other traditionalists, core traditionalists do not see an external race problem, not even a small one, and hence offer no external prescriptions. Core traditionalists are, for the most part, traditional conservatives; they believe in an impotent, minimalist government. Comcons, in contrast, are what might be called "Bush II" conservatives; they express a belief in an activist government that supports private assistance to the poor, helping the latter, many of whom are black, make lifestyle adjustments. President George Walker Bush campaigned for the 2000 presidency on a comcon platform. Despite these differences, traditionalists have one thing in common. They all believe that the race problem is essentially an internal problem, a problem of class rather than race.

## C. INTERNAL ANALYSIS

### 1. Diagnosis

When traditionalists describe the problem of disparate resources in American society today, they mainly frame it as a problem sustained by internal factors. Traditionalists do not consider resource disparity to be a problem of race; they see it as "a problem of class, one that is both cause and effect of a cultural crisis."[55] African American culture, George Will insists, "disparages academic seriousness as 'acting white,'" allows "so many black teenagers [to be] mentored [not] to think about college as a possibility and of SAT tests as important," and "celebrates destructive behaviors," such as babies born out of wedlock, broken families, drugs, and black-on-black crime.[56] Some traditionalists even allege that the internal problem includes a perceived African American practice of "hating whitey."[57]

Many traditionalists arrive at this conclusion—that culture is the condition that sustains disparate resources—by a process of elimination. Shelby Steele writes, "If conditions have worsened for most of us as racism has receded, then much of the problem must be of our own making. . . . We are in the odd and self-defeating position in which taking responsibility for bettering ourselves feels like a surrender to white power."[58] Traditionalists want African Americans to look deep into their collective soul and see hidden psychological flaws—victimization, the rejection of mainstream culture, overemphasis on racial differences, groupthink, and even hatred of whites. John McWhorter, for example, argues that African Americans are disadvantaging themselves through what he calls "the Cult of Victimology." This is a psychological condition of "infantilization," a mind-set that "condones weakness and failure." It is, McWhorter asserts, "a racewide preoccupation with victimhood, which generally entails exaggerating it, [that] gives failure, lack of effort, and criminality a tacit stamp of approval."[59] Like McWhorter, Steele believes that African Americans have a hidden investment in victimology. Steele even goes so far as to argue that African Americans see the race problem as a power struggle between themselves and whites (one between those who lack power but have innocence, and those who possess power but have guilt)[60] in which for blacks innocence, or victimology, equals power—black power. Victimology fuels white guilt, which, in turn, allows blacks to capture the high moral ground and, thus, superior power in the struggle. Black victimology, Steele continues, is expressed through a "complaining celebration" that allows blacks to sit back and wait for whites to respond to past racial injustices rather than to push forward on their own initiative without a handout from white society.[61]

In an attempt to understand the root of the problem of victimology, some traditionalists argue that the history of racial oppression in this country has conditioned African Americans to "recompose" personal fear as an external fear. Blacks have come to believe that external change in society is more important for success than personal growth and development. The focus is more on racial identity than on personal identity. In this world of identity politics, Steele maintains, racism becomes so ubiquitous that the sense of "oppression conditions [one] away from all the values and attitudes [like] individual initiative" that are necessary for personal success. Chances for advancement become missed opportunities. Steele seems to be saying that values that are necessary for personal success do, in fact, inhere in black culture, but that slavery and Jim Crow vitiated them. Remaining in a state of victimization long after the cessation of racial oppression, blacks continue to find no use for values that speak to personal initiative and responsibility.[62]

Traditionalist Thomas Sowell takes issue with Steele's historical analysis. Sowell discounts slavery in the development of what he describes as the "redneck" or "cracker" culture of poor and underclass blacks. This dysfunctional culture, he argues, was imported to the South during the time of slavery from parts of the British Isles, where aggression, braggadocio, laziness, and anti-intellectualism were glorified by people who were in fact called "rednecks" or "crackers." This is the culture that many of today's poor blacks have inherited and imbibed. As Sowell explains:

More is involved here than a mere parallel between blacks and Southern whites. What is involved is a common subculture that goes back for centuries, which has encompassed everything from ways of talking to attitudes toward education, violence, and sex—and which originated not in the South, but in those parts of the British Isles from which white Southerners came. That culture long ago died out where it originated in Britain, while surviving in the American South. Then it largely died out among both white and black Southerners, while surviving today in the poorest and worst of the urban black ghettos.[63]

While most Britons who migrated to the Massachusetts Bay Colony came from the region around East Anglia, Sowell remarks, most of "the common white people of the South" came from outside the "cultural heartland of England," mainly from "the northern borderlands of England—for centuries a no-man's land between Scotland and England—as well as from the Scottish highlands and from Ulster County, Ireland." These "were turbulent, if not lawless, regions" in which the people were referred to as a "Celtic fringe" or "north Britons."[64]

In addition to historical forces, traditionalists have identified contemporary circumstances that feed victimology. One such circumstance is "integration shock." This sociopsychological state usually occurs, Steele argues, when African Americans "move into integrated situations or face [new] challenges." Why? Steele answers that "the presence of new opportunities in society . . . triggers integration shock," because "if opportunity is a chance to succeed, it is also a chance to fail."[65] Integration shock is a "jolt of inferiority anxiety" that causes African Americans to unconsciously feel self-doubt and to consciously feel "discomfort or a desire to retreat from the situation."[66] Thus, as blacks gain more opportunities in mainstream institutions, they experience a proportional increase in integration shock.[67] Blacks become more susceptible to self-doubt and often respond with self-defeating behavior. Integration shock, Steele contends, explains why blacks give little more than perfunctory effort, opt for racial isolation within integrated institutions, and avoid opportunities for advancement.[68] According to Steele, blacks carry more internal self-doubt (a stronger antiself) than others. "The condition of being black in American means that one will likely endure more wounds to one's self-esteem than others and that the capacity for self-doubt born of these wounds will be compounded and expanded by the black race's reputation of inferiority."[69]

Steele argues that integration shock can lead to "race-holding." Race-holding occurs when one uses "any self-description that serves to justify or camouflage [his or her] fears, weaknesses, and inadequacies."[70] The person who race-holds uses his or her identity as a racial victim as an excuse for the inability to succeed. As Steele writes, "Instead of admitting that racism has declined, [blacks] argue all the harder that it is still alive and more insidious than ever."[71] Thus, according to Steele, blacks use race-holding to avoid recognizing their own self-doubt, and this is as much an obstacle to racial progress as racism ever was. With ever-increasing opportunities available to blacks during this post–civil rights era, integration shock and race-holding, Steele insists, are urgent issues for black society today.[72]

There are other cultural conditions to which African Americans must tend, traditionalists argue. For example, Bill O'Reilly maintains that there are "12 million one-parent families in the [United States]," and "single mothers run the majority of those families, and most of those mothers are poor."[73] Pointing to a related statistic, O'Reilly notes that "about 70 percent of all African-American babies are born out of wedlock, as opposed to 27 percent of whites."[74] What this means, O'Reilly calculates, is that "half of all the mothers who have kids in their teens will be poor *the rest of their lives*" (emphasis in original).[75] Because of their poverty, these kids are more susceptible than others to a life of gangs, drugs, and other criminal activity. Yet, as O'Reilly notes, criminal activity can provide opportunities, albeit illegal, for those who do not avail themselves of legitimate economic endeavors. One drug gang on the South Side of Chicago is "estimate[d] [to have] reaped about $1 million *a week* from selling narcotics" (emphasis in original). But the cost of such profits is quite high: seven hundred people within the community were murdered within a recent ten-year period.[76] O'Reilly maintains that a proclivity toward consumption—an attitude that screams "where's mine!"—is yet another misguided cultural condition in the black community. But O'Reilly notes that the internal problem he identifies is exogenous; it is at least in part conditioned by a conspicuous-consumption America culture writ large. Thus, something needs to be done about this larger problem as well as about the more immediate cultural issues facing blacks.[77]

## 2. Prescription

All traditionalists believe that African Americans cannot ultimately rely on the government, including the courts, to resolve what in the view of traditionalists is at bottom a cultural problem. Reflecting the view of his fellow traditionalists, Justice Thomas adamantly rejects "the pervasive view that the Federal Constitution must address all social ills in our society."[78] There is only so much that government can do to help African Americans or any other racial minority. What traditionalists fear is human nature. Like other human beings, African Americans will make no real attempt to resolve their problems if they know the government is going to come to their rescue. There would be no incentive to take advantage of available opportunities, no reason to even try. Equally important, traditionalists believe the government *cannot* resolve these problems. O'Reilly instructs that the main lesson of Hurricane Katrina (where the government failed to provide timely aid to thousands of poor blacks and whites who were flooded out of their homes) is that in the end we must all fend for ourselves.

Traditionalists, then, insist that the real solution to the cultural factors that sustain capital deficiencies in black society lies within African Americans themselves. They must change their culture. Specifically, blacks must adopt an individual identity rather than a racial identity. They must imbibe principles "that bring coherence and even greatness to free societies: personal responsibility, hard work, individual initiative, delayed gratification, commitment to excellence, competition by merit, the honor in achievement, and so on."[79] Blacks must maintain functional families, work hard, study assiduously in school, and build safer communities.[80] "Married parents, strong families and quality education are the primary combatants. In short, the culture of the underclass, and the values that shape that culture, ought to be the focus, and it is no longer controversial to hold this view."[81]

Reducing the number of teenage pregnancies and increasing the number of intact families is, perhaps, the principal traditionalist prescription. Parents should spend quality time with their children and model good behavior.[82] But some parents are "lousy," to use an O'Reilly word, in which case traditionalists place the onus on the individual to establish his or her own support system. Start by refusing to associate with people who will use you rather than support you, O'Reilly advises.[83] Hence, in the end, it comes down to the individual. Like Horatio Alger, blacks must pull themselves up by dint of individual initiative.

## D. SUMMARY AND REFLECTIONS

Diagnostically, traditionalists believe disparate resources are sustained not by the external factor of race but by the internal factor of class—bad behaviors and bad values—within the African American community. According to some traditionalists, two external factors do, however, indirectly sustain disparate resources by conditioning internal behaviors and values. One is the racial factor of affirmative action, and the other is the nonracial factor of "secularism." The latter refers to the American culture writ large, a culture damaged by a greedy and selfish corporate establishment, a greedy and lazy media, a greedy and morally depraved entertainment industry, and a greedy, incompetent, and sometimes corrupt government. The media and entertainment industries, for example, send negative stereotypes of blacks into the mainstream just to make a buck. Although some traditionalists, such as compassionate conservatives, prescribe governmental assistance to private institutions committed to helping blacks reshape their lives, such outside help is offered only on a class basis. Core traditionalists would not go along with this prescription. Other than eliminating affirmative action, core traditionalists believe that there is little that can be done externally to redress what is essentially an internal, or class, problem. Because disparate resources are sustained mainly by internal factors, the only way to resolves this problem is through the black community itself. Blacks must change individually—go to school and stay in school, get a job and keep a job, get married before having babies and stay married, stop doing drugs and stay out of trouble, and reject the "racemongers" like Jesse Jackson and Al Sharpton. These are the core tenets of traditionalism.

At first glance, traditionalism would seem to be a complete civil rights theory, as it appears to offer an external and internal diagnosis of and prescription for the post–civil rights race problem facing blacks. On the other hand, it is clear that traditionalism gives overwhelming attention to the internal race problem. For that reason, it could be argued that traditionalism is not a complete civil rights theory, that it is at the opposite end of the spectrum from critical race theory, which, as we shall see, is externally focused. The existence of disparate resources is as much an external job for critical race theorists as it is an internal job for traditionalists. Reformists and limited separatists are in the middle. They see a mixture of culture and race.

In my view, traditionalism's deep discounting of the external race problem is the weakest part of its critique. Given that slavery and Jim Crow caused disparate resources, it is reasonable to think that race would be a sustaining factor today. Yet traditionalists are loath to draw this analytical conclusion because they believe that, as an empirical matter, civil rights laws have effectively put an end to the race problem. But the fact is the civil rights laws changed only the *legal status* of blacks; they did nothing to repair the damage to or otherwise change the resources held by scores of African Americans wrought by slavery and Jim Crow. When, for example, the net family wealth of white America is ten times that of black America, or when the mean earnings of black males with a bachelor's degree have consistently been 65 to 75% of the mean for their white males cohorts during the entire post–civil rights period (see preface and figure 38 in the appendix), race still matters. Given that college educated blacks are doing everything traditionalists say blacks need to do to get ahead, what nonracial factor explains the racial differential that has existed all these years? How is it possible that net family wealth and at least some of the other large statistical disparities we see in the appendix (wages, occupational status, education, etc.) that have been in continuous existence since the end of the civil rights movement are not sustained by the lingering effects of slavery or Jim Crow? Trends cannot be ignored.

Brent Staples argues that slave-era barriers to black education can still be felt. The connection between nineteenth-century laws and customs that severely limited black literacy and the creation of today's black professional class begins with a study in the 1940s by sociologist E. Horace Fitchett. Fitchett found that half of the students at Howard University, the nation's leading black institution of higher education, were descendants not of slaves but of free blacks, the latter of whom had greater access to education, especially in the North. Similarly, sociologist Horace Mann Bond wrote in 1963: "I have . . .

been astonished to discover how largely the 10 percent of Negroes who were free in 1860 have dominated the production of Negro professionals (and intellectuals) up to the present day." In 2006, Staples concluded: "The black intellectual and professional classes have grown significantly since then. But studies of those groups today would probably show a strong relationship between early emancipation and membership in the present-day black elite." In other words, race still matters.[84]

It is difficult for me to accept the argument by traditionalists such as Shelby Steele, Thomas Sowell, and Justice Clarence Thomas that the government's support of affirmative action directly or indirectly sustains capital deficiencies within the African American community. Affirmative action increases rather than decreases the availability of resources for blacks. The notion that affirmative action sustains disparate resources is based on an unsubstantiated belief that racial preferences leave blacks in a state of deep despair and moral degradation, making sloughs of them all. Yet the vast majority of affirmative action beneficiaries who are black come from the striving black middle class, whom, again, traditionalists generally praise as racial role models for other blacks. Indeed, when traditionalists refer to the "class problem," they do not typically have the black middle class in mind. They usually have in mind the lower black classes, especially the black poverty class and underclass. There is, then, a contradiction between what the traditionalists say about the race problem (the problem of resource disparity is sustained by class) and what the evidence shows (the problem extends across the black classes), and between what traditionalists say about affirmative action (it hurts the lower black classes) and what the evidence shows (poor blacks are not typically affirmative action beneficiaries).

As an explanation of the exogenous nature of the internal forces that sustain the resource deficit in black society, Bill O'Reilly's indictment of what he terms a "secular" popular culture strikes me as much more persuasive than his and other traditionalists' condemnation of affirmative action. Some music, movies, and TV programs do condition dysfunctional behavior or attitudes among blacks, as well as among other young Americans. The usual suspects—such as "gangsta rap," the movie *White Chicks*, and Jerry Springer—model and validate bad behavior and bad values. These negative images of blacks come into the homes of young blacks unfiltered. There is no well-informed voice or other mediating force standing between the child or teenager and these harmful messages and images beamed into the home everyday.

The media's portrayal of blacks during Hurricane Katrina demonstrates the Fourth Estate's complicity not only in the dissemination of negative black images but, more sinisterly, in the creation of such images. Media reports regarding the aftermath of Hurricane Katrina created images that reinforced black stereotypes. For example, the caption of an Associated Press (AP) photo of a young black man clasping items in each arm walking through the flood read,

"A young man walks through chest-deep flood water after *looting a grocery store* in New Orleans on Tuesday, Aug. 20, 2005" (emphasis added).[85] In contrast, a second photo from the AP showed a young white man and woman carrying food items through the flood, and the caption read, "Two residents wade through chest-deep water after *finding bread and soda from a local grocery store* after Hurricane Katrina came through the area in New Orleans, Louisiana" (emphasis added).[86] As reformist Michael Eric Dyson and others have argued, the media captions led the reader to believe that the white residents were simply doing what they had to do to survive, just as any rational person would do under the circumstances, whereas the young black man was looting, and, hence, his actions were legally and morally reprehensible.[87] As Dyson has noted, "Words help to interpret images; language and pictures in combination reinforce ideas and stories about black identity."[88]

Although some traditionalists would attribute the media's Katrina reporting to the quest for profits and laziness rather than to racism, one must still ask whether reports such as these expose the media's unconscious racial bias. Does the fact that the media constantly frame false and negative public images of blacks reveal a bias that is at once unacknowledged and uncontrolled? What is clear, however, is that newspaper readers and TV viewers develop misconceptions of blacks based on these types of media reports. In the case of Hurricane Katrina, many Americans concluded that the government's slow relief effort in New Orleans was justified because of the perceived criminal behavior of blacks.[89]

Corporate scandals also militate against good behavior and values, not just among blacks but among the downtrodden in general. When the Securities and Exchange Commission (SEC), a federal agency, accuses the Rigas family, founders of Adelphia Communications, of using their company to secure $3.1 billion in illegal loans; when it accuses accounting giant Arthur Andersen of shredding documents relating to a client, Enron, after the SEC launched an investigation into its client's business practices; when it charges Enron with manipulating the power markets in Texas and California to boost profits and of bribing foreign officials to gain access to their markets; when it brings forth evidence that Bristol-Meyers Squibb overstated its revenue by $1.5 billion; and when it and the Department of Justice charge Worldcom with overstating cash flow by $3.8 billion and providing its founder, Bernard Ebbers, with $400,000 in secret loans, it becomes all too clear that many corporate executives are modeling the wrong behavior and values to the rest of society. The public thereby receives a strong message that the way to fame and fortune in this country is through cheating, stealing, and lying; just don't get caught—in other words, "get over."

For all their criticism of popular culture, traditionalists do not provide prescriptive details for transforming large-scale American institutions. How do blacks and other Americans change the corporate environment? Bill O'Reilly, for example, suggests that the "biased" newspapers will become more balanced in their coverage of racial matters if blacks stop buying them. But blacks constitute such a small percentage of the readership of these newspapers that their protest will hardly be noticed. O'Reilly also advises blacks to become "traditional warriors," or "T-Warriors," and actively oppose the "secular progressives," or "S-Ps." "The cornerstone of the traditional warrior's code," O'Reilly explains, "is to *do what you say you are going to do*" (emphasis in original).[90] In other words, defend traditional principles (love of country and individual responsibility) "in public—even if they are unpopular."[91] What this means, then, is that, in the end, even noncore traditionalists, such as O'Reilly, have placed all their eggs in one basket: they see the problem confronting blacks as essentially an internal one to which no real external solution can be offered.

If one looks with an open mind at the traditionalists' internal diagnosis of the resource-disparity problem, one must admit that it provides many important insights. Dysfunctional and self-defeating behavior, values, and attitudes within the African American community—including single-parent families (especially those headed by teenage mothers), poor attitudes toward education, drugs, black-on-black crime—certainly do limit available opportunities and, to that extent, sustain capital deficiencies within the community.[92] But traditionalists undercut their analysis by their tendency to oversimplify and by their concomitant failure to recognize alternate interpretations of the conditions they describe. For example, given the ubiquity of the racial stereotyping in our society today, holding on to blackness (what Steele calls race-holding) looks less like an attempt to claim victimology or evade personal responsibility than an expression of black pride and heritage in the face of racial hostility. So-called integration shock could be understood as a sociopsychological condition that is less about fear of competing toe-to-toe with whites than about the reluctance to adapt to white values that negate black worth. There is much truth in an observation made by the conservative Condoleezza Rice, a former provost at Stanford University whom President George Bush appointed as the first black female secretary of state. Contradicting Steele's notion of "integration shock," Rice asserted that "when segregation did lift they [black Americans] were more than prepared because of what blacks had done on their own."[93] Finally, separatism seems to have less to do with self-censorship than with self-support. There may be something self-limiting about each of these traits, but to see them only as indications of victimology oversimplifies.

Black-on-black crime is another example of traditionalists' oversimplification of cultural factors that sustain capital deficiencies in black America. This cultural trait is frequently cited by traditionalists as proof positive of a type of cultural degradation that is unique to the black community. But on closer inspection, this is far from the truth. In 2002, for example, 74.5% of violent crimes perpetrated against African Americans were committed by other African Americans. In that same year, however, 72.6% of violent crimes perpetrated against whites were committed by other whites.[94] Traditionalists' frequent failure to point out the white-on-white statistics when discussing black-on-black crime not only oversimplifies this internal problem but also reveals a lack of proportionality and even a punitive quality to their views about blacks. The fact is, intraracial crime is not a problem unique to African Americans.

The absence of proportionality and the presence of a punitive streak in traditionalism are most apparent in the traditionalists' prescriptive message, which is essentially that African Americans should pull themselves up by their own bootstraps. Steele places all the responsibility on the backs of blacks for dealing with the problem of disparate resources and holds the government virtually unaccountable. Similarly, O'Reilly believes that racial equality must come not through government initiative but primarily through internal transformation. Black leaders must implement a code of conduct that emphasizes relinquishing negative feelings (presumably toward whites and blacks themselves) and taking advantage of educational opportunities. This code of conduct will supposedly transform inner-city neighborhoods. O'Reilly does not, however, say how this new creed is to be implemented.[95] Educational opportunities are not plentiful, as many blacks are trapped in poor-performing public schools. Vouchers do not necessarily cover the entire cost of education, especially at high-priced private schools. And many black parents are ill equipped to handle by themselves the increasingly complex educational demands placed on striving students today. One need only look at the statistics in the appendix to get a sense of the problem: blacks are a resource-deficient people. For example, figures 1 through 16 show that blacks have among the highest (and in many instances the highest) poverty rates, and figures 22 through 45 show that blacks have among the lowest (and in many cases the lowest) income rates. Figure 38 (which reports the mean earnings of males with a bachelor's degree) as well as figure 40 (which shows earnings of persons with an advanced degree) are most instructive because they deal with individuals who possess a high level of human capital and, hence, have the ability to generate financial capital. The continuing disparity in these categories makes it unlikely that blacks will become "canon makers of the social order" anytime soon. If the statistics are overwhelming, then simply look at Hurricane Katrina. There was no dearth of blacks who lacked the financial or social capital to get out of the way of that monster hurricane in August 2005. Traditionalists, in short, do not tell us how a resource-deficient community can obtain resources on their own. Outside help is needed from either the government or the private sector.

We are left, then, with the following question: Is it fair or realistic to expect blacks to be able to change their behaviors and values without *first* doing something about the larger environment that helps condition this culture? Malcolm Gladwell has a definite answer to this question. In *Outliers: The Story of Success* (2008), Gladwell writes:

In the famous nineteenth-century novels of Horatio Alger, young boys born into poverty rise to riches through a combination of pluck and initiative. . . . In *Outliers*, I want to convince you that these kinds of personal explanations of success don't work. People don't rise from nothing. We do owe something to parentage and patronage. The people who stand before kings may look like they did it all by themselves. But in fact they are invariably the beneficiaries of hidden advantages and extraordinary opportunities and cultural legacies that allow them to learn and work hard and make sense of the world in ways others cannot. It makes a difference where and when we grew up. . . . It is not the brightest who succeed. . . . Nor is success simply the sum of the decisions and efforts we make on our own behalf. It is, rather, a gift. Outliers are those who have been given opportunities—and who have had the strength and presence of mind to seize them. . . . For Bill Gates, the lucky break was being born at the right time and getting the gift of a computer terminal in junior high.[96]

I daresay, parents have an intuitive sense that the Horatio Algers of the world need resources to succeed. It is this intuition that drives parents to fight so hard to get their children, however bright and ambitious they may be, into the best schools. Parents know that a bad school can torpedo the most heroic scholastic effort.

Yet traditionalists are asking blacks to pull success out of thin air. It might be that a few blacks can overpower strong environmental headwinds by dint of willpower. But without outside help, I doubt that the vast majority of blacks or, for that matter, any other group of Americans can play Superman. No group in the history of our republic has ever been asked to overcome even lesser burdens without outside help, private or public. Indeed, it is precisely under these circumstances that government earns its keep. It is the solemn duty of government to come to the aid of its citizens in times of need. The question, however, is whether government has both the capacity and the desire to do what it is supposed to do. I must admit that after Katrina, I have my doubts.

*Chapter 3*

# REFORMISM

## A. Overview

WITH DEGREES FROM Harvard College and Harvard Law School, Lawrence Mungin, by his own admission, made a conscious effort to be "the good black." Paul Barrett summarizes Mungin's story in his book *The Good Black: A True Story of Race in America*:

> Being the sole black attorney worried him, but he didn't want to make a stink about it. When some of the black secretaries at Katten Muchin [his law firm] went out of their way to strike up conversations with him, and he learned that they had various grievances tied to race, he did nothing to investigate or come to their aid. Indeed, he speculated in conversation with his brother, Kenneth, that the secretaries were using race as an excuse, that they might be cooking up an unjustified lawsuit. Larry sounded to Kenneth as if "he was the big company man—just work hard, everything will be fine, no complaining," Kenneth told me later. In retrospect, Larry felt chagrined that he had dismissed the secretaries' complaints so quickly. "I didn't go into the place looking for discrimination," he said.[1]

Mungin would later sue his employer, the Katten Muchin law firm, alleging employment discrimination in the firm's refusal to consider him for a partnership.[2]

What this story means for Cornel West is that "race still matters."[3] What it means for Joe Feagin is that racial fault lines created by a deeply rooted system of "white-on-black oppression," or what he also calls "systemic racism," can still be felt in American society.[4] For Glenn Loury, it means that the traditionalist refrain—"it's time to move on"—is "simplistic social ethics and sophomoric social psychology."[5] And for other reformists— Michael Eric Dyson, Ellis Cose, Tavis Smiley, Hernan Vera, Melvin Sikes, Eileen O'Brien, and scores of others[6]—Mungin's story illustrates, yet again, a basic truth about life in post–civil rights America: race continues to play a significant role in the African American struggle for worldly success and personal happiness. The inertia of discriminatory traditions—"historic inequalities and longstanding cultural stereotypes"[7]—makes race a potent, if often invisible, force in the distribution of resources throughout the post–civil rights period.

Thus, while both reformists and traditionalists agree that slavery and Jim Crow created the capital-deficiency problem in black America, they disagree about what sustains the problem all these years after the end of the civil rights movement. Traditionalists see the civil rights movement, which they believe gave us racially enlightened laws and attitudes, as an intervening agent that has effectively overridden any continuing impact slavery or Jim Crow might have exerted on the well-being of blacks today. Class or culture, they calculate, is the only remaining plausible explanation for the extant resource deficit in the African American community. Reformists, in response, adamantly maintain that slavery and Jim Crow continue to have lingering effects that limit opportunities for resource development. In addition, they insist that white racism has simply moved from the "frontstage" to the "backstage," and societal discrimination is a force to be reckoned with. Reformists, however, concede that some elements of black culture (not the whole of black culture) do in fact limit opportunities for capital development within the African American community. Having made that important concession, reformists are, nevertheless, quick to stress the exogenous nature of this internal problem. Bad behaviors and bad values, they argue, are conditioned by the external factor of race. The dysfunctional cultural orientation that we see in some black communities is, in other words, racialized. Most important, reformists, unlike traditionalists, strongly believe that the internal factors are no match for the external ones, that the latter are the major factors that sustain disparate resources.

Consistent with their race-still-matters belief, reformists do not hesitate to prescribe race-conscious remedies. These remedies are tendered with a single purpose in mind—to lower, if not eliminate, racial barriers. Thus, to redress racism and racial discrimination in their manifold forms, reformists propose an ongoing regime of civil rights reforms ranging from doctrinal changes in civil rights law to more aggressive use of racial preferences, from job training to job creation, and from child care to welfare—in other words, a whole slew of legal and economic remedies from the government. For the internal factors of bad behavior and bad values, reformists prescribe a household-based self-help program. This program is markedly different from the traditionalists' self-help program in two ways. First, it is intended to coexist with governmental assistance. Hence, the government has a significant presence in redressing both the internal and the external factors that sustain disparate resources. "Discrimination and segregation in employment and housing, institutional discrimination, poor primary education, and low African American college enrollment cannot be ended without government assistance."[8] Second, unlike the traditionalists' unstructured, individual-focused self-help program, the reformists' concept of self-help is designed to operate as a family project that draws heavily upon the black middle class for support and the black ethos for substance and inspiration. This raises an important question: Is the reformists' adopt-a-family approach to black self-help potentially more effective in bringing about a cultural transformation within certain segments of black society than the traditionalists' ad hoc, Horatio Alger approach?

Reformists, like traditionalists, are not monolithic. For this reason, I shall attempt to preserve the diversity of thought among reformists as I did in my discussion of traditionalists in the last chapter. Nuances will be observed, and major reformists with distinct voices will be heard throughout the chapter.

## B. External Analysis

### 1. Diagnosis

The reformist analysis of the American race problem begins with the same dispositive question with which every other post–civil rights theory begins— namely, why have African Americans failed to achieve racial equality decades after the end of the civil rights movement? In answering this question, reformists cannot simply point to racism and leave it at that. They must respond to the traditionalists' charge that racism and racial discrimination are not inhibiting factors in these post–civil rights days. Traditionalist Dinesh D'Souza made this very point in an important debate he had with the Reverend Jesse Jackson. D'Souza recalled that debate as follows:

> I did not deny that racism exists, and conceded that in a big country like the United States one could find many examples of it. But I asked Jackson to prove to me that racism today was potent enough and widespread enough that it could prevent me or him, or my daughter, or his children, from achieving their basic aspirations? Where is that kind of racism, I said—show it to me.[9]

In his book *Enough*, Juan Williams echoes this sentiment. Sounding less like a reformist than a traditionalist, Williams remarks:

> There is no discounting the damage done by slavery and racism. They are a tragically heavy weight of history on black people. And while much of the burden has lifted, it can still be found weighing on the black people, through stereotypes and negative images, leaving us at a real disadvantage. But with the *Brown* decision and the passage of civil rights and voting rights laws, the historic damage done by slavery and racism is no longer heavy enough to stop most black people from fighting through the static and making their way to a better life.[10]

Thinking as a traditionalist, one might throw another log onto the fire. Black income has risen since the end of the civil rights movement.[11] The black poverty rate has, in fact, been cut in half since the 1960s. At the time of the passage of the 1964 Civil Rights Act, nearly one half (49.6%) of all blacks lived in poverty.[12] Today, that number is down to just over 20%.[13] With so much improvement among blacks, how can one reasonably claim that race still matters? Does the existence of disparate resources in the African American community really come down to the inability of certain segments of that community to take advantage of available opportunities? Reformists have answers to these questions.

They contend that the problem of disparate community resources is a racial problem, plain and simple. Resource disparity, in other words, is sustained by the external factor of race. Neither racism nor racial discrimination, reformists insist, is a relic of a bygone era. Both are very much alive today, and both not only limit opportunities but also harm blacks psychologically. Reformists have attempted to catalogue the various ways in which racism and racial discrimination operate today. They use terms like "frontstage" and "backstage" racism, "individual" and "structural discrimination." Frontstage racism is old-fashioned racial antipathy or racial stereotyping expressed overtly in public places. In contrast, backstage racism is expressed overtly in private settings, that is, behind closed doors among family and friends. Individual discrimination (sometimes called "individual disparate treatment") is intentional discrimination that usually takes place in one-on-one or small group settings. In contrast, structural discrimination (sometimes called "systemic disparate effects") is unintentional discrimination embedded in the practices or policies (standard operating procedure) of institutions (institutional discrimination) or society at large (societal discrimination). Individual discrimination and institutional discrimination are connected to an identifiable discriminator, or perpetrator, the presence of which gives legitimacy to the sense that an actionable wrong has been committed. In contrast, societal discrimination, which can be defined as the cumulative effects of all forms of prior discrimination (including the lingering effects of slavery and Jim Crow) or current discrimination, has no identifiable perpetrator. It has too many perpetrators to count—the whole of society.[14] Reformists, in short, believe that disparate resources are sustained externally by racism (frontstage and backstage) and racial discrimination (individual as well as structural in the forms of institutional and societal discrimination).[15]

## A. RACISM

African Americans, reformists argue, experience frontstage racism mainly in the form of racial stereotyping. Frontstage racism occurs in public places, including restaurants, shopping malls, hotels, parks, highways, streets, and the workplace. Racial profiling is a clear example of racial stereotyping that takes place in the public arena. Police officers across the country engage in racial profiling. "African American motorists are stopped and prosecuted for traffic stops more than any other citizens," according to one federal judge. The judge's findings are consistent with a report published by the Justice Department's Bureau of Justice Statistics (BJS) in 2007. The report concludes that while drivers of all colors are pulled over by the police at approximately the same rate, black and Latino drivers are more likely to be searched and arrested. After being stopped, blacks are searched 9.5% of the time, Latinos 8.8% of the time, and whites 3.6% of the time. Blacks are arrested after being stopped more than twice as often as whites (4.5% vs. 2.1%), whereas Latinos are arrested 3.1% of the time. One of the coauthors of the report, BJS statistician Matthew Durose, argues that these findings do not prove the existence of racial profiling because there could be nonracial explanations for the statistical disparities. But what are they? Do black and Latino drivers speed more than white drivers? Do they drive around with more illegal substances or weapons or open containers of alcohol than white drivers? It may be that black drivers are less willing to cooperate with police officers who stop them—while three-quarters of Latinos and whites stopped for running a traffic light or stop sign concede the legitimacy of the stop, nearly one-half of black drivers believe they did not commit an infraction—but that does not adequately explain the matter. These nonracial explanations seem especially dubious considering that older middle-class blacks and Latinos are included in the statistics. What is most telling is the fact that although blacks are more likely to be arrested than whites, blacks are also more likely to be released from jail without so much as a traffic warning. This strongly suggests that there was no probable cause for arresting them in the first place, and that police officers are arbitrarily rummaging through the personal effects of black motorists. The BJS findings, it should be noted, are similar to those produced in a 2004 study by the RAND Corporation, which found that black drivers are more likely to experience discretionary pat downs and are more likely to have longer stops by police.[16]

There are other oft-cited examples of frontstage racial stereotyping. One involves the well-dressed, well-mannered, middle-class black (or wealthy black, as in the case of the actor Danny Glover) who is unable to catch a cab in cosmopolitan New York City. So widespread is the practice that seven cabdrivers were nabbed in the first day of "Operation Refusal," a program implemented by New York City in an attempt to crack down on cabdrivers who refused to pick up African American passengers.[17] Even Larry Mungin's determined effort to be "the good black" could not protect him from frontage racism. As Paul Barrett recounts:

> Despite his alienation from his past and membership in the contemporary version of DuBois's talented tenth, Mungin wasn't immune to infuriating stereotypes in middle-class white circles. When he returned from work dressed in a suit, he got friendly nods from neighbors in his apartment complex in Alexandria, Virginia. Later the same evening, however, wearing sweat clothes on his way to the gym, he found that the same neighbors would visibly tense up. On the elevator, some women would punch the control panel and get off at the next floor, or clutch their handbag to their chest, as if Mungin were about to rip it away from them.
>
> "I understand what's going through their minds, but how do you think that makes me feel?" Mungin asked angrily. "I'm black, so they think I'm going to rob or rape

them. But I'm the same person who walks in with the Armani suit. Don't they see me? The answer is no. They see a black man. *I* am the one who is robbed. I am robbed of my reputation because of the color of my skin."

Race had crept up on Mungin and forced its way into his life. In his youth, he had avoided the issue—amazingly—and had few *visible* racial scars from that period. But he encountered isolated examples of hostility as soon as he arrived at Harvard. As a rule, he didn't react outwardly; he walked away. But by the time he reached his mid-30s, he had accumulated enough unhappy experiences that it was becoming difficult to contain his building anger. The effort made him weary. It left him confused about his black identity. He couldn't ignore it anymore, as was illustrated by his asking the question at his job interview about the number of black [attorneys] in Katten Muchin's Washington office.[18]

Racism can also be found in the delivery of emergency medical services. Studies at hospitals in two major cities found that black patients with bone fractures were significantly less likely to be given pain medication than their white counterparts.[19] Dr. Lewis R. Goldfrank, the director of emergency services at a New York City hospital, argues that "racism, flat out," is the only way to explain this disparity in medical treatment.[20]

There are more "hate crimes"—crimes in which the perpetrator intentionally selects a victim or a victim's property based on race, religion, sexual orientation, ethnicity/national origin, or disability—based on race than on any other characteristic. Recent figures reported by the Federal Bureau of Investigation pursuant to the Hate Crime Statistics Act reveal that 7,489 hate crime incidents were reported in forty-nine states and the District of Columbia in 2003 alone. Fifty out of 100 hate crime offenses were motivated by racial hatred, nearly 20 out of 100 involved religious bias, and 16 out of every 100 crimes evidenced bias based on sexual orientation. Additionally, 14 out of 100 hate crimes occurred because of an ethnicity or national origin bias.[21]

Given these experiences, reformists quite understand the African American comedian Chris Rock when he tells his white audiences: "Ain't one of you would change places with me. And I'm *rich*!" Reformists also know what Arthur Ashe, the legendary and well-assimilated black tennis star who died of AIDS at age forty-eight, meant when he told an interviewer six months before his death that "living with AIDS is not the greatest burden I've had in my life. Being black is. No question about it." Finally, reformists believe it is still the case that blacks must make unusual efforts to succeed only because they are black, and that if a black person fails, whites will not think, "He doesn't have what it takes." Whites will say, "Blacks don't have what it takes."

Although reformists argue that frontstage racism in post–civil rights America is mainly manifested as racial stereotyping, they also see evidence of old-fashioned racial antipathy. For example, during the 2008 presidential primary campaign, Senator Hillary Clinton played to antiblack sentiment among certain white voters. She consistently charged that African American senator Barack Obama, her chief opponent in the primary campaign, did not have the support of "hard-working white Americans."[22] These voters, she saw, still harbored old-fashioned, Jim Crow–style racial antipathy. What Senator Clinton saw was later affirmed by a *Washington Post*/ABC News poll taken at the end of the primary campaign in June 2008: "30 percent of white voters . . . admitted to harboring racial prejudice."[23]

Reformists maintain that overt racism today takes place less often in the frontstage than in the backstage. There is, in other words, a spatial variation in the expression of this form of white racism. As Leslie Houts Picca and Joe Feagin assert, "Much of the overt expression of blatantly racist thoughts, emotions, interpretations, and inclinations has gone backstage—that is, into private settings where whites find themselves among other whites, especially friends and relatives."[24] Thus, the argument is that there is "significantly divergent racial performances by white Americans in public (multiracial) and private (all-white) areas."[25]

Picca and Feagin base this argument—"closed-door performances" (backstage) differ from "outside performances" (frontstage)—on their review of extant research conducted by other sociologists and on their own fresh research on the subject. Their research assistants, most of whom were white graduate or college students, were asked to interviewed their cohorts and family in various venues. A typical report read as follows:

> Most white families like to say that they're not prejudiced. They like to say that they don't discriminate, that they want true equality, that they want all these things, but if you ever put them to the test there is a lot that will back off. A lot of whites still, the majority I'd say, will say the right, politically correct things at the right times, but behind closed doors, or with their friends, their small circle of friends, will be extremely bigoted in their comments.[26]

Commenting on other interviews conducted in their study, Picca and Feagin observed:

> In this research study, several white respondents indicated that they or their acquaintances think consciously of protecting some racist performances by doing them "behind closed doors" in circles of friends and relatives. Reflecting on white behavior, one educator in this study spoke about the "racism no one wants to talk about . . . because it is not accepted to be racist." He continued by noting that "a lot of white people have some feelings that they won't even say," clearly referring to such holding back in multiracial settings. In this study another college student said that he knew "a lot of people who are very racist," and backed this statement by citing white friends who regularly use the word "nigger" in conversations among themselves. He indi-

cated that he himself uses that racist epithet only in *private* contexts with white friends.[27]

Although backstage racism is directed toward all people of color, Picca and Feagin believe that black Americans are the main targets. They maintain that an "antiblack perspective is central to and deeply embedded in the white-racist framing" that informs backstage racism. This framing consists of "cognitions, images, emotions, and inclinations." The old-fashioned stereotype of the "dangerous black man" and the "oversexed" black woman combine with the belief in a "morally questionable" black culture and other newer expressions to give content to backstage racism. The point Picca and Feagin wish to make is that while white Americans who harbor these sentiments know that blatant racism "is generally inappropriate or frowned upon" in the frontstage, they view the backstage "as a space that is safe from certain frontstage expectations about interpersonal politeness on racial matters."[28]

Picca and Feagin's findings on backstage racism are supported by others who are not sociologists. Looking at numerous studies of racial dynamics in American institutions, from TV game shows to retail markets, Steven Levitt, an economist, and Stephen Dubner, a journalist, argue in their book, *Freakonomics*, that racial discrimination may appear to have been "practically eradicated during the twentieth century, like polio ... [but], more likely, it has become so unfashionable to discriminate against certain groups that all but the most insensitive people take pains to at least *appear* fair-minded, at least in public. This hardly means that discrimination itself has ended—only that people are embarrassed to show it" (emphasis in original).[29] The racist comments of Senator Trent Lott (R-Miss.) would seem to illustrate this contention. Senator Lott got into trouble for publicly supporting segregation in a speech he gave in 2003 at the hundredth birthday celebration of retiring senator Strom Thurmond (R-S.C.). Lott's segregationist views were well known around Washington, D.C., but his colleagues and the press said nothing. Was this because they had grown accustomed to hearing racist comments in private? Was it because these comments had seemed "normal" to them? How many listeners actually shared Lott's views at some level?[30] Obviously, reformists and traditionalists draw different conclusions from the Lott incident.[31]

Whether frontstage or backstage racism, a complex array of negative white attitudes toward blacks sustains capital deficiencies within black America, according to reformists. Cornel West, in particular, argues that it is white America's resistance to fully accepting the humanity of blacks that sustains disparate resources. Whites see blacks as a "problem people," West insists, rather than as fellow American citizens with problems. These racist attitudes are not new; they have been around since slavery. While acknowledging the civil rights movement and the undeniable progress blacks have made over the centuries, reformists argue that racism remains a serious problem in post–civil rights America.[32]

## B. RACIAL DISCRIMINATION

Reformists maintain that disparate resources are sustained not only by negative racial attitudes held by whites in various manifestations but also by negative racial acts, some of which flow from racist mind-sets. Like racism, discrimination comes in different forms; it is not just one thing. It consists of individual discrimination and structural discrimination, the latter of which includes institutional discrimination and societal discrimination.

Individual discrimination is easy to comprehend. A black person is treated "less favorably" (not just differently) than a white person because of his or her race. In other words, discrimination is motivated by a racial animus or racial stereotype.[33] Mungin's claim of discrimination against his employer, the Katten Muchin law firm, discussed at the beginning of this chapter, is an example of individual discrimination. So is the claim, discussed later in this chapter, made by Pat Washington against her employer.[34] Another illustration of individual discrimination often given by reformists involves the use of the peremptory challenge in jury selection. This device allows lawyers to exclude potential jurors from sitting on a jury. The discriminatory use of this device is illustrated in *Miller-El v. Dretke*, a case decided by the U.S. Supreme Court. Thomas Joe Miller-El was being tried for capital murder in a Texas state court. Dallas prosecutors used peremptory challenges to eliminate 91% of the eligible black jurors. The Court found the prosecutors' explanations for these eliminations to be pretextual and granted Miller-El federal habeas relief, noting that the prosecutors' selection of the jury along racial lines amounted to "state-sponsored group stereotypes rooted in, and reflective of, historical prejudice."[35] Miller-El was lucky. Most legal claims of this type fail because it is very difficult to prove discrimination in the prosecutor's use of the peremptory challenge. Peremptory challenges are by their very nature subjective; that is, unless it is obviously directed to a specific racial group, the lawyer using a peremptory challenge is not required to state a reason, or "cause," for using it.[36]

Although acts of individual discrimination can be found throughout society,[37] reformists seem more concerned with structural discrimination, institutional and societal, than with individual discrimination. Structural discrimination is discriminatory effects. Unlike individual discrimination, the less-than-favorable, or discriminatory, treatment is not motivated by an antecedent racial animus, and to that extent it is "facially neutral."[38] Structural discrimination can arise from a particular institution's normal operating practices or policies, in which case it is institutional discrimination,[39] or it can come from the accumulated effects or totality of all forms of prior or current dis-

crimination (less-than-favorable treatment) in society, in which case it is societal discrimination.[40] The SAT is an oft-cited example of institutional discrimination. I have attempted to capture the essential reformist charge against the
SAT and other standardized test in the following passage:

> The real culprit in the ... [disproportionately low percentage of black students at
> elite colleges is] overreliance on the SAT and similar standardized tests. Blacks sim-
> ply do not score as well as whites and other groups on these tests. During the twelve-
> year period between 1976 and 1988, the black/white racial differential on the SAT
> declined significantly, going from an average of 240 points to an average of 187
> points. But since 1989, the racial differential has actually widened, even though black
> scores have increased slightly. In 2001, the average point difference was 201 points.
> Worse, the test gap extends beyond the SAT. . . . [I]t appears even before kindergar-
> ten and persists into adulthood.[41]

Like all forms of institutional discrimination, the SAT was not intentionally
designed to discriminate against blacks. It is facially neutral. But its effects are
quite disparate.

Societal discrimination, the other form of structural discrimination, has
been defined by the Supreme Court as "discrimination not traceable to its own
actions."[42] It is, in other words, what Michael Selmi calls "discrimination in the
air."[43] But this is not the only way to define the concept. As Selmi explains:

> Societal discrimination might be defined as discrimination for which there is no
> identifiable responsible party, public or private. It might alternatively be defined as
> discrimination that occurred at some time in the past with an identifiable party that
> is no longer legally culpable because the statute of limitations has run or the effects of
> the discrimination are now too attenuated to trace. . . . [S]ocietal discrimination . . .
> [might include] the lingering effects of past discrimination. The term may also serve
> as a surrogate for identifiable discrimination in the circumstance where a govern-
> mental entity is reluctant to admit or prove its own discrimination. Finally, . . . soci-
> etal discrimination might best be seen as the cumulative effects of multiple acts and
> actors—a combination of all the factors identified above.[44]

I would submit that the latter definition—in which societal discrimination is
defined as the cumulative effects of all forms of prior or current discrimination, including the lingering effects of slavery and Jim Crow—is perhaps the
most coherent. It clarifies the concept in several ways. First, it suggests that
even though societal discrimination focuses on discriminatory effects in the
here and now, these effects may well have begun with an intentional discriminatory act in the past. Second, it makes clear that societal discrimination incorporates the effects of current discrimination. Third, it offers that societal
discrimination is more amorphous than institutional discrimination in that
the former is not tied to any particular institutional practice or policy, although
it can certainly affect what goes on in an institution.[45] Finally, whereas institu-

tional discrimination identifies a particular institution as the perpetrator of the discriminatory effects, societal discrimination, consisting of the cumulative effects of all discrimination in society, past or present, identifies society as the perpetrator. This is tantamount to saying societal discrimination has no identifiable perpetrator, and that, according to the Supreme Court, is why societal discrimination is not subject to legal redress. The problem, in other words, is that societal discrimination is "ageless in [its] reach into the past, and timeless in [its] ability to affect the future."[46] Critical race theory's concept of racial subordination, in contrast, carries no expectation or requirement that one must first identify a perpetrator before bringing a legal action. It does not matter who the perpetrator of racial subordination is—society, institutions, or individuals.[47]

Reformists believe that societal discrimination is a major contributor to disparate resources. Joe Feagin, for example, argues that the capital deficiencies we see in the black community are sustained by societal discrimination, which he calls "systemic racism." These deficiencies, in other words, were put in place by America's historic system of white-on-black oppression, and they are held in place by the continuing power of that system. As Feagin explains:

> The perpetuation of systemic racism requires an *intertemporal* reproducing of a variety of organizational structures and institutional and ideological processes. These structures and processes are critical to sustaining racial inequalities. Reproduced over time are racially structured institutions, such as the economic institutions that embed the exploitation of black labor and the legal and economic institutions that protect that exploitation and extend oppression into other arenas of societal life. Each new generation inherits the organizational structures that protect unjust enrichment and unjust impoverishment (emphasis in original).[48]

Ours is a "totally racist society," Feagin continues, because "every major aspect of life is shaped to some degree by the core racist realities."[49] Self-generating systemic racism includes an assortment of racialized practices, such as the unjustly gained economic resources and political power of whites (see the poker game allegory in the introduction), as well as "white-racist ideologies, attitudes, and institutions created to preserve white advantages and power."[50]

Reformists do provide specific examples of societal discrimination. Leonard Baynes attempts to show how societal discrimination works in housing, that is, how a congeries of discriminatory traditions come together to sustain housing segregation:

> The hypersegregation of African Americans and Latinos is caused by income disparities between African Americans and Latinos, exclusionary zoning practices that limit the quantity of affordable housing in suburban neighborhoods, blatant housing discrimination against racial minorities, and "white flight" from integrated communities. This hypersegregation relegates many African Americans and Latinos to

neighborhoods where work has disappeared and in which transportation options to suburban jobs are either unavailable or unaffordable.[51]

Another discriminatory tradition that contributes to hypersegregation is what Thomas Shapiro calls "asset poverty" among African Americans.[52] Because slaveholders during slavery and employers during Jim Crow prevented previous generations of African Americans from accumulating wealth, blacks today have not inherited the types of "transformative assets" (large assets such as stocks and bonds) that can be used for a down payment on a house. This is but another way of identifying the lingering effects of financial capital deficiencies caused by slavery and Jim Crow.

Shapiro also points out that the absence of transformative assets—the lingering effects of prior racial oppression—adversely affects black education. Without transformative assets, it is difficult for students to pay for college without going deeply into debt, take lower-paying jobs or jobs with fewer hours that do not interfere with classes or studying, and, perhaps most important, grow up in affluent communities with high-quality schools. While most blacks (54%) do not even have sufficient assets to survive at the poverty level for three months if they were without income, only a quarter of white families are this asset poor.[53] In fact, one study shows that "white middle-class families had on average 113 times more financial assets than black middle-class families."[54]

As these illustrations show, most reformists' claims of structural discrimination, whether institutional or societal, are based on findings of statistical disparity. For example, Gary Orfield argues that the statistical distribution of curricular resources in our public schools is too reminiscent of the dual system of education that existed during the days of Jim Crow to be ignored. School districts formulated discriminatory policies during Jim Crow, policies regarding the allocation of educational resources between black and white schools. The effects of these policies linger today because the damage they cause has never been fully repaired. The racial differential created during Jim Crow is with us today. Thus, it is no wonder, Orfield concludes, that today "suburban schools offer three times more high-ability classes than low-ability classes, whereas poor urban schools offer the same number of each of these kinds of classes."[55] This is not simply different treatment; it is less-than-favorable treatment, what the Supreme Court defines as "discrimination."[56]

Statistical arguments are subject to traditionalist Thomas Sowell's charge that statistical disparity does not necessarily equate with racial disparity. Any number of nonracial factors, not the least of which is culture, may explain away the disparities. Reformists have two responses to Sowell's important argument. The first is the analytical device called "intraclass racial disparity," which I developed during my days as a reformist. Intraclass racial disparity is designed to detect race-based disparities in a racial community stratified along class lines; in other words, it attempts to separate racial discrimination from class discrimination. Rather than simply looking at undifferentiated statistical disparity, intraclass racial disparity compares the distribution of racial burdens and advantages class by class, not unlike comparing apples with apples. Thus, in looking at racial disparity against the grid of class stratification, one is able to separate the class element, with which traditionalists are rightly concerned, from the racial element. One finds, for example, middle-class white families have on average 113 times more financial assets than middle-class black families, as just mentioned, and that middle-class blacks experience more employment discrimination than middle-class whites as measured by the number of employment discrimination cases filed by blacks and by the Equal Employment Opportunity Commission (EEOC) on behalf of blacks as well as by the quotidian experiences of middle-class blacks working in high-level jobs.[57] Middle-class black students experience more racism on college campuses as measured by, inter alia, the number of racial incidents reported each year. (The *Journal of Blacks in Higher Education* performs a useful service by running a nationwide tally of these incidents.)[58] Working-class blacks experience more housing discrimination than their white counterparts as measured by the number of U.S. Department of Housing and Urban Development (HUD) investigations. And disproportionately more blacks than whites experience intergenerational poverty in geographically isolated communities (inner city or rural), which cultivate behaviors and values that are both dysfunctional and self-defeating. This "underclass" phenomenon is rarely associated with the white poverty class. There is hardly ever any talk of a "white underclass." Unlike poor whites, who experience class disadvantage, poor blacks suffer both class and racial disadvantage.[59]

The factors that sustain intraclass racial disparity, then, differ from class to class. External factors such as racial discrimination tend to impact the black middle class and working class more directly than they impact poor blacks. In contrast, internal factors, such as teenage pregnancy or criminal behavior, tend to sustain racial disparities in the black poverty class, underclass, and, to a lesser extent, the working class more so than they do in the middle class.[60] These cultural traits, as Brent Staples correctly points out in his essay "A Short History of Class Antagonism in the Black Community," have often been severely criticized by the black middle class.[61] Many of these black critics, such as the actor and activist Bill Cosby,[62] were, at one time, reformists.

The second response to Sowell's argument regarding the usefulness of statistical disparity is that reformists for the most part concede Sowell's point. That is, they acknowledge the difficulty of establishing a "quantitative attribution of causal weight to distant historical events" such that one could not say with certainty that disparate resources are (or are *not*) sustained by societal discrimination, especially the lingering effects of prior racial oppression.[63] For this reason, they do not argue that statistical disparity conclusively constitutes racial disparity. They argue instead that statistical disparity gives rise to a *rebuttable pre-*

*sumption* of racial disparity. Our shameful racist past, our proximity to Jim Crow, and our continuing experiences with racism justify this presumption in the Age of Obama, reformists argue. This evidence, in effect, shifts the burden of proof to doubters, such as traditionalists, to come forward with credible and substantial evidence tending to show the absence of racism or racial discrimination, including the cessation of lingering effects. At the very least, Glenn Loury argues, evidence of the continuation of "past racial injustice is relevant in establishing a general presumption *against indifference* to present racial inequality" (emphasis added).[64] There is no moral or logical basis for "simplistic applications of liberal neutrality that issue in mandates of colorblindness."[65]

Reformists, then, have answered D'Souza's question—whether racism today is potent and widespread enough to sustain disparate resources—by citing multiple episodes of frontstage and backstage racism plus many examples of individual and structural discrimination. The reformists' decision to use the black middle class as the basis for demonstrating the existence of debilitating racism and racial discrimination is quite important; for it involves a class of blacks who do *not* possess the internal liabilities to which traditionalists point as the primary reason for resource disparity in the black community. If race can limit opportunities for the Lawrence Mungins (or individuals like Pat Washington, whom I shall discuss in a moment)[66] of black society, race can surely limit opportunities for working-class and poor blacks, even as the latter also have nonracial issues with which to deal. For reformists, the racial experiences of well-educated African Americans explain the racial gaps in income for persons with a college or postgraduate degree, especially those involving black males (see figures 34–45). Thus, in answer to D'Souza, reformists maintain that race *is* potent and widespread enough to sustain disparate resources.

## 2. Prescription

Reformists prescribe a variety of governmental measures to redress racism and racial discrimination. Race-based affirmative action is the principal reformist prescription. Other prescriptions are equally familiar but less controversial, such as protest marches, economic boycotts, and other tried-and-true civil rights demonstrations. Still others involve vigorous enforcement of and doctrinal changes to extant civil rights laws, government-supported job-training and job-creation programs, and reparations for slavery and Jim Crow. Some reformists prescribe much deeper remedies, such as a new constitutional convention and government-supported child care. This section of the chapter covers most of these prescriptions. For a more detailed and comprehensive discussion, I recommend *The Covenant with Black America*[67] and *Whitewashing Race: The Myth of a Color-Blind Society*.[68] The latter is particularly noteworthy because it deals with the legacy of "disaccumulation" in black America and "accumulation" in white America caused by slavery and Jim Crow. The book also has something to say about current discrimination and proposes more affirmative action, more public money for inner-city schools and job-skills programs, and more employment opportunities. A massive wealth redistribution effort is also on the menu.[69]

The external prescriptions tendered by reformists rest upon an important assumption regarding the role of whites in resolving the American race problem. Contrary to traditionalists (and limited separatists, but very much like critical race theorists), reformists believe white Americans must take an active role in redressing the external factors that sustain disparate resources. Whites, reformists maintain, give present-day meaning and vitality to racism and racial discrimination, especially societal discrimination, by simply ignoring them. Reformists believe that when racial stereotyping is ignored or seen as harmless play, and when racial patterns in education, housing, employment, and the criminal justice system are ignored, disparate resources are sure to continue unabated. Thus, as a first step in resolving the race problem, whites must increase their racial awareness. Both Cornel West and Joe Feagin suggest that educational programs in schools and colleges must teach about the realities and effects of racism and help build interracial relations. The media must also help by stressing our "commonality and collective aspirations" rather than portraying blacks as outsiders.[70]

Joel Kupperman captures the essence of the reformists' position on their principal prescription—racial preferences. Affirmative action, Kupperman observes, is a "timely" rather than a "timeless" prescription.[71] Indeed, it is on this basis that onetime traditionalist Glenn Loury is able to accept racial preferences. Although Loury recognizes the "intuitive appeal of 'blindness,'" he "cannot abide the imposition of abstract strictures of neutrality upon a game in which systematically nonneutral practices have left so many raced and stigmatized outsiders with so few good cards to play."[72] The goal is to have a color-blind society, but we must get there through procedural fairness—"race-egalitarianism before race-blindness."[73] For this reason, reformists, unlike traditionalists, find compelling the distinction between benign discrimination (remedial or inclusionary color-conscious policies) and invidious discrimination (exclusionary color-conscious policies). It is morally wrong, reformists argue, for the government to maintain a "race-neutral" stance while blacks have not been given a realistic opportunity to overcome historic racial disadvantage caused by the government and society. There is, in fact, no race neutrality, let alone equal opportunity or racial fairness, in such a stance, they insist.[74]

Unlike other reformists, Cornel West does not believe race-based affirmative action offers a solution to poverty, which he believes constitutes a large portion of the American race problem. Instead, West embraces class-based affirmative action. He contends that class-based affirmative action is much more redistributive than race-based affirmative action.[75] This does not mean, however, that West opposes race-based affirmative action programs. Indeed, he believes eliminating existing affirmative action programs would be disastrous for blacks because there is no indication that in the absence of such programs white employers would make decisions based purely on merit. Race still matters. Hence for West, a somewhat flawed program of affirmative action is better than no program.[76]

In addition to affirmative action, reformists prescribe vigorous enforcement of extant civil rights laws as well as specific doctrinal changes to make these laws more effective. One major area of concern is employment discrimination law. Reformists propose wide-ranging prescriptions designed to deal both with procedural hurdles that typically arise in the prosecution of employment discrimination cases and with substantive concerns that often make it difficult to win these cases on the merits. For example, prosecuting structural discrimination cases or individual discrimination cases (cases in which the discrimination is face-to-face, person to person) presents myriad procedural problems. These problems arise from the way in which Title VII of the 1964 Civil Rights Acts, the nation's principal employment discrimination law, was originally conceived by Congress and subsequently interpreted by the Supreme Court. A large and recurring procedural problem involves the impotence of the EEOC, the federal agency charged with statutory authority to enforce Title VII. The story of Pat Washington provides a first-person account of the feeble state of the EEOC's enforcement powers.

Pat Washington filed a complaint with the EEOC after allegedly suffering through several forms of sex and racial discrimination from her colleagues in the Department of Women's Studies at San Diego State University (SDSU). She was denied tenure in May 2001 and in July filed a complaint with the EEOC alleging employment discrimination. A year later, the EEOC sent Washington its findings regarding her charge of discrimination. The EEOC informed Washington that it found "reasonable cause" to believe that SDSU had in fact discriminated against her in violation of Title VII. The report suggested (the EEOC could not command) that SDSU reinstate Washington and grant her "tenure, promotion, back pay, and benefits." For the EEOC to tell a complainant that there is "reasonable cause" to support her claim of discrimination is quite unusual. Less than 10% of the nearly eighty thousand complaints filed per year with the EEOC are found to have "reasonable cause."

SDSU did not, however, accept the EEOC's findings. Instead, it dismissed them by claiming that the EEOC case manager (who was a black female) was biased and that the university did not have an opportunity to "tell its side of the story" (even though the EEOC allowed it to respond to Washington's complaint). One would think that Washington's lawyers would have been emboldened by the EEOC's findings. Instead, they backed down from their initial positive outlook on the case. In fact, they "downplayed the significance of the findings." Washington soon realized that her lawyers and SDSU's lawyers wanted the same outcome: an easy settlement. All Washington wanted was to get her job back. After spending six years getting her Ph.D. and another six years "jumping through all the hoops I was told I needed to jump through to get tenure," Washington wanted vindication rather than a settlement. Walking away with a cash settlement would only have meant that both the university and her lawyers would win. SDSU could deny any liability and would be free to continue its discriminatory practices.

What Washington needed most was vigorous lawyering. She did not get it from her lawyers, which is all too typical in complex employment discrimination cases. Nor could she receive it from the EEOC, because it has no enforcement powers against state entities like SDSU. Nor could she get it from the Department of Justice, which, although it does have the power to sue state entities, was "too busy" with bigger lawsuits to get involved with this small-fry case. The EEOC's lack of enforcement power against state entities makes it the subject of ridicule, contempt, and negative stereotyping by Title VII defendants. This point was made clear to Washington during a conversation she had while waiting for a plane at the Oakland airport. As Washington tells it:

> The conversation got around to my tenure and promotion battle. When I mentioned the EEOC reasonable cause finding, my new acquaintance stopped me and said, "Wait. Let *me* tell *you* how the university responded. The university said that the EEOC didn't do a thorough investigation, that the investigator didn't interview the appropriate campus individuals, that they didn't get a chance to present all of their evidence, and that the investigator was biased for whatever reason."
>
> I was stunned. His summary was right on target. When I asked how he knew what my institution had said, he told me that he had worked for the EEOC until retiring a few years ago, and that the response SDSU had made regarding the EEOC findings in my favor was the standard response to a favorable finding for the plaintiff. He then commented wryly, "If the finding is for the university, it's a press opportunity, but if it's for the charging party, then it's a flawed investigation."
>
> Go figure.[77]

To strengthen the prosecution of employment discrimination cases, reformists prescribe several measures.[78] For example, they propose that the EEOC should be given authority to do more than simply attempt to conciliate charges brought against state defendants like SDSU. The EEOC should be authorized to sue state defendants in federal court in the event that conciliation fails. Currently only the U.S. Department of Justice can sue state and local governmental agencies for employment discrimination. In addition, private attorneys are often too incompetent, too greedy, or plainly unethical to prosecute these complex cases.[79] So it falls upon the EEOC to become the primary enforcement agency for Title VII. All it can do now is attempt to facilitate a settlement, or reconciliation, between the parties. But reconciliation typically fails because, without the power to sue, the EEOC is neither feared nor respected by state defendants.

Some reformists have worked out rather detailed economic prescriptions designed to buttress the internal self-help program, described in the next section of this chapter.[80] These prescriptions essentially entail the creation of a government-sponsored employment opportunities program that would include job training and job creation, income transfers, and child care services. Some of these resources would be available on a needs-only-basis rather than on a race-specific-basis.[81] Other reformists would extend this program, albeit without specifying how, to include "housing, food, health care, education," and other basic goods and services.[82]

Joe Feagin strongly believes that a new constitutional convention must also be included in the external prescription. Feagin argues that our current Constitution is defective because it was crafted by a small group of individuals who did not represent the broad sweep of American society. All were white males, and most were overtly racist and slave owners at one time or another. It is not surprising, Feagin notes, that a nation founded on such a constitution would be systemically racist. Thus, Feagin believes that our government should convene a new constitutional convention that would include drafters who are truly representative of the current demographic composition of the nation.[83]

The demand for black reparations is a recent addition to the reformist prescriptive regime. Feagin and other reformists argue that blacks should be given restitution for capital deficiencies created during slavery and exacerbated by Jim Crow. Feagin proposes reparations in the form of wealth transfers, government programs to improve income and education, and the guarantee of representation and participation in the political arena. Additionally, Feagin believes that reparations should include asset-building programs, job training, improved housing conditions, and seed capital for small businesses to restore wholeness to individuals and to communities.[84] Other reformists prefer strictly noncompensatory reparations. Glenn Loury, for example, conceives of reparations in "interpretative terms," that is, as a way to "establish a common baseline of historical memory—a common narrative, if you like—through which the past injury and its continuing significance can enter into current policy discourse." Loury has in mind something like the South African Truth and Reconciliation Commission.[85]

Although reformists believe that disparate resources are primarily sustained by the external factors of racism and racial discrimination, and that, consequently, an external prescription is needed, they do concede that internal factors contribute to the problem. Like traditionalists, they believe that culture can sustain or exacerbate capital deficiencies within the African American community. But, unlike traditionalists, reformists insist that the internal race problem is conditioned by external factors. They place most of the blame on "the racist system" rather than on the backs of blacks, even though they do criticize black culture.

## C. INTERNAL ANALYSIS

### 1. Diagnosis

There is substantial agreement between reformists and traditionalists as to the internal factors that sustain or otherwise contribute to capital deficiencies within the African American community. Family disintegration, poor education, black-on-black crime, babies born out of wedlock, and other self-defeating and dysfunctional behaviors and values are cited by reformists and traditionalists alike. Bill Cosby may have expressed views held by a few black reformists and more than a few traditionalists when, in 2004, he "harangued inner-city parents for doing too little to educate their children. He threw salt in the wound by saying those parents were spending too much on expensive sneakers and not enough on books."[86] But what Cosby failed to do, according to reformist Michael Eric Dyson in *Is Bill Cosby Right?*, is give a complete and accurate account of the problem. Cosby missed the structural barriers that give shape to the black culture he criticized, used racial stereotypes in describing some of these misdeeds, and, in criticizing the way in which young blacks dress, correlated ethical standards with sartorial splendor.[87]

As Dyson suggests in his criticism of Cosby, reformists believe the internal problems blacks face are exogenous. While some traditionalists also believe the internal race problem is shaped by external factors, the external factors they cite—especially affirmative action—are not ones to which reformists would point. Reformists believe that racism and racial discrimination are the chief external phenomena that condition bad behaviors or bad values in the black community. "True," Loury declares, "the so-called underclass in the ghettos of America is behaving badly, in self-destructive and threatening ways. But those patterns of behavior, embodied in those individuals, reflect structures of human development that are biased because of a history of deprivation and racial oppression."[88] Goodwin Liu argues that hypersegregated communities only intensify a sense of privation, which is a breeding ground for black-on-black violence.[89] William Julius Wilson argues that the high percentages of female-headed households, teenage pregnancy, high-school attrition, and incarceration among blacks are due in large part to the lack of employment opportunities for black youth in many cities.[90] The aggregation of capital deficiencies feed into angst, rage, and despair, causing blacks to lash out at others within their own communities. Seeing no hope, many African Americans direct their hostilities against others who are within reach and even more vulnerable than themselves, especially black women.[91]

Reformists believe that the traditionalists' "Cult of Victimology" is too simplistic to adequately describe the internal race problem. They would characterize the problem as a deep malaise within black society. Cornel West provides a very useful description of the problem, insisting that

> the most basic issue now facing black America [is]: *The nihilistic threat to its very existence.* This threat is not simply a matter of relative economic deprivation and political powerlessness—though economic well-being and political clout are requisites for meaningful black progress. It is primarily a question of speaking to the profound sense of psychological depression, personal worthlessness, and social despair so widespread in black America (emphasis in original).[92]

West is using the term "nihilism" in its philosophical sense, meaning a spiritual and cultural voidness, rather than its psychiatric sense, meaning a self-delusion that the world, including oneself, does not exist.

Thus, for West, Loury, and other reformists, the internal race problem is one of black nihilism conditioned by racial circumstances. These circumstances include the historic failure of our society to ensure racial justice, to fully accept the basic humanity of blacks, and to see blacks as "fellow American citizens with problems" rather than as "a problem people." The external forces that condition bad behaviors and bad values in the black community are, in short, the ceaseless assaults on "black intelligence, black ability, black beauty, and black character."[93]

But not unlike traditionalist Bill O'Reilly, at least one reformist, Cornel West, also believes the internal factors that sustain disparate resources are shaped by nonracial external circumstances. West contends that the destructive nature of modern American culture sets a poor example for good behavior and values. Motivated by greed, public officials and corporate America sow the seeds of distrust and pessimism throughout society. Market-driven popular culture (TV, radio, films) "has taken sex, violence, and consumption to a dangerously attractive level, reinforcing a dog-eat-dog mentality, wherein self-destructive methods of violence and abuse of power are condoned to achieve self-gratification."[94]

Like O'Reilly, West also criticizes black leadership. He singles out Jesse Jackson and Al Sharpton (as does O'Reilly), faulting them not because they play the race card too much, as O'Reilly claims, but because they do not play it enough.[95] Contextualizing his view of modern black political leadership in the black ethos, West, unlike O'Reilly, argues that black leaders today are not perpetually "upset about the condition of black America" as were Malcolm X, Martin Luther King Jr., Adam Clayton Powell, and other giants of the civil rights movement. Today's black leaders, West insists, lack anger to fuel "boldness and defiance." Far too many black political leaders today have distanced themselves from a vibrant tradition of resistance and a community bonded together by ethical ideals. West concludes: "Most present-day black political leaders appear too hungry for status to be angry, too eager for acceptance to be bold, too self-invested in advancement to be defiant."[96]

## 2. Prescription

What do reformists prescribe as a solution for the internal race problem they boldly describe? West sets the prescriptive baseline by observing, "The fundamental crisis in black America is twofold: too much poverty and too little self-love."[97] While the government must have a hand in resolving the former,[98] blacks must take the initiative in resolving the latter. Blacks must, in other words, engage in a program of self-help.

Joe Feagin reminds us that self-help is a venerable tradition in black America.[99] Perhaps traditionalists were thinking of this custom when they offered their own prescription of black self-help. I doubt it, because the two prescriptions are quite dissimilar, starting with the meaning of the term "self-help." The traditionalists' concept is taken in the Western or European sense—meaning the "individual"—and therefore has no structure apart from the individual's own initiative. In contrast, the reformists' concept of "self-help" borrows from African American heritage wherein the term has a collectivist quality. It is a group-centered concept that is more complex and more familiar to blacks than the traditionalists' individual style of self-help. Indeed, while reformists give great deference to black heritage, traditionalists, especially black traditionalists, do not. The former are running toward black heritage; the latter seem to be running away from it.[100]

To redress black malaise or nihilism, a disease of the soul, blacks as a group must embrace what West calls a "love ethic." More than mere sentimentality, an ethic of love is heightened spirituality that seeks to generate a sense of agency among the downtrodden by instilling not only love of oneself but also love of others.[101] West's love ethic is similar to traditionalist O'Reilly's call for greater spirituality and less secularism in American society. But, unlike O'Reilly's undirected prescription, West's program digs deep into the black religious tradition—spirituals, fellowship, service to the community as well as reverence for God—to find spirituality. He also draws spirituality from the secular realm: the civil rights movement—protest marches, sit-ins, and the black church as a wellspring of black social and political leadership (Martin Luther King, Adam Clayton Powell, Vernon Johns, and other black civil rights leaders). The source of West's spirituality, in other words, is "authentic blackness." West is preaching the "politics of conversion."[102] This strategy for black self-help would seem to resonate with the black community much more than O'Reilly's.

Other reformists have suggested additional content for a program of black self-help. For example, when I was a reformist I proposed that middle-class blacks work with underclass and working-class blacks to expose them to the behaviors, values, and attitudes necessary for a black person's success in American society. These cultural traits include not only what might simply be called life skills (such as the fundamentals of money management and how to improve employment opportunities) but also middle-class black survival skills (such as how to deal with racial angst and despair, or, in other words, black nihilism).[103]

I also suggested a structure for effectuating black self-help. Rooted in the historic role the black middle-class has played in resolving problems, large and small, in the black community, this structure consists of "institutional" and "household" support—in other words, ad hoc support for black institutions and especially black families. Institutional support envisions, for example, black corporate executives spending some of their working days with inner-city schools or convincing their companies to finance computers or books for such schools or community centers.[104] Institutional support directed at black schools not only will give black students a sense of importance but also will help resolve an external condition that is a holdover from Jim Crow—the scarcity of textbooks. African Americans have even filed a class action lawsuit against the state of California alleging that "textbooks are so scarce at some schools that children often . . . don't have books for homework."[105] This twenty-first-century condition is reminiscent of the substandard conditions in segregated schools established for African Americans during Jim Crow.

Although supporting black institutions is important, helping black households is the primary means of delivering the reformists' notion of black self-help. This is a kind of "adopt-a-family" program in that it envisions middle-class blacks working one-on-one in long-term relationships with less fortunate African American families and individuals. In this arrangement, the black middle class is asked to lay open and coach the behaviors, values, and attitudes of mainstream society plus the techniques of African American survival "in a racist society."[106] For example, middle-class African Americans can help other African Americans, especially young African American males, deal with black nihilism by saying to their racial kin: "You have the right to be angry about centuries of racial exploitation as well as present-day racism and racial discrimination. But you do not have the right to dwell on that anger, to feel guilty about these matters, to suffer low self-esteem, or to react in other self-destructive ways."[107] This black middle-class cultural tradition is sometimes referred to as the "black survival maxim." It would be difficult for a nonblack, however well intended, to have the credibility or moral standing needed to convey such a message to an African American, especially a young one.

Finally, Joe Feagin, who strongly favors external reforms over internal ones,[108] suggests, along with West, that blacks should attempt to strengthen their political voice by building coalitions with other minority groups and with progressive whites. Feagin argues that a national coalition of antiracist organizations, which should include members of all oppressed groups, can prove to be important in the fight against systemic racism. Blacks must be able to understand that such coalition building serves their material interests.[109]

The internal prescription is intended to work in conjunction with the external one. Its ultimate goal, particularly the adopt-a-family self-help program, is to move as many blacks as is possible into position to take full advantage of opportunities created by external prescription.[110] Everyone is to move up the socioeconomic ladder and into the American mainstream. Thus, there is symmetry between the reformists' external and internal prescriptions.

## D. SUMMARY AND REFLECTIONS

Diagnostically, reformists assert that race still matters. But they also maintain that black behavior and values matter as well. Racism (frontstage and backstage) and racial discrimination (individual, institutional, and societal) are the primary external factors that sustain disparate resources, according to reformists. These external factors, in addition, condition a proclivity toward dysfunctional and self-defeating behavior and values (nihilism) among blacks, particularly the black underclass and poverty class, which in turn sustain disparate resources internally. Given these circumstances, reformists believe that the best way to develop resources within the black community is through both external and internal measures. Externally, reformists primarily call for more affirmative action and strengthening extant civil rights laws for middle-class and working-class blacks, and job training, child care, and other economic remedies for the lowest black classes. A family-based self-help program, rooted in the black ethos, is the primary internal prescription.

Reformism offers a complete civil rights theory. All the elements for an external and internal analysis of the American race problem are present, both diagnostic and prescriptive. Unlike traditionalism and critical race theory (as we shall see), the weight between the external and internal is more evenly distributed. The analysis is not skewed in one direction or the other.

The arguments that underpin the reformists' external and internal analyses do, however, vary in strength. For example, the studies demonstrating the existence of racism and racial discrimination plus the plight of middle-class blacks like Larry Mungin and Pat Washington leave little doubt about the existence of racism and racial discrimination. But whether race still matters—whether it is potent enough, even though widespread, to deny opportunities—cannot be answered categorically one way or the other. On the one hand, one can certainly argue that, given the anemic state of our civil rights laws, there is nothing to prevent backstage racists from indulging their tastes for discrimination. Race probably mattered in Larry Mungin's denial of a partnership even though he lost his discrimination lawsuit. The defendant law firm won because of a legal technicality, namely, the burden of proof was placed on the plaintiff,

Mungin. Had the burden of proof been on the defendant, the outcome of the case would have been different. On the other hand, did race matter in Mungrin's or Pat Washington's educational success? Did race matter in the extraordinary educational successes of Barack and Michelle Obama (Columbia undergraduate, Harvard law school; Princeton undergraduate, Harvard law school, respectively)? Perhaps race would have mattered but for the internal drive each demonstrated in achieving their undergraduate and postgraduate degrees. Or maybe race mattered in a positive way. What I am suggesting is twofold: whether race still matters depends on the specific circumstances of each case, and the fact that it has been shown to matter repeatedly is cause for concern.

Traditionalists are right to raise the issue of class. Intraclass racial disparity gives us a more sophisticated way of understanding how race still matters notwithstanding class stratification. Separating racial discrimination from class discrimination, intraclass racial disparity compares the quotidian experiences of blacks and whites class by class: middle-class blacks with middle-class whites, working-class blacks with working-class whites, and poor blacks with poor whites. It posits that one must look *inside* the classes to see the problem of race, that simply looking at class structure per se, comparing, for example, middle-class blacks with poor whites, misses the race problem. Comparing apples with apples and oranges with oranges, one finds disparate resources at every socioeconomic level. Poor blacks are not the only blacks who face capital deficiencies. Other black classes also have deficiencies that are specific to their particular socioeconomic environment. The existence of intraclass racial disparity, then, challenges the traditionalist assumption that the advent of an African American middle class in this post–civil rights period signifies the end of a race problem and the beginning of a class problem.

Finally, intraclass racial disparity offers a response to the suspicion some traditionalists have for the reformists' use of statistics as a basis for calculating racial discrimination. Sowell and other traditionalists argue that disparate resources as measured by statistical disparities do not necessarily establish racial discrimination. To be sure, there is theoretical truth to this argument. The shortage of interested applicants for a particular position can certainly skew the statistics and ultimately skew the allocation of societal resources. But this is less likely to happen when one considers the kinds of jobs that highly educated individuals usually pursue. If one goes to law school, then one is likely to be interested in practicing law at its highest level.

In my view, reformists are demonstrating a degree of reasonableness in treating statistical disparity as a rebuttable presumption, rather than as conclusive evidence, of institutional or societal discrimination. Indeed, the statistical assumption that underlies the reformists' claim of structural discrimination is the very same assumption the Supreme Court uses when it determines the existence of employment discrimination, namely, "*absent explanation*, it is ordi-

narily to be expected that nondiscriminatory hiring practices will in time result in a work force more or less representative of the racial and ethnic
composition of the population in the community from which employees are
hired" (emphasis added).[111] There is remarkable symmetry between this statement by the Court and the statement by Loury, a nonlawyer, that evidence of
the continuation of "past racial injustice is relevant in establishing a general
presumption against indifference to present racial inequality."[112]

Affirmative action is the reformists' main external prescriptive formula. In
their view, affirmative action is the only proven means of remedying racial disparities in such crucial areas as education and employment. Traditionalists, on
the other hand, argue that affirmative action is too high a price to pay for what
they regard as an ill-advised, "cosmic" attempt to even out the distribution of
community resources. I might agree with that argument if traditionalists could
produce an effective alternative to affirmative action. Having failed to meet this
challenge, traditionalists seem content to permit disparate resources to persist
in perpetuity. This would effectively relegate blacks to a kind of second-class
citizenship, which is simply unconscionable. I suspect traditionalists would not
countenance such a position if they were on the bottom. They, too, would be
arguing for affirmative action. Even reformist Cornel West, who has reservations about race-based affirmative action, counters with a substitute. But because there are numerically more poor whites than poor blacks in this country,
West's proposal of class-based affirmative action has never been proven to be
as effective as race-based affirmative action in helping blacks overcome racial
barriers.[113]

There is no doubt, as traditionalists remind us, that the government in a liberal, democratic society must remain neutral on matters of race. That is precisely why reformists believe so strongly in affirmative action. Given the history of racism and racial discrimination in this country and the continued
existence of disparate resources, reformists argue that the government does, in
fact, play racial favoritism. When the government simply does nothing about
racial disparities, it gives tacit consent to the status quo. Benign neglect favors
the existing resource distribution by default. The government, in short, does
not act in a racially neutral fashion by simply taking a hands-off, color-blind
approach.

I see little difference between the reformist and traditionalist understanding
of the internal factors that sustain disparate resources. Both see patterns of social pathology within the black community that limit opportunities. Teenage
pregnancy, drugs, and black-on-black crime are some of the pathologies on
which both reformists and traditionalists focus. Traditionalists describe this
internal problem as a "Cult of Victimology." Reformists describe it as black nihilism. A few traditionalists and all reformists consider the internal problem to
be exogenous, although for different reasons—traditionalists see affirmative
action or secularism as the external conditioning agent, reformists see race as

the culprit. Putting aside these differences, there is remarkable symmetry between reformists and traditionalists on the internal problem. Indeed, Cornel West and Bill O'Reilly, with their mutual criticism of black leadership and deep concern about market-driven popular culture and corporate-driven consumption, could easily hang out together—not a bad idea.

One might ask: If both O'Reilly and West believe that pernicious elements of the American culture—whether secularism, commercialism, or corporatism—are bad for all Americans, how is it that blacks are more adversely affected by these elements than other Americans? Why aren't poor whites falling apart in the same way as poor blacks or other blacks? O'Reilly's answer, I believe, is that black culture is more susceptible than even poor white culture to these "isms" because it has been weakened by victimology, a psychological state peculiar to blacks. West, I believe, would answer that black culture is uniquely susceptible because it has been vitiated by the cumulative effects of racism and racial discrimination, which, in turn, have produced no dearth of self-hatred among blacks. I do not believe these explanations tell the whole story. In other words, I take slight issue with the way in which traditionalists and reformists characterize the internal race problem.

Whether Cornel West's black nihilism, John McWhorter's "Cult of Victimology," or Shelby Steele's integration shock, blacks (particularly inner-city young adults) are seen as a dispirited, crestfallen people, a people mired in "a pervasive spiritual impoverishment." But in numerous instances, defiance and not despair is a more appropriate description. Many blacks who engage in self-destructive behavior seem to be more angry and defiant than spiritually spent or "culturally regressive." This condition, which might be described as racial sensibility, arises from the fact that, unlike other racial minorities, African Americans did not come to this country of their own free will looking for a better way of life. Unlike other black groups—Africans, Caribbeans, and the like—African Americans were enslaved en masse by *this* society. Many slave descendants therefore have, at best, mixed feelings about this country. There is the desire for worldly success, to be sure, but not on the terms set by "the man." These mixed feelings can be manifested in the form of low self-esteem and even self-hate, but they also give rise to angry defiance, which can overwhelm the drive to succeed.

Racial sensibility seems particularly strong among the young. Black youth manifest racial sensibility in such misguided social conventions, studied most assiduously by scholars such as Michael Dyson and Randall Kennedy, as the use of the "revisionist self-denigrating" term "nigga" or the pursuit of "thug life."[114] Disaffected young blacks take the racism they feel and use it to soothe their pain. "Nigga" is used as a term of endearment. It serves the purpose of differentiating friends and other blacks who are "down" from the rest of society. Although a vile term, "nigga" is worn as a badge of honor or defiance. But one wonders whether this attempt to commandeer the word "nigga," nullifying its power to harm, has been successful. The fact is even these "down" African Americans would still be angry if a white person were to use the word.

Thus, I merely wish to suggest that one should not overlook racial sensibility, or angry defiance, as a cultural trait that helps to sustain disparate resources. The late rapper and hip-hop legend Tupac Shakur gave insight into this sociopsychological condition that grips so many young blacks when he said to a white woman who had complained about the language he was using in front of her daughter while attending a public event: "I'm sorry if my language offends you, but it can't offend you any more than the world your generation has left me to deal with."[115]

In addition to the spiritual impoverishment that traditionalists and reformists see and the racial sensibility that I see, there is yet another side to the bad behavior and bad values that inform bad black culture, especially among the young. The terms "ghettoism," "ghettocentricity," and "ghettofabulous" have been used to describe this internal condition. It is the phenomenon of celebrating ghetto life. While previous generations of blacks have denounced ghetto life, and even attempted to burn down the ghettos in the 1960s, the current generation of black youth celebrates this life. Criminal behavior, excessive materialism, disrespect for authority, irresponsible sex, and exaggerated masculinity "all become self-identifying features of an authentic 'blackness' for these young [blacks]."[116] Erin Kaplan further explains this phenomenon in an article that analyzes Bill Cosby's criticism of this dysfunctional side of black culture:

> It doesn't help that Cosby refuses to expand the boundaries of what he's really talking about, which isn't the dereliction of the black poor but something bigger: ghettoism. Ghettoism is about the manners and mores of all black people and how they play to white folks, and it used to be that being deemed "ghetto" was a high insult. But with the explosion and exploitation of hip-hop and thug life, there has been such a mad rush to ghettoism through music, fashion, slang and the like that it has become awfully tough—and more than a little hypocritical—to argue that people living the reality are doing, or being, anything wrong. The promiscuity and materialism that Cosby seems to think are emanating exclusively from the black poor are the raw ore of what I call the American ghetto-industrial complex, a vast array of entertainment-related businesses that includes record labels, movie studies, advertising companies, book publishers and video producers.
>
> . . . [T]oo many poor blacks buy into "defective cultural narratives" that tell them the only way to be authentically black and socially significant is to live poor and in a ghetto. But as [Michael Eric] Dyson says, that's a statement that has the benefit of being true without being informative. Let's be real: The "defective cultural narrative" is not a story that blacks are telling each other, but that the ghetto-industrial complex is telling the world every day. Everybody, it seems, wants to be black. We—and I'm speaking of black folk too—affect the rebel gangsta qualities we attribute to the black poor casually and shamelessly; Simon & Schuster just issued "Hold My Gold: A

White Girl's Guide to the Hip-Hop World," a sprightly sounding how-to book that is nothing less than old-fashioned fetishistic racism dressed up in the thin clothes of modern-day irony. As Dyson says, if we are going to parcel out blame for the blasé acceptance of the black poor and prison-bound, please, let's do it fairly. Surely a celebrity such as Cosby, who has played the game of image all his life, can see the role of the media in this mess.[117]

I am in great sympathy with Michael Eric Dyson, who also observes, "A juvenocracy that thrives on violence, the political economy of drugs, and the culture of the gun must be viewed, in part, as a symptom of economic and racial injustice. It must be seen as a moral surrender of black youth to the seductions or excessive material gratification."[118]

Synthesizing all these cultural critiques, I see three distinct lines of criticism. The first is spiritual impoverishment (as taken from John McWhorter's "Cult of Victimology," Shelby Steele's integration shock, and Cornel West's black nihilism). The second is racial sensibility, or angry defiance (as seen in the political side of hip-hop culture expressed in some of Tupac Shakur's work). The third is thuggery, misogyny, and instant gratification (as brought to light most prominently by Michael Eric Dyson). In short, despair, defiance, and ghettofabulosity are what I see as the negative elements of black culture that help sustain disparate resources.

In my view, reformists owe a debt of gratitude to traditionalists not for the latter's discovery of an internal problem in black America—the Talented Tenth broached this problem long ago—but for having the courage to bring the problem into mainstream civil rights discourse. Although traditionalists do not connect the internal problem to race, there is little disagreement between them and reformists concerning the existence of a cultural problem. That agreement by itself is an important convergence of thought in post–civil rights theory.

There is also general agreement between traditionalists and reformists as to what to do about the cultural problems within black society. Both prescribe black self-help. Despite this basic symmetry, there are prescriptive differences between the two groups. The reformists' black self-help program (adopt-a-family) is much more developed and ambitious than the traditionalists' view of black self-help ("just-say-no"). Unlike traditionalists, reformists draw upon black institutions and cultural traditions for material and spiritual support.[119] Middle-class African Americans are asked to work one-on-one with less successful African Americans to "coach" the behaviors, values, and attitudes that are necessary for a black person to succeed in "a still racist America." The question is whether today's black middle class has a level of commitment to the cause of racial justice that will inspire a substantial number to adopt a family. This raises the delicate question of black solidarity in the Age of Obama, a question that sits at the center of the next post–civil rights theory.

## Chapter 4

# LIMITED SEPARATION

## A. OVERVIEW

IN HIS MEMOIR, *Colored People*,[1] Henry Louis Gates Jr. reminisces about a rich personal and communal life growing up in a pre-integrated community in West Virginia. Teachers cared about their students, families functioned well, and blacks looked out for one another. Things changed after integration. The black high school and the corn mill, where many blacks worked, were shut down. They were considered "too segregated" and, hence, illegal under the ruling in *Brown v. Board of Education* and its progeny.[2] With each closing of a black institution, the community's "womblike colored world" disappeared. Forced to jettison the identity that had bonded them together for so long, young blacks found it difficult to adapt. Integrated schools were alien and unwelcoming, jobs became hard to find, and sharp divisions developed in the black community of Piedmont, West Virginia. None of the blacks wanted segregation, but none regarded their high school or the corn mill as "segregated." As the 1970s unfolded, blacks began to realize that the community's "most beloved, and cementing, ritual was doomed to give way."[3] What was lost was a "colored world [that] was not so much a neighborhood as a condition of existence."[4] To Gates and other blacks in this sweet community, "the soul of the world was colored"—the mainstream was black.[5]

The virtues of black-mainstream communities have been recognized by none other than Condoleezza Rice, who served as secretary of state and national security adviser in the Bush II administration. Born and raised in the segregated South, Rice resents the white-shaped narrative of pre-integrated black communities: "What I always disliked was the notion that blacks were somehow saved by people who came down from the North to march. You know, black Americans in Birmingham and in Atlanta and places like that were thriving and educating their children and being self-reliant and producing the right values in those families and in those communities."[6] One of the best discussions of black values can be found in *The African American Book of Values*, a collection of writings on the black experience edited by Steven Barboza.[7]

This awareness of the benefits derived from black-mainstream communities provides the inspiration for a post–civil rights theory called "limited separation." This theory envisions voluntary racial isolation that is *racially nonexclusive* and available to all racial groups, not just to blacks. Thus, limited separation is not total separation or racial segregation. Total separation is a form of racial isolation that, although voluntary, is racially exclusive. It denies whites access to black institutions, cuts blacks off from the rest of the world, and, as such, is an illegitimate form of racial isolation. Marcus Garvey's return-to-Africa campaign in the early twentieth century is one form of total separation; the Nation of Islam's call for a black nation within a nation created out of five southern states is another expression of total separation and, hence, an illegitimate form of racial isolation. Groups other than blacks, such as Native Americans on casino-rich reservations and the Amish in pastoral communities, practice their own brand of total separation. Although Americans seem to accept these forms of total separation, limited separatists deem them to be illegitimate because of their exclusionary features.[8]

Like most Americans, limited separatists also regard racial segregation to be an illegitimate form of racial or ethnic isolation. Racial segregation is government-enforced racial isolation that has the intent and effect of disadvantaging and stigmatizing blacks. This form of racial isolation is nothing less than racial bullying by the government. It gives the government license to tell blacks where they can go and what they can do, treating them as second-class citizens. Although it is racial isolation, limited separation is not racial segregation. As Justice Clarence Thomas has noted, "Racial imbalance is not segregation."[9]

In the context of the African American community, limited separation consists of "cultural and economic integration" among the black classes.[10] In other words, "African Americans of all socioeconomic classes com[e] together as financiers, entrepreneurs, employees, and customers."[11] Limited separatists believe that such intraracial integration is "necessary for economic independence for African Americans as individuals, as families, and as communities."[12] Thus, as a post–civil rights theory for African Americans, limited separation's fundamental idea is that African Americans should be allowed to come together for the collective goal of establishing a nurturing and self-supportive environment within a larger, racially hostile or racially indifferent environment. This will enable blacks to achieve racial justice without relying on a governmental rescue or the kindness of whites, and without suffocating individual autonomy in the process.[13] Limited separation gives blacks a choice between living and working within black communities and institutions or living and working within white or other nonblack communities and institutions.

Limited separation has a spiritual side, called "Black Liberation Theology." BLT, as it is sometimes called, received a great deal of public attention during the 2008 presidential campaign when it was revealed that then-Democratic presidential candidate Barack Obama had been a longtime member of a black church in Chicago that practices BLT. Obama quit the church after racially charged remarks by his former pastor, the Reverend Jeremiah Wright, were made public and made an issue by his political opponents. Reverend Wright was a disciple of the Reverend James Cone, who founded BLT in 1969. In a

2005 interview, Cone stated that he "sees God as concerned with the poor and the weak," and the gospel as "identical with the struggle of blacks for justice." He declared that BLT combines the teachings of Martin Luther King (an oppressed people must love their enemy) and Malcolm X (an oppressed people must love themselves). BLT holds that it is possible to be "unapologetically black and Christian at the same time." It was the failure of the white Christian church in the 1960s to embrace these teachings that gave rise to BLT.[14]

In sum, limited separation offers a kind of "black nationalism." It signifies racial solidarity but without nation building, as the term "black nationalism" often suggests.[15] In discussing the external and internal dimensions of limited separation, this chapter will focus on its secular rather than its spiritual side.

## B. External Analysis

### 1. Diagnosis

One central claim of limited separation is that a principal reason blacks continue to suffer resource deficits so long after the end of Jim Crow is because society, including blacks, has placed too much faith in racial integration or assimilation. Designated the chief vehicle for the delivery of racial justice in our post–civil rights society, racial integration, limited separatists insist, cannot carry (and, indeed, has not carried) the full weight of that struggle. Limited separatists offer several arguments in support of this assertion. For those in a hurry, here is a cursory overview.

Limited separatists strongly believe that it is simply not within the self-interest of whites to cede power or to otherwise disadvantage themselves to help blacks. No amount of "we-are-all-Americans" rhetoric is going to change this very human condition. Somebody has to be on the bottom—better them than us. Given human nature, limited separatists continue, it is not difficult to understand why racial discrimination is part of the quotidian experiences of so many blacks who work or live within racially integrated settings. Limited separatists also contend that racial integration depletes scarce resources from black communities by encouraging the exodus of stable families and talented individuals. They argue, in addition, that within racially integrated institutions, blacks constitute a "society of one," a stranger in racially integrated settings. Finally, racial integration demeans blacks by judging them by "white" standards. This last argument is a good place to begin fleshing out limited separation's external diagnosis.

One of the principal problems with racial integration, limited separatists argue, is that it diminishes black Americans by insisting that they "be like" white Americans rather than just be themselves—"unapologetically black." The point limited separatists are making, I believe, is simply this: no one can accomplish anything for himself or herself while trying to be someone else. It is difficult for blacks to be themselves while in hot pursuit of racial integration because racial integration is not racially neutral; it is not color-blind. American color blindness is a myth. "When Americans think of 'color blind,' they see white, not black or even monochrome."[16] White values constitute the "'default' cultural standard" in American society. As examples, limited separatists point to situations in which there is racial conflict in matters ranging from the prevailing standard of beauty (blond vs. ebony) to the role racism plays in explaining African American disadvantage. The mainstream American culture usually resolves these issues in favor of white values and not African American values, limited separatists maintain. John Brown, for example, is viewed in the mainstream American culture as a nefarious type—"sadistic" or "insane," even a "terrorist."[17] This view of the slave abolitionist, who was captured at Harpers Ferry and later hanged, overshadows the African American perspective captured in David Reynolds's book *John Brown, Abolitionist*,[18] in which Brown is portrayed more sympathetically, in other words, as a savior and one of the few nonracist whites in America during the antebellum period. Although some black abolitionists were wary of Brown's proclivity toward violence, most blacks, whether enslaved or not, saw him as a visionary: "I John Brown am now quite *certain* that the crimes of this *guilty land will* never be purged *away*, but with Blood"[19] (emphasis in original). Ralph Waldo Emerson and Henry Thoreau were among the few whites who held a positive view of Brown.[20]

In Don Quixote fashion, African Americans, limited separatists assert, have invested an inordinate amount of energy pursuing racial integration's imaginary promise of racial justice. Blacks still suffer disparate resources decades after racial integration received the government's and society's imprimatur. But could the problem be that there has not been enough racial integration?

The fact is, post–civil rights America remains largely segregated. Supreme Court justices Ruth Ginsburg and Stephen Breyer have noted the prevalence of de facto segregation in our public schools. Referring to data for the years 2000–2001, the justices observed that "71.6% of African-American children and 76.3% of Hispanic children attended a school in which minorities made up a majority of the student body."[21] Similarly, Sheryll Cashin argues in *The Failures of Integration* that housing segregation is ubiquitous in our society.[22] She offers several explanations for this condition: "integration exhaustion" among blacks; the premium whites place on homogeneity; racial steering by the real estate industry; private institutional practices; and public policy choices made by the federal government throughout the twentieth century. As to her first explanation, Cashin believes that African Americans are reluctant to move into neighborhoods without a significant black presence—a critical mass—because of the hostilities they may faced in being "pioneers." Cashin also speculates that the premium whites place on homogeneity stems from the fact that whites are, and have been, the dominant group in American society. Those in power often fear losing power. Such fear, Cashin argues, motivates whites to value homogeneity strongly. As she notes, "Whites are less likely than blacks to want to live in diverse neighborhoods."[23] Racial steering, Cashin's third explanation, occurs when real estate agents, whether consciously or subconsciously, direct (or steer) potential home buyers into residential areas or zones they determine to be best suited for the potential home buyer based on the buyer's race. Although against the law, racial steering, Cashin insists, is widespread. Cashin likewise maintains that private institutional or corporate practices fuel housing segregation by promoting the value of homogeneity. For example, "financial institutions, insurance companies, retailers, and . . . land use planners" all rely upon a certain amount of racial and economic profiling to determine how best to invest in and develop land as a business, according to Cashin.[24] Finally, public policy choices made throughout the twentieth century have promoted homogeneity, Cashin argues. Local governments "fueled the proliferation of new, homogenous communities" through their zoning powers. In tandem, the federal government, through the Federal Housing Administration (FHA), "adopted and propagated the orthodoxy that homogeneity was necessary to ensure stable housing values." The FHA chose to underwrite mortgages, primarily for detached, single-family homes, almost exclusively in white suburban neighborhoods.[25]

Limited separatists have a response to the paucity of integration in America. The answer, they assert, is not more integration but less integration. Racial integration is not a good thing for all blacks. Limited separatists argue that where integration has taken root it too often has had deleterious consequences for black communities and black individuals alike. It has depleted black communities of precious resources. It has ignited an exodus of stable black families and talented individuals who pursue the dream of racial nirvana through integration. Answering the siren song, many blacks are not happy in integrated institutions:

> So much fuss has been made about affirmative action hiring that little attention has been given to what happens to African American employees (whether or not they are beneficiaries of affirmative action) *after* they are hired. A closer look reveals no dearth of racial disparities hounding the African American corporate manager or professional. Loneliness, disaffection, stress and hypertension (or "John Henryism"), "complex racial discrimination" (sophisticated or unconscious racial discrimination frequently accompanied by nonracial factors), and de facto segregation in high-level jobs are the principal problems. . . .
>
> . . . Being the only African American—or, at best, one of only a few—results almost by definition in feelings of loneliness. Such feelings may be heightened by maladroit professional and semi-social interactions with well-meaning white colleagues. An awkward remark ("blacks seem to have a natural ability for basketball") or a racist joke can be very painful. Insulting remarks can cause one to feel relegated to "solitary confinement" on the job.[26]

The story of Lawrence Mungin, the black lawyer with a double Harvard degree discussed in the last chapter,[27] illustrates the treatment scores of African Americans receive in integrated institutions, according to limited separatists. No limited separatist, Ellis Cose strikes the same theme in his book *The Rage of a Privileged Class: Why Are Middle-Class Blacks Angry? Why Should America Care?,*[28] as do reformists Joe Feagin and Melvin Sikes in their book, *Living with Racism: The Black Middle-Class Experience.*[29] Feagin and Sikes recount the poignant story of a young black journalist who committed suicide due to the pressures of being what some have called "a society of one." Leanita McClain was only thirty-two years old at the time of her suicide. Shortly before her death, *Glamour* magazine recognized her as one of the outstanding women in corporate America. But McClain simply could not deal with "the white-normed corporate environment [in which] 'Black women consciously choose their speech, their laughter, their walk, their mode of dress and car. They trim and straighten their hair. . . . They learn to wear a mask.'"[30]

Limited separatists point with alarm to a report on black students attending integrated elementary schools as further demonstration of the "wrath of integration." The report, in relevant part, reads as follows:

> Twelve-year-old Nicole Hayman has some special talents, but none allows her to shine where it seems to matter the most—in the classroom. She can jump rope double-dutch style for long stretches without tangling her feet. She is slightly bigger than her mostly white fifth-grade classmates. . . . But for all her strengths, in the classroom Nicole feels powerless. She frequently stumbles over words when reading aloud. When the teacher allows her white classmates to do things, and not her, she feels that the teacher dislikes black people. "Sometimes, I feel like I can't do anything right," Nicole says. "Sometimes, I feel like a failure."
>
> [Our] survey of those living in some of the communities involved in the *Brown* case found many Nicole Haymans—still haunted by the sense that the world is inherently unequal and views them as worthless.
>
> Jerome Robinson, 12: "I don't like school. [My white teacher] doesn't treat me like a student. She acts like I'm not even here." He's a sixth grader at Alexis I. DuPont Middle School in Wilmington, Del.
> Dilip Nyala, 12: "I don't show respect if I don't get respect." He's a student at DuPont School.
> Stephanie Fells, 11: "I don't really like white people that much. They are just beating black people at everything." She's a student in Farmville.
> Chiriga Howie, 10: "A lot of the white girls just look at me and start staring and whispering. Sometimes, they act like I'm not even there."[31]

These sad voices are hard to ignore despite one's theoretical leaning. They underscore a point Derrick Bell makes in *Silent Covenants*: "For years, advocates assumed that integration, on its own, would improve the educational prospects of black children."[32]

Limited separatists frequently mention the dignity harms (a.k.a. "the black tax") African Americans sustain in integrated settings as further evidence of racial integration's failure. Even middle-class African Americans experience these harms, they contend. As an example, they often tell the story of the African American partner in a law firm who arrived at work early one morning. As he fished for his key card, a young white associate in the firm stood in front of him, blocking the way and asked, "May I help you?" The partner tried to by-pass the associate but was again stopped. Finally the partner identified himself to the associate, and the associate stepped aside.[33] Another story is that of an African American college student who, while walking home one night through a predominantly white neighborhood, was followed by the police and avoided by white pedestrians. The area had been terrorized by a rapist, a white rapist.[34] In another example of racial humiliation, Isabel Wilkerson, Chicago bureau chief for the *New York Times*, was racing through the airport trying to make an appointment when white Drug Enforcement Administration agents began fol-lowing her. The agents followed Ms. Wilkerson onto an airport bus and pro-ceeded to interrogate her. This was pre-9/11. Experiencing this "dignity harm had reduced her from a respected journalist to a suspected criminal."[35] Limited separatists believe that "dignity harms are inevitable in an integrated American society. They are as permanent as taxes. But unlike other forms of taxation, dignity harms discriminate on the basis of race."[36]

Finally, limited separatists maintain that whites do not consider it to be within their material interest to change how racial integration has operated since the end of Jim Crow. Relative to black Americans, white Americans are doing quite well within racially integrated institutions. Blacks do not pose a threat to their control of these institutions or to other material benefits whites derive therefrom. It is simply not in the best interest of whites to give up their racial advantage. And, limited separatists continue, no other group, including blacks, would give up their privileged position if they stood in the same shoes as whites. More than any other factor, that simple fact of human nature ex-plains why integration sustains resource disparity, limited separatists insist.[37]

Limited separatists are quite clear regarding what should be done about this external race problem. They strongly believe that blacks must primarily look neither to whites nor to the federal government but to themselves for help in digging out of a hole that they did not dig. The best place to find a helping hand is at the end of your own arm.

## 2. Prescription

Limited separatists believe that the only prescription that has a proven record of success in redressing the external factors they identify as sustaining dispa-rate resources—overreliance on racial integration as a strategy for achieving racial equality—is the creation of beneficial forms of racial isolation (i.e., lim-ited separation). The Supreme Court must constitutionalize limited separation so that blacks can create institutions of self-support. To get started, blacks would have to accept a certain amount of public funds, which would be used to support educational programs and business endeavors. Thus, the external prescription entails a change in the extant law as well as some federal financial assistance.

The threshold question, as Albert Samuels suggests in the title of his book *Is Separate Unequal?*,[38] is how can racial separation be made legal? How can it be constitutionalized given the dictates of *Brown v. Board of Education*? Limited separatists have, in fact, suggested a way to recognize the constitutionality of beneficial forms of racial isolation. They maintain that black self-help institutions that receive public funds (including funds from black taxpayers) are constitutional under the Equal Protection Clause of the Fourteenth Amendment provided that the clause is read as a vindication of the "nonsubordination principle" rather than the color-blind principle, as it typically is.[39] The nonsubordination principle invalidates racial classifications only if they subordinate and stigmatize a social group. Beneficial forms of racial isolation do not subordinate or stigmatize whites or any other racial group, limited separatists insist. Black businesses, Historically Black Colleges and Universities (HBCUs), black public schools K–12, and similar black institutions do not subordinate or stigmatize any group. Ergo, they should be constitutional under the Equal Protection Clause, limited separatists maintain. This argument is supported by the fact that "it was not until *Croson*, decided in 1989, that a majority of the Supreme Court justices began to consistently interpret the Fourteenth Amendment as a vindication of the color-blind principle, rejecting in the process truly benign racial classifications—those that neither subordinate nor stigmatize."[40]

Under the nonsubordination principle, then, African Americans would be able to use public funds in combination with their own resources to develop community resources similar to what blacks did not only in Henry Louis Gates Jr.'s Piedmont, discussed at the beginning of this chapter,[41] but also in Tulsa, Oklahoma, in Durham, North Carolina, and in other black communities under worse circumstances—namely, Jim Crow. Indeed, limited separatists envision the creation of myriad "T-Towns" across the United States. T-Town is the name given to the Greenwood section of Tulsa, Oklahoma, during Jim Crow. The story of T-Town was told most famously in a 1985 PBS documentary titled *Goin' Back to T-Town*, narrated by David McCullough, the renowned presidential biographer and narrator of *The American Experience* series on PBS. *Goin' Back to T-Town* tells the story of how blacks, who were once enslaved by whites and Indians alike in what became the state of Oklahoma, made Greenwood into one of the most prosperous and self-contained communities in all of America. Blacks of all classes worked and lived together. They experienced worldly success and personal happiness, as much as blacks could under Jim Crow, even after a terrible race riot decimated their community in 1921. In fact, the community grew even more prosperous after the riot, so much so that it enhanced its reputation as "the Black Wall Street."[42]

But whereas the T-Towns established during Jim Crow were completely self-sustaining, that would not be possible today, limited separatists believe. Capital deficiencies in black America are so great and society so much more complex today that federal financial assistance is needed to help blacks help themselves. For example, providing financial assistance to black businesses, Timothy Bates observes, would help black entrepreneurs create new businesses within the black community beyond the myriad "mom-and-pop" shops (such as beauty parlors and barbershops) that have historically been a steady source of the business activity in the black community. Set-aside programs or other forms of federal financial assistance, Bates argues, would enable black-owned businesses to get a toehold in construction, wholesaling, high-tech, and emerging businesses. Federal financial assistance would also help black businesses broaden their markets citywide, statewide, nationwide, and even internationally. Always, though, the money comes back into the black community where entrepreneurs retain their home bases, live, and shop.[43]

Establishing limited separation as an official post–civil rights policy also means that African American students attending public schools would be given the *option* to attend an integrated school or a "black" school. The latter is in reality a predominantly black school, because limited separation does not permit total racial exclusion. As the internal prescription discussed later in this chapter will show, other racial groups can establish cultural institutions as well, provided that they adhere to certain conditions.

Although publicly financed, black public schools established under limited separation would operate very differently from today's de facto segregated schools. As Justices Ginsburg and Breyer have observed in describing the latter, "Schools in predominantly minority communities lag far behind others measured by the educational resources available to them. . . . However strong the public's desire for improved education systems may be, . . . it remains the current reality that many minority students encounter markedly inadequate and unequal educational opportunities."[44] In contrast to these failing schools, limited-separate public schools would be patterned after successful black private, or "independent," schools, many of which are associated with the Council of Independent Black Institutions or the Institute for Independent Education. These institutions, which grew out of the black educational activism movement of the 1970s, stress academic excellence and African American heritage in the education of black students.[45] Limited-separate public schools, it is urged, would be separate *and* equal. In other words:

> They are "separate" rather than "segregated" as they are chosen by African Americans because of the quality of their educational programs rather than imposed on them by default; because they are controlled by African Americans rather than

whites; because they have educational programs tailored to the special needs of African American children rather than to those of children in general; and because they educate and nurture African Americans without subordinating or stigmatizing white children. They are "equal" because their academic programs are first-rate and they are funded adequately.[46]

Limited separatists also insist that their schools, unlike de facto segregated schools, would have parental and community involvement, strong leadership, prepared and committed teachers, and a comprehensive curriculum. These schools, they argue, would look to parents and the community for both spiritual and material support; to principals to take the initiative in identifying and articulating goals and priorities, and to select the staff, evaluate teachers, and perform other leadership duties; and to teachers (most of whom will be African American) to "understand the needs and conflicts the children face . . . [and to] have the ability to infuse African American children with pride through positive reinforcement and high expectations of academic and personal excellence."[47] Rather than adopting an Afrocentric curriculum, these schools would teach "traditional Eurocentric philosophies and ideas, in addition to knowledge about the culture and heritage of all ethnic minorities in this country."[48] Although a private school, Marva Collins Westside Preparatory School is an example of this type of limited-separate school. Founded in Chicago's inner city in the 1970s, Westside Prep teaches classical literature in addition to black literature. Racial solidarity and pride are built around strong parental involvement, black heritage, high academic expectations, self-esteem, morality, and perseverance. Academic achievement is the rule rather than the exception.[49]

Some limited separatists would, however, strongly emphasize an Afrocentric curriculum.[50] They have in mind a school less like Marva Collins Westside Prep, with its Eurocentric core curriculum, than a school like the African American Academy in Seattle. The latter's mission is "to meet the needs of African American and all children, providing them with an academic and African-centered education: nurturing them, in order to meet their emotional needs, while helping them to develop positive social and cultural skills which will enable them to become leaders of tomorrow. Instruction at the Academy places an emphasis on the history, culture, and heritage of African and African American people."[51] The school operates upon the Seven Principles of Nguzo Saba, which "have their roots in a rich African cultural history: UMOJA (Unity); KUJICHAGULIA (Self-Determination); UJIMA (Collective Work and Responsibility); UJAMAA (Cooperative Economics); NIA (Purpose); KUUMBA (Creativity); and IMANI (Faith)."[52]

Whether Afrocentric or Eurocentric, limited-separate public schools would have a common goal: academic excellence. Indeed, it is wrong to suppose that academic excellence is not the primary goal of Afrocentric schools. The African American Academy states that its "primary goal" is academic excellence. More important, this K–8 school reports that it has, in fact, achieved its goal, that a student body that is 99% nonwhite has "produced test scores 'higher across all grade levels in reading, writing and math.'"[53] These results would not be possible without a degree of pluck among the parents and students. Limited separatists insist that blacks themselves have an indispensable role to play in resolving the American race problem.

## C. Internal Analysis

### 1. Diagnosis

The limited separatists' internal critique is, for the most part, coextensive with the reformists' internal critique. "Black nihilism"—what reformist Cornel West defines as "the profound sense of psychological depression, personal worthlessness, and social despair so widespread in black America"[54]—is the primary internal factor sustaining disparate resources. In addition, both groups of post–civil rights theorists connect black nihilism to external conditions, but not to the same ones. Limited separatists do not deny the influence of racism and racial discrimination on black culture, and to that extent they are consistent with reformists. They then go on to connect black nihilism to white self-interest, the treatment of blacks in integrated institutions, and society's color-blind rhetoric that blames blacks for the lack of racial progress. I begin with the color-blind rhetoric.

Society's pervasive rhetoric of color blindness, limited separatists argue, contributes to black nihilism because it measures civil rights success "by the extent to which society transcends race-consciousness."[55] Given the death of Jim Crow, blacks have only themselves to blame for their problems.[56] Unfortunately, limited separatists continue, many African Americans have imbibed this narrative and, as a result, think less of themselves and less of other blacks with each failure of the race. Fed by white self-interest, white ignorance, and white racism, the narrative, limited separatists insist, leaves blacks with a kind of collective depression. This depression is so widespread among black students that one black educator described it as a "crisis of self-hatred."[57]

Additional conditions for black nihilism are created when blacks are required to fit into the good ol' boy network in integrated institutions, limited separatists maintain. They argue that the requirement to fit in is considerably more onerous than the normal amount of conformity imposed on all persons climbing the corporate ladder. Fitting in is more onerous for blacks than for whites or nonblack minorities because the jump from black to white is greater than the jump from yellow to white or brown to white, limited separatists argue. Phenotypically and sociohistorically, blacks are farther from whites than any other racial minority.[58]

It is also argued that the requirement to fit in undermines the essential claim of black equality—the hope, the desire, indeed, the expectation that blacks will be recognized as the true equal of whites. When blacks are made to understand that their promotion or success in predominantly white institutions depends on the extent to which they are perceived to be "like whites" or at least not a threat to whites, limited separatists contend, the message is clear: blacks are being judged on the basis of white standards. How demeaning is that? they ask. According to limited separatists, when racial integration operates in this way, which is most of the time because of human nature, it "begets a low-grade or second-class equality for African Americans."[59] Other civil rights theorists who could not be described as limited separatists have come to the same conclusion. "At best integration demean[s], compromise[s], [and makes African Americans] eternally dependent," insists John Edgar Wideman.[60] Similarly, Henry Louis Gates Jr. notes the detrimental psychological effect integration has visited upon many blacks. African American attitudes about skin tone and hairstyles demonstrate the extent to which African Americans associate positive qualities with "whiteness" and negative qualities with "blackness."[61] In short, limited separatists maintain that black nihilism is a psychological state that results in part from the manner in which blacks are treated in integrated institutions.

In addition to the color-blind rhetoric and the maltreatment of blacks in integrated institutions, white self-interest, limited separatists urge, also conditions black nihilism. Most whites act not out of racism but out of a perceived self-preservation, limited separatists insist. Fearful of losing their competitive advantage over blacks and other racial minorities or wishing to acquire greater racial advantage, white Americans in all social classes are reluctant to disadvantage themselves for anyone, blacks included. For example, forced integration may be beneficial to black students, but it is not going to happen because it disadvantages white students. Black educational interests are secondary to the educational interests of white students. Limited separatists wish to make the point that it is difficult for a black student to feel good about herself knowing that in her educational experience white interests trump black interests. Limited separatists have a plan for dealing with this problem.

## 2. Prescription

Despite their severe indictment of integration, limited separatists have not abandoned integration as a partial prescription for the American race problem. The reason, I believe, is because racial integration is working for *some* African Americans. That seems reason enough to retain it as a strategy to maximize individual success and happiness. Indeed, limited separatists seek to create choices for African Americans.[62] Racial integration is one option; limited separation is another. The challenge for this unique group of civil rights theorists is to convince blacks of the value limited separation has to offer. This endeavor consumes much of the internal prescriptive analysis that one finds in limited separation.

If, as Wendy Brown-Scott insists, racial integration and color-blind policies prevent "both individual African-Americans and African-American communities and institutions from being accepted as equal partners in the struggle for racial justice," then, limited separatists argue, African Americans should not hesitate to pursue a different strategy.[63] Such a strategy is one in which blacks, in effect, create their own civil rights by strengthening institutions within the black community. The black church, which historically has been the black community's most powerful resource, can be the fulcrum on which such institutions are strengthened. In his article "The New Agenda of the Black Church,"[64] Lloyd Gite explains how the black church, in addition to providing spiritual guidance, could enlarge its traditional role as resource developer, which, in turn, could make jumping from chocolate to vanilla unnecessary. Because the black church is one of the most creditworthy institutions in the black community, it is positioned to provide credit or collateral for start-up businesses. Gite notes that "'90% of all black giving is channeled through the church,' making it the one enduring institution in low-income black communities with the ability to secure major credit."[65] Gite also observes that some black churches have already established microloan programs that secure loans from larger financial institutions to invest in small business entrepreneurs in the black community. This method of self-sufficiency can be replicated in black communities across the country, limited separatists believe. Here is how. As a condition for receiving financial assistance through black churches, black entrepreneurs would have to agree to maintain a significant business presence within the community (even after expansion into other markets) and to continue to live in the community. Limited separatists want to provide incentives to reverse the exodus of resources from the black community that has marked the post–civil rights era. When stable, middle-class black families and skilled individuals leave black communities for white communities, they take with them financial and human capital. Keeping middle-class families and jobs in the black community builds community cohesion, strengthens racial identity, and augments intragroup support.[66]

Long underfunded and frequently ridiculed by some traditionalists as inferior institutions that "award Jim Crow degrees that do not meet the standards of the average traditionally white colleges,"[67] HBCUs also play an important role under limited separation. These institutions of higher education continue to occupy a key place in African American communities long after Jim Crow's demise.[68] Limited separatists contend that a report by the Carnegie Commission on Higher Education issued just after the end of the Jim Crow era still holds true today:

The Colleges founded for Negroes are both a source of pride to blacks who have attended them and a source of hope to black families who want the benefits of higher learning for their children. They have exercised leadership in developing educational opportunities for young blacks at all levels of instruction, and, especially in the South, they are still regarded as key institutions for enhancing the general quality of the lives of black Americans.[69]

Thus, the significance of HBCUs extends far beyond their local communities.

In addition to developing economic and educational resources, limited separatists envision buttressing black political power through the creation of black political action committees (PACs) and the establishment of cross-racial political coalitions. Black PACs would

> operate as other political action committees do and in conjunction with them. It would be similar to the Susan B. Anthony List, which funnels money to both Democratic and Republican candidates who support abortion rights and other women's interests, the Jewish federations that provide financial support to local and national politicians who take pro-Jewish stances, and GOPAC, an interlocking network of political action committees created by Newt Gingrich that raised money and refined a political ideology that sowed the seeds of the Republican [Party's rise during the 1990s].[70]

Financed mostly by African American businesses and wealthy individuals, such as Oprah Winfrey and Bill Cosby, black PACs would not only support African American candidates for office but also fashion African American political ideology and strategy, including finding ways to "influence white candidates and office-holders at all levels."[71]

Limited separatists stress the nonexclusivity of their theory. Although designed specifically for African Americans, limited separation is applicable to other groups, including white men, women, and homosexuals. When writing about limited separatists many years ago, I developed a three-prong test that could be used to determine eligibility for limited separation. The first prong requires the group employing limited separation to demonstrate a need to create a supportive environment free of debilitating racial disadvantage. For example, African American law students on a predominantly white college campus shaken by racial turmoil or racial insensitivity would be able to justify the establishment of BALSA, a black American law student association found in most major law schools, on this very ground. In contrast, African American law students attending Howard University Law School would not be allowed to establish a BALSA; because Howard is the leading historically black law school in the nation, black students have the home court advantage there.[72] The second prong requires institutions that operate under limited separation to grant access to individuals from outside the group, so long as these individuals are willing to support the institution's mission, which, for black institutions, is to tend to the special needs of African Americans. Thus, white law students would be permitted to join BALSA under this condition.[73] The final prong permits a limited-separate institution to deny access to an individual belonging to another group only when his or her race would destroy the institution's identity. In this case, race would be a bona fide selection qualification "reasonably necessary to the normal operation of that particular [institution]."[74] The bona fide selection qualification (BFSQ) requirement borrows from the bona fide occupation qualification (BFOQ) test that is a well-established concept in employment discrimination law under Title VII of the 1964 Civil Rights Act.[75] If, for example, the addition of more white law students to BALSA would change the character or identity of the organization, these additional students could be denied membership on grounds that race was a BFSQ.[76]

Limited separatists believe this three-prong test is a fair way to strengthen or construct culturally identified, self-help institutions without unnecessarily trammeling the interests of others, both within and outside the institution. The thinking is that African Americans, like other ethnic groups, would benefit from reinvestment in their communities and in themselves. Group solidarity through cultural identity "has provided immigrant groups with a springboard from which to achieve individual success and a certain level of personal satisfaction in American society."[77] Cuban Americans in Miami and Chinese Americans in the many Chinatowns across the country have all done well without obliterating their cultural identity and traditions. Limited separatists believe that African Americans should also be given the option of blending into or standing apart from mainstream society.

## D. Summary and Reflections

Limited separatists offer a complete post–civil rights theory. Externally, they argue that disparate resources persist so long after the death of Jim Crow because society, including blacks, has placed all its eggs in one basket. Racial integration has been anointed the chief vehicle for generating resources within the black community. But racial integration has not succeeded, limited separatists argue, less because whites are racist than because whites, no more or less than other racial groups, are self-interested. It is simply not within the self-interest of whites, collectively or individually, to cede power or to otherwise disadvantage themselves to help blacks. In the cold calculation of self-interest, there is no reason why whites should cede power or privilege. Limited separatists also contend that racial integration depletes scarce resources from black communities by encouraging the exodus of stable families and resourceful individuals. Finally, racial integration has not worked well for blacks in most places where it has been tried. Far from approaching racial nirvana, "integrated blacks" face loneliness, disaffection, and hypertension as they are required to look, talk, and think in ways that are not in conflict with white mores. To resolve these external problems, limited separatists prescribe the legalization of a community-based black self-help program—one that involves the construction of beneficial forms of racial isolation—plus governmental financial assistance for black educational institutions and new businesses.

Internally, limited separatists adopt the reformist diagnosis of black nihilism. Like the latter, limited separatists believe that this sociopsychological problem is conditioned by the external factor of race, that is, racism and racial discrimination. But unlike reformists, limited separatists also argue that nonracial external factors—white self-interest, conformity pressures placed on integrated blacks to be "like whites," and society's blame-the-victim color-blind rhetoric—are even more responsible for conditioning black nihilism. Prescriptively, these post–civil rights theorists insist that cultural and economic integration within black society—that is, limited separation—is the only proven way to effectively counteract black nihilism. This community-based form of black self-help will create or reintroduce culturally defined institutions and traditions of black society from which young blacks in particular can acquire self-respect, a sense of purpose, and spirituality. Although culturally identified, beneficial forms of racial isolation spawned by limited separation, including black schools and black businesses, are racially nonexclusive. Nonblacks can participate in black institutions. More than that, limited separation is available to whites and other nonblack social groups under certain conditions.

Despite its vow of racial nonexclusivity, limited separation is a hard pill to swallow. Many individuals, particularly whites, have a visceral reaction against any form of black separation. Even though other social groups have pursued limited separation—including Italian Americans in Little Italys, the Amish, and women in single-sex schools—there seems to be something about black Americans coming together, even if for mutual support, that some whites find threatening or otherwise unacceptable. This, in itself, is evidence that Americans still have a problem with race, that race still matters. The fact that a large percentage of blacks—perhaps as many as 25%[78]—are unwilling or unable to assimilate is reason enough to take limited separation seriously as a civil rights theory.

By focusing on the unique needs of blacks, limited separation certainly increases the chances for a cultural and economic transformation of the black community. Programs and institutions—such as schools, churches, businesses, and professions—specifically tailored to address the needs of blacks offer the best hope for a successful campaign of self-help. This, indeed, has been the particular strength of the most successful black institution, namely, the black church. It is not unreasonable to speculate that the black church has been the most successful black institution in the history of this country because its focus has not been compromised or diluted by the demands of racial integration.

Unlike other black institutions, such as HBCUs,[79] the black church was left untouched after the demise of Jim Crow. This may be because religious freedom is one of our core constitutional protections.p[80]

Limited separation offers an it-takes-a-village self-help program that is much more complex and ambitious than the it-takes-an-individual self-help program put forth by traditionalists or even the it-takes-a-family self-help program offered by reformists. Clearly, blacks are thinking seriously about the it-takes-a-village self-help program. A large percentage of blacks, some "integration exhausted," have lost faith with racial integration.[81] Black Liberation Theology, discussed at the beginning of this chapter, remains as popular as ever among even middle-class blacks. Limited separation's underlying theme of black solidarity has even made it to the silver screen.

Black solidarity was the theme of a critically acclaimed motion picture, *Akeelah and the Bee*, that appeared in 2006. Famed black actor Laurence Fishburne produced and starred in the movie. *Akeelah and the Bee* tells the story of an eleven-year-old black girl, Akeelah, from a black community in Los Angeles who becomes the cochampion of the National Spelling Bee, sharing the title with an Asian boy from an affluent family in a Los Angeles suburb. Luckily, a few middle-class black families also live in Akeelah's community. One neighbor, a black English professor who teaches at UCLA, helps her study for the competition, but he can take her only so far. She then has to turn to her community for help. Everyone from the mailman to the street hustler helps her learn thousands of words in preparation for the national competition. Her mother, who was widowed when a stray bullet killed her husband on his way home from work years earlier, finds time in her busy schedule to help, as does Akeelah's sister and delinquent brother. The movie's message is clear: it takes an African American village for African Americans to succeed. Individual, Horatio Alger–style self-help is important, as traditionalists maintain. So is family-based self-help, as reformist contend. But both can only go so far. Community solidarity is needed to seal the deal.

The film's message is exactly what limited separatists teach. Community-based self-help is the only logical response not only to the internal race problem (black nihilism) but also to the external race problem (too much racial integration). Limited separatists seem to be suggesting that it will take nothing less than an all-out effort by the black community for blacks to overcome the external and internal race problems, as they define them. Cultural resources will have to be marshaled through collective action to guide and support blacks, especially black youth, who are dispirited about the racial environment into which they were born. Living and working together in the same community, the black classes can create a synergistic force from which all will benefit. Middle-class blacks are key to the success of the program. They bring stability, know-how, wealth, and hope in the form of role models into full view of other blacks. Only they have the credibility to impart the black survival maxim, discussed in the last chapter,[82] to disaffected black youth. When black youth can see role models walking the streets of their neighborhoods, they begin to have dreams that are not only bigger but also reachable.

Although the concept of community-based self-help is not alien to blacks—witness, for instance, not only Piedmont, West Virginia, the Greenwood section in Tulsa, Oklahoma, Durham, North Carolina, and black public schools in the District of Columbia that thrived under Jim Crow,[83] but also the collective action blacks took in the civil rights movement—some blacks who might otherwise be sympathetic to limited separation may reject it. These blacks may prefer a model that emphasizes private over public start-up funds. This is the path taken by one of the most successful demonstrations of limited separation today, which appropriately is located in Harlem, "the spiritual capital of black America." As the late CBS News correspondent Ed Bradley reported on *60 Minutes* in 2006:

> In its heyday during the Harlem renaissance, it was a wellspring of politics, music and art. But over the years, the neighborhood suffered a steady decline and came to symbolize the worst of urban poverty and decay. Today, there's a new renaissance under way in Harlem, with the construction of new buildings, businesses and schools.
>
> One of the people leading the charge is [an African American,] Geoffrey Canada.... [H]is vision, quite simply, is to save children.... His testing ground is a 60-block area in central Harlem that he calls "The Harlem Children's Zone."
>
> The Harlem Children's Zone is an area that covers less than one square mile and is home to some 10,000 children. On the ground, the neighborhood is slowly coming back to life, with newly renovated townhouses standing side by side with buildings that have fallen victim to violence and despair, local businesses next to national chains. But despite all the renewal, nearly all the children live in poverty —and two-thirds of them score below grade level on standardized tests. That's why Canada, a graduate of Bowdoin College and the Harvard School of Education, has claimed this territory as his own and is trying to save it, block by block, child by child.
>
> Canada's ambitious experiment [is to have all his students go on to college]. [He] aims to prove that poor kids from the inner city can learn just as well as affluent kids from the other side of America. He has flooded the zone with social, medical and educational services that are available for free to all the children who live here.
>
> "They get what middle-class and upper middle-class kids get," Canada explains. "They get safety. They get structure. They get academic enrichment. They get cultural activity. They get adults who love and them and are prepared to do anything. And I mean, I'm prepared to do anything to keep these kids on the right track."
>
> ... Classes have a ratio of one adult for every six kids as well as state-of-the-art science labs, a first-class gym, and a cafeteria that looks more like a restaurant. Only healthy food is served here, to help fight obesity.[84]

Canada believes that if he is to succeed, he must save the children's parents first. To accomplish this threshold goal, he established the "Baby College," which is "a nine-week workshop that literally teaches new parents how to raise their kids so that they will enter school ready to learn." Canada posits that "middle-class families know education begins at birth. Poor parents don't know that." Parents are also taught other parenting skills, such as how to discipline their children without using "physical force."[85]

In addition to social services and health care for the students, the Harlem Children's Zone also provides direct financial assistance to families. This financial support is, however, quite limited, such as money to purchase food when family funds run out. Some parents are also referred to adult education classes where they can pursue a GED. Starting in its preschool program, the Harlem Children's Zone opens a $250 college fund for each student and adds to that fund each year thereafter.[86]

Operating the Harlem Children's Zone is not cheap, as one might expect. CBS reports that "it costs $16,000 a year to educate a student at the Promise Academy," one of the charter schools in the zone. Approximately $10,000 comes from the city, while the remainder comes from the school's own coffers. The total budget of the Harlem Children's Zone is about $36 million a year. According to Canada, "Only a third of it comes from the government; the rest comes from private donations." Overall, Canada "has amassed a staggering amount of *private* money—more than $100,000,000—to realize his goal" (emphasis added).[87]

Canada's practical idealism is an exquisite modification of limited separation in that financial support from the private sector is emphasized over taxpayer dollars. Like Canada's construction of the Harlem Children's Zone, the creation of self-supporting black communities will have to begin with outside money. These funds, like Canada's, should be private rather than public to the extent possible because of government interference, inefficiency, and incompetency. I am reminded of the government's mishandling of the relief efforts for Hurricane Katrina but also of the small-business owner's admonition: if a small business wants to stay in business, it must stay away from the government.

Whatever the form (private or public), outside funding is problematic. It often comes with strings attached. These conditions can force black institutions to act in ways that are not within the best interests of blacks. Indeed, it was the fear of "calculating altruism," "dangerous donations and degrading doles," and "conflicting agendas" that caused many African American educators in the postbellum South to passionately oppose the "new philanthropy" that poured into the region from northern industrialists as well as federal and state governments.[88] This begs the basic question of whether blacks ever really exercise self-determination if they rely on outside help. Is that really *self*-help?

If funding is a serious problem facing limited separation, balkanization is not. Limited separation is not total separation. Its three-prong test prohibits racial exclusion. Nonblacks are not excluded from black institutions any more or less than they are excluded from black churches or HBCUs today. In fact, a white student was the valedictorian for the class of 2008 at Morehouse College, one of the most prestigious HBCUs. Black communities formed under limited separation will balkanize America no more than Native American reservations, Little Havanas, Little Italys, and Chinatowns do so today. In addition, integration will not cease to exist; it will coexist with limited separation.

Although limited separation retains racial integration as an optional strategy, it offers no solution for the problems of loneliness, racial humiliation, and limited opportunities blacks face in integrated institutions. What is to become of "integrated blacks"? Unless something is done, blacks in integrated institutions will continue to face racial subordination. Perhaps limited separatists offer no solution here because, given the pull of white self-interest, if not racism, they do not believe any such solution is possible. Indeed, if a solution were possible, there would be no need for limited separation.[89]

One of the most sustained and impressive attacks on limited separation comes from Tommie Shelby. While not denying the absolute importance of black unity as a condition for achieving racial justice in our society today,[90] Shelby rejects limited separation and other expressions of black separatism in favor of a more relaxed form of black solidarity. He endeavors to construct a form of black solidarity that is appropriate for our post–civil rights era. After describing Shelby's argument in greater detail, I will critique it and then speculate on how limited separatists might respond.

Following in the footsteps of Martin Delaney, the "father of black nationalism," Shelby divides the traditional strategies for cultivating black solidarity into what he calls "strong" and "weak" black nationalism. Strong black nationalism, sometimes called "classical black nationalism," is based on the belief that black unity in the fight for racial equality is best achieved by emphasizing not only a distinct black cultural and political identity but also a common language, heritage, and religion that are separate from those of other groups.[91] Familiar expressions of classical black nationalism include Marcus Garvey's return-to-Africa movement in the 1920s, the Nation of Islam's desire to build a nation within a nation using five southern states with the highest black population, and Malcolm X's black power nationalism in which Malcolm "argued that the U.S. government should be viewed as a colonial power in relation to blacks in America and that blacks should oppose this illegitimate control over their communities."[92] Classical black nationalism entails total racial isolation—cultural purity, economic self-containment (not just self-sufficiency), and political autonomy (not just identity)—or, in other words, racial exclusion, total separation. Shelby rejects this form of black nationalism, as do limited separatists.[93]

In contrast to strong black nationalism, weak black nationalism (weak black unity) is voluntary racial isolation that is neither totally isolated nor racially exclusive. It incorporates several diluted, or weakened, forms of nationalism—cultural identity, political identity, and economic identity, or self-sufficiency. Each of these weak nationalisms contemplates some level of interaction with whites and other racial groups. Although these limited nationalisms are typically supported by blacks in the context of "group self-organization," Shelby believes they can be supported by blacks on an individual, or ad hoc, basis and that only one, ad hoc political nationalism, should be pursued by blacks. Thus, Shelby divides weak black nationalism into two broad forms: group self-organization and individual, or ad hoc, solidarity. Both forms of solidarity can be expressed culturally, politically, or economically.[94] Limited separation is about black communities, and for that reason, it falls within the group self-organization category

Shelby rejects all forms of black nationalism with the exception of ad hoc political nationalism. He does so on the basis of a philosophical belief in what he calls "pragmatic nationalism." This is "the view that black solidarity is merely a contingent strategy for creating greater freedom and social equality for blacks."[95] More important, pragmatic nationalism argues "against the familiar claim that it is necessary and politically useful for blacks to develop a positive shared identity—to collectively define a group-affirming conception of blackness."[96]

In addition to this general indisposition toward racial identity, or "essentialism,"[97] pragmatic nationalism is responsive to what Shelby terms the "collective action problem." This problem rests upon the view that intraracial differences of class, culture, gender, and religion undercut any attempt to achieve robust black identity and unity in post–civil rights America.[98] Shelby notes that "African Americans have been able to improve their socioeconomic position, sometimes quite substantially, despite continuing racial barriers and sometimes with the help of affirmative action and minority set-aside programs. Although anti-black racism negatively affects all blacks, its specific impact on blacks' life prospects can vary considerably—in scope, degree, and kind—across different sectors of the [black] population."[99] Proceeding from the philosophical perch of pragmatic nationalism, Shelby sees fatal flaws in classical nationalism (including its most diluted form, black power), limited separation (weak nationalism in its group self-organizational form), and ad hoc solidarities based on cultural and economic nationalism (weak nationalism in its individual form). Each of these nationalism is essentialistic, and each founders on the shoals of the collection action problem. Thus, in Shelby's view, ad hoc political nationalism is the only expression of black nationalism that can survive the realities of black life in contemporary American society—namely, the manifold stratifications within contemporary black society, particularly the self-interests of well-to-do blacks.[100]

It is necessary to delve deeper into Shelby's embrace of limited political nationalism and rejection of limited separation. According to Shelby, "concerted action as a political strategy to uplift or resist oppression" is the only type of unity blacks are capable of achieving these days, provided that it is done on an ad hoc basis.[101] He argues that it is simply not in the best interests of well-to-do blacks, especially affluent blacks like Oprah Winfrey and Michael Jordan, to embrace anything more than an ad hoc political solidarity. Political unity, Shelby emphasizes, is driven by individual initiative rather than by "institutional autonomy."[102] Hence, his theory of ad hoc political nationalism envisions "trans-institutional black solidarity—a form of group unity that does not depend on organizational separation but rather extends across social organizations within which blacks (could) participate."[103] Blacks will only unite on these terms, Shelby contends, to fight for racial justice. Why? Because this is the one thing in which all blacks have a stake. Regardless of class or gender, blacks are adversely affected by racial injustice—"the stigma of race and racial inequality"[104]—albeit to different degrees. Thus, Shelby presents his theory of ad hoc political nationalism as an "emancipatory tool"—a device that is needed in the protracted struggle for black freedom and equality.[105] Black political unity is "a joint commitment on the part of individual blacks to maintain solidarity with one another regardless of the racial composition of the political organization in which each participates."[106]

To illustrate how his theory of black political solidarity might work, Shelby points to the Congressional Black Caucus (CBC). He assets, "Though members of the CBC form only a small minority in a white-dominated legislative body, their unity with one another and with other black citizens enables them to influence federal legislation and to ensure that black interests are not ignored. They work individually, together, and with other egalitarians in Congress to push for full employment, raising the minimum wage, . . . tax cuts for low-income families, and other measures that advance the causes of racial and economic justice."[107] Of course, a limited separatist would ask, how effective has the CBC been in creating beneficial legislation specifically for blacks? If ad hoc black political solidarity was at work in the election of President Barack Obama, it remains to be seen whether that form of racial solidarity is sufficient incentive for the president to push for legislation that will benefit blacks specifically.

Shelby's philosophy of pragmatic nationalism, as we have seen, rejects limited separation's organizational-based program of black self-help on grounds that it is essentialism and cannot resolve the collective action problem—such as, middle-class blacks will not move back to predominantly black communities because these communities tend to have "high concentrations of poverty."[108] Yet Shelby concedes that "maintaining some black-only unity or black-controlled organizations is still useful and has its place within the larger social reform effort."[109] This is a bit puzzling, for one would think that pragmatic nationalism embraces traditionalism's it-takes-an-individual approach to black self-help. But Shelby insists that it does not. "Pragmatic nationalism," he writes, "is not a group-undermining form of 'liberation individualism.'"[110] Perhaps, then, pragmatic nationalism would accept reformism's adopt-a-family strategy. Shelby seems to suggest this when he notes that "it is imperative that more-affluent blacks extend special concern to the least advantaged."[111] On the other hand, the adopt-a-family prescription relies on racial identity for its implementation. Although not organizational, this may be too much group identity (too much "blackness") to suit pragmatic nationalism. The fact is, Shelby seems to be uncertain as to how much blackness is necessary for black unity to succeed, even on an ad hoc basis in the political realm. Reformists believe a lot of black identity is needed (namely, at the group family level); limited separatists insist more than that is needed (namely, at the group organization level). This highlights one of several problems inherent in Shelby's notion of black unity.

Pragmatic nationalism, as conceived by Shelby, downplays the importance of "a positive shared identity" for black success.[112] Limited separatists and reformists like Cornel West would argue that this may be well and good for the striving black faculty and students at Harvard (where Shelby teaches) and other elite universities, but it is not an antidote for the internal problems that plague most of black society. In fact, a positive shared black identity is precisely the type of identity young blacks need to fight black nihilism.[113] Furthermore, group identity, whether at the institutional or family level, is not only part of the black ethos; it is also part of the heritage one finds in white ethnic groups. Group identity has, in fact, played an important role in the success of America's white ethnic groups.[114] Although today it may be less important to some members of ethnic groups that have assimilated into the American mainstream, identity remains an important dynamic in the lives of America's struggling immigrants. For example, Latinos coming across the southern border share a strong racial identity even as they embrace the opportunities the country affords. Why should African Americans be any different? Shelby does not answer this question. Instead, he seems to be operating under a traditionalist assumption—to wit, there is something wrong, something negative about group identity.[115] But a commitment to group identity is socially and morally neutral. It is the content of the identity that counts.[116] Reformists and limited separatists are asking blacks to embrace something good: "a positive shared identity." Striving for group excellence frees the individual from the prison of selfishness and thereby makes him or her more altruistic, more human and humane. I saw this phenomenon firsthand during the civil rights movement. There would have been no Martin Luther King Jr. without group identity. King, in fact, had commitments to overlapping identities—such as religion, activism, and fatherhood—all of which were firmly rooted in an underlying black identity.

By downplaying the importance of "a positive shared identity" for black success, Shelby misses the fact that many assimilated Americans deem "a positive shared identity" to be all-important. That is, although group identity may be less important to some members of ethnic groups that have assimilated into the American mainstream, identity remains an important dynamic in the lives of many whites who hold positions of power or influence in our society. Bill O'Reilly, Rush Limbaugh, Sean Hannity, Sarah Palin, and other white traditionalists see themselves as "cultural warriors," protectors of an American identity defined in terms of their view of what counts as patriotism, Christianity, good governance, racial equity, economic fairness, and other cultural values. Limited separatists would argue that it is naive for blacks to think that group identity is not important in post–civil rights America.

A limited separatist would also note that Shelby fails to explain how his theory of black political solidarity overcomes the collective action problem. Ad hoc political solidarity is at least as susceptible to individualism, self-interest, class, gender, and other intraracial divisions as limited separation or ad hoc nationalism based on cultural or economic unity. What is so special about ad hoc political nationalism that exempts it from the strictures of intraracial divisions? Why is ad hoc political nationalism any more empowered by the desire for racial justice than other forms of black nationalism, ad hoc or systemic?

Shelby, in fact, is caught in a catch-22. He argues that the desire for racial justice will motivate ad hoc political unity among blacks. But without a sense of shared racial identity, which Shelby dismisses, the drive toward racial justice can miss the mark. The idea of racial justice rings hollow if infused with a watered-down notion of black identity. Indeed, it can be downright dangerous, much like supporting democracy in new regimes without paying attention to what the voting might bring. The results, although democratically produced, may not be in a country's best interest. In the past, black identity—be it a strong commitment to freedom during slavery or to equal treatment under the law during Jim Crow—guided the struggle for racial justice, even in the face of strong opposition from other groups that did not identify with the black perspective. There was a symbiotic relationship between racial justice and black identity. Blacks knew what racial justice meant at the time; they could feel it in their bones. There is no reason to think that this dynamic relationship should not hold true in the Age of Obama and beyond.

The real problem with Shelby's theory of black unity, his concept of pragmatic nationalism, is that it has no beef. It asks too little of blacks, especially well-to-do blacks. It assumes that blacks can only go as far as political solidarity, and even there only on a limited, or ad hoc, basis. If the struggle for racial justice has only enough gas in the tank to motivate ad hoc black political solidarity, then blacks are in a world of trouble: the struggle for racial justice will run out of gas before its reaches the finish line.

Shelby gives us many reasons why blacks, particularly middle-class blacks, may not embrace the robust form of black solidarity limited separation offers. But what about the reverse side of that question, namely, are there any reasons for middle-class blacks to respond affirmatively to the challenge presented by limited separation? Are there reasons why they should choose to return to a black-centered life as many have done in communities like Harlem? Are there reasons why they might want to take the lead in creating jobs in African American neighborhoods, improving education in African American schools, and transforming the lifestyles of working-class and poor blacks living within African American communities?

Limited separatists believe that the incentive for all this effort is not racial kinship but naked self-interest. Some of the reasons in support of this position come from an unlikely source, namely, Sheryll Cashin, an integrationist who seems opposed to any form of racial separation. Cashin believes that many middle-class blacks are "integration exhausted" and, hence, prefer racially and economically separate communities. A limited separatist would argue that integration-exhausted blacks are the most likely candidates among middle-class blacks to create limited-separate communities. But what about their desire for economic homogeneity? Cashin also provides an answer to this question. She argues that middle-class blacks who endeavor to establish their own communities can run from poor blacks and the crime associated with them, but they cannot hide from them. Poor blacks are bound to enter "chocolate" near-suburbs that ring many inner cities.[117] Indeed, Mary Patillo McCoy observes that many middle-class blacks living in the near-suburbs have similar experiences to blacks in the inner cities, such as drugs and crime.[118] Thus, while naked self-interest may cause well-to-do blacks to reject limited separation, it might also cause them to embrace limited separation.

There is, however, little doubt that limited separation is a hard sell to make in these post–civil rights times. Notwithstanding successful applications in the past or in the present, and notwithstanding the pain and humiliation so many blacks experience in integrated institutions, many well-to-do blacks will have a difficult time warming up to the idea of limited separation. I am reminded of the black TV producer in the film *Crash*, which won the Oscar for the best movie of 2005. In this largely accurate portrayal of the complex web of racism in post–civil rights Los Angeles, the black TV producer, portrayed by Terrence Howard, was willing to tolerate a degree of racial humiliation, which scores of integrated blacks experience in professional workplaces, because of the lifestyle his high salary afforded him, including a fancy automobile and a spacious house in the suburbs. He also seemed to genuinely love his work. Limited separatists would have a difficult time convincing even this spiritually wounded person to give up his material comforts for a new life in a modern-day version of T-Town.

Difficult, but not impossible. If limited separatists are to win the hearts and minds of more middle-class blacks, the self-interest argument must be enlarged to mean not only material and personal gains but also spiritual and racial gains. In other words, I do not think that the self-interest argument can be completely divorced from spirituality or even racial kinship. It must be an *enlightened* self-interest, one that incorporates personal satisfaction, happiness, material wealth, black heritage, and racial altruism as well. Middle-class blacks must be shown that it is in their long-term self-interests to reach back to help other blacks, and that this can be done without excluding or otherwise subordinating whites or nonblack racial minorities. In addition, limited separatists must make clear that they are not asking middle-class blacks to move in next to a crack house. Community reconstruction will accompany the moving-in process. Limited separation, therefore, is best conceived, it seems to me, as a small operation (such as the Harlem Children's Zone) that gains momentum over time. These points must be emphasized in the marketing of limited separation.

In spite of all the problems identified here, limited separation is still to be admired for its spirit and truthfulness. As I said on another occasion, limited separation avoids the kind of "Rousseauist romanticism that underpins ... [other civil rights theories] in which it is naively expected that whites will act more nobly than African Americans or any other group would act under similar circumstances. It is an extraordinary person who can look beyond her own self-interest when matters of family and financial security are at stake. As luck would have it, the world is made up of mostly ordinary people. Limited separation, then, is a civil rights theory for ordinary people."[119]

When I think about limited separation, I do not see nationhood, such as the Native American nations that exclude blacks and other non-Indians from membership.[120] Instead, I think of black churches, Jewish synagogues, and women's colleges. I think of communities like Little Havana in Miami and the Chinatowns and Little Italys throughout the country. None exclude outsiders from their places of worship, schools, communities, or jobs. Each creates a supportive environment for its main constituency, and each works well within the context of our larger social order. Still, limited separation certainly challenges received traditions in post–civil rights theory. Limited separatists maintain that orthodox civil rights thinking is stuck in a kind of intellectual paralysis. Traditionalism and reformism, both of which reject racial isolation, would have us believe that a theory that teaches racial integration and one that espouses racial separation are mutually exclusive—Martin Luther King Jr. to the right, Malcolm X to the left. Limited separation attempts to demonstrate that Martin and Malcolm can coexist.

*Chapter 5*

# CRITICAL RACE THEORY

C RITICAL RACE THEORY often uses narrative, or storytelling, to convey its complex messages and simultaneously raise racial awareness.[1] So it is quite appropriate that this chapter begins with a story that attempts to capture the core teaching of critical race theory. The story unfolds outside the highly contentious context of race, a place wherein racial truths are sometimes hard to see, and proceeds as follows. Jane and Alice are soon to be roommates in a new apartment. Jane is the first to arrive at the apartment. She instinctively arranges her furniture in a manner she finds both aesthetic and functional. As she moves the chairs, tables, and other pieces of furniture around the apartment, Jane is conscious only of her own sensibilities. She has no thought of disadvantaging Alice. In fact, Jane is not even thinking about Alice. Her only immediate desire is to make the apartment's interior reflect her personality, comfortable and pleasing. Alice arrives after Jane's furniture is firmly in place and immediately expresses her dissatisfaction with the layout of the apartment. She is dissatisfied not only with the type of furniture Jane has selected but also with its placement in the apartment. She insists that the arrangement of the furniture neither affirms, acknowledges, nor validates her personality and needs. Alice finds the furniture arranged in a way that makes movement around the apartment uncomfortable and inefficient for her. In response to Alice's complaints, Jane moves one or two chairs a few inches but does not otherwise rearrange the apartment or make room for more than a few pieces of Alice's furniture. Hence, the apartment's design remains fundamentally unchanged. Clearly, Alice has influence over the apartment, but Jane has dominion.

If Alice were a critical race theorist, she would use one word to describe her inability to exert sufficient power to change the basic design of the apartment: "subordination." Jane, not Alice, exercises control or hegemony over the apartment. Her needs and tastes are privileged; they are given priority over the needs and tastes of Alice. Significantly, Alice's subordination occurs notwithstanding the fact that her roommate has *not* acted with antipathy or malice toward her. If Alice were black and Jane white, Alice, the critical race theorist, would use a more pointed word or two to describe the same situation: "racism" or "racial subordination." Although using the term "racism" in this manner does not comport with the quotidian language of whites (Jane certainly does not think of herself as a racist, a person motivated by an invidious animus), it makes perfect sense from Alice's perspective. From the victim's perspective it matters little what motivates her mistreatment. The critical factor is that she (Alice) is disadvantaged no matter what.

Critical race theorists can be understood as insisting that the arrangement of resources in our society along racial lines, not unlike the arrangement of furniture in the story, is "racist." It is racist because it is racialized. Whites have most of our country's resources and have had them from the very beginning. They did not acquire them "fair and square." And being in control, whites will always be at the top and blacks at the bottom. Racial inequality is locked in—there will always be racial differentials in the distribution of resources in our society. If we as a society are serious about doing anything about disparate resources—about resolving the nation's longest running moral problem—then we must first do something about white hegemony.

Although critical race theorists, or "race crits," believe that racism exists despite the absence of invidious intent, this does not mean they are unconcerned with malicious intent or that, like traditionalists, they see old-fashioned racism (racial antipathy) as nothing more than a racial inconvenience in post–civil rights America. By focusing so intently on racial subordination, critical race theorists simply wish to crystallize what may be their most important contribution to post–civil rights theory—to wit, an unflinching insistence that white hegemony, even though it may not be motivated by racial hatred or have an identifiable perpetrator, is every bit as pernicious, or racist, as the "white only" signs that hung over Mr. Smith's restaurant during Jim Crow. From the *victim's* perspective, racial antipathy and the perpetrator's identity are irrelevant. The issue is not about racial discrimination; it is about racial subordination. "Less important for critical race theory . . . is the effort to define 'discrimination'—much less to produce a 'unifying' definition of the phenomenon—in part because . . . the subject of critical race theory is no longer 'discrimination' but 'subordination.'"[2]

Critical race theorists, in short, argue that disparity resources in black society are sustained by white hegemony. Whites have power and, hence, control over the nation's resources; blacks do not. Whites use their power to stay in control, not to intentionally hurt blacks. Whites exercise control through individual, institutional, and societal filters that privilege "insiders" (straight white males, especially white elites) and subordinate "outsiders" (not only blacks but also other people of color, women, and homosexuals). Filters that privilege whites are what sustain disparate resources.

Race crits have different ways of describing these subordinating filters. Some use "structuralism" to describe, or "deconstruct," them. Disparate resources are sustained by society's structures—economic, educational, political, and so on. Other race crits see the matter through a "postmodernist" perspective. Disparate resources are sustained by society's superstructure—its stories, public images, and attitudes (i.e., culture writ large)—manifested in multiple places rather than hardwired to a single place or font of subordination. For postmodernists, there is no "hegemony," only "hegemonies." Similarly, "idealists," who, like postmodernists, believe racial subordination is rooted in ideas, suggest that disparate resources are sustained by "attitudes and social information"— the stories insiders tell or, in other words, "discourse"—including the silencing of opposing voices. In contrast, "realists," or "materialists," who, like the structuralists, believe subordination is rooted in the pursuit of profit and power, can be read as suggesting that disparate resources are sustained by the avowed or unconscious desire of insiders to allocate privilege to further their own material interests. I do not attempt to reconcile these fissures in critical race theory (except to note that they are perhaps more complementary than contraposed) because, for present purposes, it is unnecessary to do so. All critical race theorists believe that disparate resources are sustained externally by individual, institutional, and societal filters that privilege whites and subordinate blacks. All say that the inertia of the hegemonic traditions is what sustains resource disparity in post–civil rights America. All contend that insiders are responsible for creating an unmistakable slant or built-in bias in society that favors them and concomitantly disadvantages outsiders. Finally, all hold that the relationship between power and race—whites on top, blacks on the bottom—is ancient history in our country and, like the furniture in Alice's apartment, shows no signs of changing fundamentally if left alone.[3]

For the most part, critical race theorists believe that it is sufficient just to unpack the complex relationship between power and race for all the world to see, that the job of the critical race theorist is less prescriptive than diagnostic.[4] Given critical race theory's discursive mission, it may seem unfair to impose on it the intellectual framework advanced in this book, namely, the theory of completeness. Yet in my view there are certain strictures to which any post–civil rights theory should adhere if it is to be taken seriously. Indeed, some race crits are now giving attention to prescriptive discourse, including the notion of "praxis"—activism or, more precisely, "the idea ... that analysis should not lead to paralysis."[5] Adhering to the theory of completeness is important for yet another reason: it provides a basis for comparing major post–civil rights theories. In examining critical race theory closely, one can, indeed, find some prescriptive measures. These measures, however, lack the sense of urgency and imagination that one finds in the theory's diagnostic revelations, or deconstruction.

Because critical race theorists believe resource disparity is fundamentally sustained by external factors (subordinating filters that act as social narrative or social structure), they pay little attention to internal factors that might contribute to the problem. Criticism of black culture does not figure into the meat of the race crits' post–civil rights analysis. Race crits mainly believe the American race problem is sustained by the actions of insiders. Accordingly, there is very little internal diagnostic or prescriptive analysis offered in critical race theory, certainly less than in the other theories.

## A. External Analysis

### 1. Diagnosis

Critical race theory's external diagnosis of the American race problem is predicated upon a belief that individual, institutional, and societal filters sustain disparate resources by privileging whites (or whiteness) and subordinating blacks (or the other). These filters, it is argued, exist not because white elites hate blacks, although some of that still exists, but because they simply want to retain their power and control in society, that is, white hegemony. White hegemony is all about the relationship between power and race in American society—whites have considerably more power than blacks. Thus, resource disparity between whites and blacks is inextricably linked to power disparity between whites and blacks.

Whites did not acquire their power fairly or squarely, critical race theory holds, they acquired it the old-fashioned way—that is, by stacking the deck in their favor. Much of this deck stacking was directed toward blacks specifically, as in the case of slavery and Jim Crow. That is racism. But a good deal of the deck stacking was generic, something that cultural elites do in all societies, which critical race theory still regards as racism. The argument is as follows: cultural elites typically construct their societies in their own image, meaning they typically give themselves all or most of the power; straight white males are America's cultural elites; ergo, American society is constructed in the image of straight white males (they have most of the power), which makes America a racist society—intent has nothing to do with it.[6] Thus, personal, institutional, and societal filters that privilege whites were constructed for reasons of either racial hatred or social cloning by cultural elites. I shall attempt to unpack this argument.

First and foremost, critical race theorists do not think it matters why the subordinating filters came into existence. For analytical purposes, they are quite willing to recognize that there are different reasons (racial antipathy and social cloning) for the social construction of racial subordination. But in the end, the results are the same: power in America is racialized—American society is racist. Resource disparity will always exist so long as racism, or white hegemony, exists. This, I believe, is the critical race theorist's basic argument as to what sustains disparate resources.

Implicit in this argument is the belief that racial disadvantage in our post–civil rights society is based not on truth or merit; it is based on the social construction of race and nothing else. White elites took control of our resources from the beginning and have not relinquished it. Hence, America, critical race theorists assert, is not objective, or neutral, when it comes to matters of race. It is, in fact, "antiobjective"; it privileges insiders and subordinates outsiders.

It is important to emphasize that critical race theory is concerned less with discrimination than with subordination, although some crits still consider the former to be an important subject for discussion. Richard Delgado and Jean Stefancic define discrimination as the "practice of treating similarly situated individuals differently because of race, gender, sexual orientation, appearance, or national origin."[7] This definition captures the concepts of individual and institutional discrimination, both of which require the identification of a perpetrator.[8] It does not, however, reach societal discrimination, a form of structural discrimination that has many perpetrators (some distant, others contemporary) but none that can be readily identified.[9] Delgado and Stefancic, in contrast, define subordination as the "process of holding or rendering of lesser importance, as through racial discrimination, patriarchy, or classism."[10] So defined, subordination is inclusive of, or broader than, discrimination in that it is not necessarily tied to a perpetrator, whether in the past or in the present. Subordination mainly focuses on individual, institutional, or societal processes that discount outsider interests or values, that is, private and public forces that create and maintain insider hegemony for whatever reasons—racial hatred or insider cloning. As Delgado instructs, "You can always find another reason why things are the way they are."[11]

Delgado illustrates the point by noting that George Wallace's son has said that his father opposed civil rights so persistently during his tenure as the governor of Alabama in the 1960s "not because he disliked black people or wanted to resist desegregation. It was rather because he was trying to preserve Southern culture."[12] Many white South Carolinians claim that far from being a symbol of slavery, the Confederate battle flag, which once flew over the South Carolina state capitol, is a symbol of their heritage.[13] Yet the flag was raised over the capitol for the first time in 1962 as a symbol of "states' rights" in defiance of the federal push for civil rights.[14] (In 2000, the flag was removed to another part of the state capitol grounds—a case of "moving the furniture.") What critical race theorists seem to be saying, then, is that racialized conditions—whites having the best jobs, salaries, education, housing, and so on society has to offer, as the appendix shows—constitute racial subordination, or racism, whether or not they are preceded by a discriminatory motivation. From the victim's perspective, the perpetrator's state of mind makes little difference, because the victim is disadvantaged either way.

Does this argument justify the broad use of the term "racism"? Critical race theory uses the term in a manner that departs not only from conventional American usage, which connotes racial antipathy or invidious animus, but even from the manner in which the term was used by progressives during the civil rights movement. For example, Stokely Carmichael and Charles Hamilton, the former of whom was among the first black leaders to bring the term "black power" into mainstream civil rights discourse, defined "racism" as the "predication of decisions and policies on considerations of race *for the purpose* of subordinating a racial group and maintaining control over that group" (emphasis added).[15] By removing the element of purpose or intent from the concept of racism in any form, by essentially equating racism with disparate resources, critical race theorists have taken the concept in a different direction.

Some scholars have criticized this new development. While acknowledging the long history of racial disadvantage in our society, Daniel Farber asks, "What vocabulary do we have left with which to talk about Rodney King [who was beaten by white police officers while handcuffed and on the ground] when we have used up the word racism to talk about a dorm residence rule [that unintentionally disadvantages blacks]?"[16] Farber reminds us that a "black congressman from Harlem" chaired the congressional committee that gave us the crack cocaine sentencing law, which has had such a devastating impact on African American communities.[17]

Privileging the victim's perspective, critical race theorists would probably argue in response that the difference lies in the cultural meaning blacks (the victims) would attach to both events. The cultural meaning African Americans would attach to the Rodney King beating is very different from the cultural meaning they would assign to the dorm residence rule. Even though the latter might disadvantage black students, it does not appear to privilege insiders, stereotype blacks, or otherwise harm the racial status of black students. It is not "racist" in the critical race theory sense. In contrast, the Rodney King incident reinforces insider status, stereotypes blacks, and visits no dearth of racial status harms on blacks.[18] As to black involvement in creating the crack cocaine sentencing law, it is important to remember that state of mind counts little in critical race theory's analysis of racism. Black elites in predominantly white institutions can be racist toward other blacks (i.e., exercise control in a way that privileges whites, stereotypes blacks, or otherwise harms their racial status) even if they do not intend to do so.

In addition to its nonmotivational, or cognitive, feature, racism, as conceptualized by critical race theorists, has another quality: permanence. As Delgado states: "There is change from one era to another, but the net quantum of racism remains exactly the same, obeying a melancholy Law of Racial Thermodynamics: Racism is neither created nor destroyed."[19] This does not mean that there has been no racial progress since the end of Jim Crow. What it does mean is that even though blacks are better off today than they were at the end of the civil rights movement, most of the significant racial differentials between blacks and whites have not narrowed much, and in some instances have even widened.[20] This has prompted Derrick Bell to charge: "Black people will never gain full equality in this country. Even those herculean efforts we hail as successful will produce no more than temporary 'peaks of progress,' shortlived victories that slide into irrelevance as racial patterns adapt in ways that maintain white dominance. This is a hard-to-accept fact that all history verifies."[21]

Race crits advance two different diagnoses to explain the permanency and pervasiveness of racism—the operation of the subordinating filters—in the American social order. Some critical race theorists make a structuralist, or "structuralist determinist," argument while others offer a poststructuralist, or postmodern, argument. I shall briefly touch upon this dichotomy and delve more deeply into the contrasting filters when I look at the modern-day division between realists and idealists.

The structuralists contend that racial hierarchy is sustained through subordinating filters embedded in the very structure of our society. These filters operate at various levels: individual, institutional, and societal. Let us take institutional filers as an example. Political, economic, legal, educational, residential, and other organizational structures contain filters that privilege whites and subordinate African Americans. Law firm recruiters, for example, tend to favor applicants who basically look and think like them, that is, white males. So they look to see if the applicant "fits in," such as plays golf or surfs, has graduated from the "right" law school, or belongs to the "right" organizations. There is no attempt on the part of the recruiters to discriminate against black applicants. They might, in fact, even accept a token few so that the firm's bottom line looks nondiscriminatory. But there is no real commitment to diversity here because diversity is just not important to the people who run the law firm—elite white men. Rather than looking at institutional filters, some structuralists focus on an overarching societal filter, that is, a single structure of subordination. Marxists, or economic determinists, for example, see society's means of production—capitalism—as the main filter that privileges whites of a certain class and subordinates the vast majority of blacks. Racial subordination is rooted in the existing social ontology. It is interesting to note here that much of the structuralist thinking in critical race theory comes from critical legal studies, a precursor to critical race theory.[22] I shall delve into these filters in greater detail when I discuss the racial realists later in this chapter.

Postmodernists characterize the subordinating filers quite differently. Unlike struturalists, poststructuralists argue that racial subordination mainly operates as discourse, which includes the silencing of alternative perspectives or narratives. Following Michel Foucault and other Continental scholars, postmodernists are less concerned with social structure than with social narrative. Under their influence, the operative terminology of hegemony shifts from social arrangement to hidden discourse. Individual and institutional filters that privilege whites also operate through discourse.[23] Postmodernists reject the idea of a "single font" of subordination in American society. Unlike the class, or Marxist, structuralists,[24] postmodernists argue that subordination is "diffused at multiple sites (schools, the military, factories, universities)."[25] There is no "hegemony," only "hegemonies." The focus, then, is not a single, overarching societal subordinating filter. It is on multiple individual or institutional (discursive) hegemonies. Furthermore, "there is no necessary connection between the marginalization experienced by various subaltern groups, so [marginalization] can occur independently on several fronts along lines of gender, race, age, physical ability, and so on."[26] Thus, postmodernists like Kimberlé Crenshaw and Paulette Caldwell focus on intersecting subordinations, such as the intersectionality of race and gender.[27] Postmodernist Patricia Williams also focuses on "multiple subjectivities."[28] Postmodernism, as Angela Harris correctly observes, is an attack not only on structuralism but also on essentialism.[29]

A refinement of the structuralists' and poststructuralists' contrasting views has developed among critical race theorists. Influenced by the postmodernists, some crits, called "idealists," "work almost entirely in the realm of discourse,"[30] analyzing such matters as intersectionality, essentialism, hate speech, census categories, and the Western canon. For them, subordinating filters operate mainly through narrative.[31] Others, called "realists," "materialists," or "economic determinists," while not denying that "text, attitude, [cognition,] and intention may play important roles in our system of racial hierarchy," maintain that "material factors such as profits and the labor market are even more decisive in determining who falls where in that system."[32] Hence, they believe that racialized disparate resources are sustained by filters that privilege white material interests. Both arguments merit a closer look.

The idealists argue that our understanding of the hegemonic ideology of white racism is essential to our understanding of why resources are racialized in the way that they are. We must, they insist, focus on "racial ideologies and the damage they have caused. . . . Apart from wars, the two most shattering ordeals of modern times have been the forced transportation of Africans and the mass murder of European Jews. Both events are products of ideas."[33] Idealists would agree with the writer Charles McGrath, a non-crit, who observes that our actions are influenced by "all the bric-a-brac we carry around in the attic of our minds: imagery, quotations, movie dialogue, advertising jingles, song lyrics, snatches of overheard conversation."[34] Thus, the racial judgments we make and actions we take are corrupted by the biases we bring to the table, whether avowed or unconscious.

Idealists, particularly those with a background in literary criticism, emphasize narrative, including the denial of narrative. The argument is that the "master narrative" subordinates, or discounts, the stories of outsiders—the "other." It does so by not allowing their counterstorytelling to reach a wider audience. The master narrative succeeds because it is "louder" than the voice of the other, and because we are not always aware of its racially subordinating message. As Charles Lawrence elaborates, "Because racism is so deeply ingrained in our culture, it is likely to be transmitted by tacit understandings."[35] The master narrative is reproduced through individual or institutional filters. For example, insiders control the media, an important medium for storytelling, and consequently are in a position to impugn the legitimacy of outsider narratives and prevent them from reaching a wide enough audience to make a difference. By denying the legitimacy of outsider discourse, insiders are forcing assimilation and, thereby, refusing to give other narratives a role in constructing the nation's collective identity.

Stereotyping—generalizations about a group based on perceived attributes of members of the group—is one of the most insidious forms of subordinating discourse. It is a subordinating filter that operates through individuals (e.g., the newspaper editor who believes a black reporter is better suited to cover the inner city rather than Wall Street) or institutions (e.g., racial profiling by the police). Stereotyping functions as a means of understanding difference and determining otherness. It gives the dominant group the power to create and shape public images in ways that reinforce norms and define other groups. Outsiders are virtually powerless to counter these damaging images as such images become "the bric-a-bac" carried "around in the attic of our minds."[36] The consequences of stereotyping are, indeed, major.

Realists do not deny the power of discourse but argue that, despite cultural ideology, power in American society has always been determined, first and foremost, by material conditions. Subordinating filters that take the shape of institutional arrangements determine the quality or quantity of resources in the black community. It is "the shifting tides of white desire, now for labor, now for land, now for cannon fodder, now for political loyalty and Americanism, [that] underlie most major shifts in minority fortunes."[37] Public officials often place sewage treatment plants and toxic dumps in outsider communities not because they hate blacks or Latinos but because it is *convenient* for them to do so. As the world becomes more globalized, jobs will shift to people of color in other countries where labor is relatively cheap. This new economic arrangement subordinates the economic interests of blacks and other outsiders. Specifically, it undermines the job market for outsiders as the jobs left at home shift toward technology and other skills many outsiders do not have.[38] These and other types of material concerns of insiders, more than anything else, sustain capital deficiencies in black and other outsider communities. Public discourse merely reinforces extant forms of social arrangements.[39]

In support of their position, realists often point to Derrick Bell's "interest-convergence principle," more commonly known as the "white self-interest principle." This principle, they contend, not only offers proof of the realist claim that material concerns carry the day but also helps to explain how racial progress materializes in our "permanently racist" society.[40] Bell's principle asserts that "the degree of progress blacks have made away from slavery and toward equality has depended on whether allowing blacks more or less opportunity best served the interests and aims of white society."[41] Racial progress for African Americans and other outsiders occurs only when white elites believe they can benefit from it in some material way. The deal must be a win-win situation; otherwise there is no racial progress.

Bell is not the first person to articulate the white self-interest principle. Malcolm X, and perhaps others before him, articulated the principle during the civil rights movement. White Americans, he declared, "don't know what morals are. They don't try to eliminate an evil because it's evil, or because it's illegal, or because it's immoral; they eliminate it only when it threatens their existence."[42] Is there evidence to establish the validity of the white self-interest principle? Bell asserts that President Lincoln's motivation for issuing the Emancipation Proclamation is a classic illustration of the principle. Although Lincoln personally hated slavery and was, in fact, the first president to invite an African American (Frederick Douglass) to the White House, Lincoln issued the proclamation solely for military purposes, in other words, to save the Union, rather than to save African Americans from slavery. Hence, the argument goes, Lincoln was willing to permit slavery— perhaps the worst form of human debasement and oppression ever seen on American soil—to continue if necessary to preserve the Union. As he wrote to newspaper editor Horace Greeley: "If I could save the Union without freeing any slave, I would do it."[43] In the same letter, Lincoln asserted: "I have stated my view of *official* duty; and I intend no modification of my oft-expressed *personal* wish that all men everywhere could be free."[44]

Of course, the strength of this illustration is somewhat undercut by the fact that the Union's purpose for fighting the Civil War had changed by the beginning of Lincoln's second term. By then, Lincoln and many Union soldiers and civilians came to see the war's chief purpose as freeing the slaves. This was an avowed position. Indeed, many Union soldiers reenlisted for that reason alone. They experienced a change of heart after seeing African American soldiers fight bravely. As James McPherson writes: "By the war's last year, the example of black soldiers fighting for the Union as well as liberty had helped convince most white soldiers that they should fight for black liberty as well as Union. There were some holdouts, to be sure. . . . But these were distinctly minority views among Union soldiers by 1864. When Lincoln ran for reelection on a platform pledging a constitutional amendment to abolish slavery, he received almost 80% of the soldier vote—a pretty fair indication of army sentiment on slavery at the time."[45]

Finally, it should be noted that the white self-interest principle finds support in the work of scholars who are not critical race theorists. Philip A. Klinkner and Roger M. Smith, for example, argue that significant racial progress occurs in our country only with the convergence of three circumstances: (1) large-scale wars, which require extensive economic and military mobilization and, hence, African American assistance; (2) an enemy whose repressive regime inspires American leaders to advocate inclusive, egalitarian values in order to justify the war; and (3) domestic political organizations that are able to pressure American leaders to follow through on their rhetoric.[46] Klinkner and Smith's work augments the validity of Bell's white self-interest principle.

The final point to make about the realist perspective concerns the term "realism" itself. Critical race theory's use of the term is somewhat uncertain. It does not appear to refer to the "racial realists" or "feminist realists" who have abandoned the belief that "equality can be obtained through law."[47] The debate between the idealist and the realist seems more reminiscent of the age-old debate between the Marxist idealists and economic determinists. In fact, Delgado uses the term "economic determinists" as a synonym for "realists."[48] Thus, the idealist/realist debate has been in progress for quite some time. Revisiting its origin can help to clarify its current reincarnation.[49]

The debate first arose during the late nineteenth and early twentieth centuries when European intellectuals sought to explain the failure of the Marxist prediction of a proletarian revolution and the concomitant decline of capitalist societies. Marxism is a complex system of thought.[50] At its most basic level, Marxism analyzes anything and everything from a particular intellectual framework, namely, a "scientific law" of "historical materialism," or "dialectical materialism." This concept incorporates two main features. The first comes not from Karl Marx directly but from his predecessor, the German philosopher Georg Wilhelm Friedrich Hegel. Hegel posited a "theory of ideas," or consciousness: the best of opposing thoughts (the "thesis" and the "antithesis") merge into a higher level of consciousness (the "synthesis"). The main objective of history is to create synthesis after synthesis after synthesis—in other words, new knowledge moving toward "absolute knowledge." In this way, our ideas are constantly turning into higher forms of consciousness.[51]

Hegel described an "idealist" dialectic ("the mind contemplating itself"). Marx then set this dialectic on top of a materialist foundation, ultimately shifting the focus to class struggle. Thus, the second feature of Marxism, sometimes referred to as "economic determinism" or "economism," posits that all societies (whether socialistic or capitalistic) have a basic structure that consists of an economic base or "infrastructure" (the means of production, e.g., slave-based, mercantile, or capitalistic) that *determines* its "superstructure" (law, education, religion, politics, the arts, morality, and all other cultural or ideological phenomena).[52] Hegel's dialectic and Marx's materialism—together, dialectical materialism—yield the Marxist proposition that history is a story of economic struggle between the oppressor and the oppressed (such as the slaveholder vs. the slave and the lord vs. the serf). In capitalist societies, the class conflict is between the bourgeoisie and the proletariat. Thus, capitalism, like all economic systems, is always in a state of crisis. Marx predicted that the conflict between capital and labor would result in the working class rising up and overthrowing the system of capitalist exploitation.[53]

The trouble with Marx's dialectical materialism was that the subordinated classes seemed quite content to go along with this system of exploitation. Why did they not see that revolution was manifestly within their material interests as Marx had predicted? Why did the dominated classes in advanced capitalist societies seem so complacent? Why did socialist revolutions fail to materialize in these societies as Marx had predicted?

Marx's followers sought to answer these questions. They argued that Marx presented an undertheorized, or perhaps a wrongly theorized, notion of class domination.[54] Marx's materialism overshadowed his (or Hegel's) idealism. Economic determinism, the hidden process by which economic reality engenders idealism (culture, ideas, or "what is in your head"), had less explanatory power than Marx had supposed. Idealism (superstructure) was more important in explaining class domination and, more precisely, why socialist revolutions failed to come into being, than Marx had theorized.

Later Marxists, then, rejected the crude deterministic notion of their teacher on the ground that social ideology, or message, was too powerful to downplay. Marxist economic determinism missed an important point: the ruling ideology "disguises" itself through media, religion, and other social institutions, and hence becomes unrecognizable as exploitation. People walk around with preconceived, unexamined notions about life shaped by the elite class. Economic determinism, then, failed to see that the very ideology that subserves the interest of the ruling class, that allows them to stay in power, was "internalized and endlessly reinforced in schools, churches, institutions, scholarly exchanges, museums, and popular culture."[55] Whereas crude determinism treated these and other institutions as merely epiphenomenal (as secondary and resultant), the later Marxists treated them as primary elements essential to an understanding of how class domination is accepted at many levels in a society.

It appears that Delgado and perhaps other racial realists are introducing crude determinism into critical race theory. Although Delgado concedes the value of superstructure, he clearly treats it as epiphenomenal, not nearly as important as the structure. I shall weigh in on this feature of the debate in my reflections at the end of this chapter.[56]

Adding to the confusion concerning the meaning of idealism and realism is the fact that some critical race theorists move back and forth between the two camps. For example, Bell, the realist, sounds idealist when he writes about the "'ideological hegemony' of white racism."[57] He also asserts that "*Brown* [*v. Board of Education*] teaches that advocates of racial justice should rely less on judicial decisions and more on tactics, actions, and even attitudes that challenge the continuing assumptions of white dominance."[58] This could be a declaration of realism (challenge social conditions directly rather than indirectly through the courts) or idealism (challenge social attitudes, which, because of First Amendment concerns, are beyond the reach of courts).

Although the distinction between idealism and realism is somewhat clouded, one thing is quite clear. All critical race theorists, whether idealist or realist, see in society what Delgado characterizes as an unmistakable slant that favors insiders.[59] They believe that insiders have a constructed, unnatural, and permanent advantage in our society, and that this set of circumstances, this built-in bias, is what sustains disparate resources.

## 2. Prescription

As one might expect, idealists and realists have different views as to how best to respond to racial subordination. Given their belief that the most powerful external factor sustaining disparate resources is the silencing of outsider voices, idealists prescribe, first and foremost, that outsider voices be brought into mainstream discourse. Once mainstreamed, these voices should work to identify the fallacies filtered into the insider's narrative, thereby changing the mainstream narrative. Ultimately, insider and outsider voices should be intertwined, idealists seem to suggest, to create a truer sense of the American experience and identity.[60] One way to begin changing the national narrative is through storytelling. By simply telling their stories, outsiders can break down the insider narrative as well as provide insiders with a vehicle for understanding the life of the "other." Thus, idealists believe racial subordination can be eliminated "by ridding ourselves of the texts, narratives, ideas, and meanings that give rise to it and that convey the message that people of other racial groups are unworthy, lazy, and dangerous."[61] Kimberlé Crenshaw argues that by purging ourselves of such stereotypes, our society will be able to "maintain a distinctly progressive outlook that focuses on the needs of the African American community."[62]

The realists, perhaps surprisingly, would not prescribe a Marxist or class-based overthrow of capitalism. Indeed, their prescription looks very reformist. For example, they propose eradicating barriers to upward mobility by doing away with conventional tests and other traditional standards of merit. These material filters privilege whites and subordinate blacks. But what about things like candor and truth? "For the critical race theorists, objective truth, like merit, does not exist, at least in social science and politics. In these realms, truth is a social construct created to suit the purposes of the dominant group."[63] Since merit has no inherent warrant, it can be set aside. This seems to suggest that hiring and even curricular selection should be based less on merit than on racial design, overturning subordination.[64] At the very least, it means more affirmative action. Indeed, realists embrace ongoing affirmative action as a basic remedy.[65] Finally, critical race theorists believe in "rectifying racism" in the criminal justice system so that young men of color will have a better chance of going to college than to jail. Unfortunately, they do not explain how this is to be done.[66]

Realists would use interest convergence to win insider approval of specific materialist prescriptions. They would, in other words, convert interest convergence from a negative to a positive, a kind of sword that can be used to ensure the success of their prescriptions. Interest convergence, then, is used to help insiders understand that it is within their material interests to embrace the interests of outsiders. The challenge for critical race theorists is to demonstrate how insiders will benefit materially from the former's prescriptive measures.

## B. Internal Analysis

For all their penetrating analysis and originality in diagnosing the external factors that sustain disparate resources, for all their theorizing about the American race problem in our post–civil rights era, critical race theorists have surprisingly little to say about internal factors that might contribute to capital deficiencies within the African American community. Unlike traditionalism, reformism, and limited separation, there is very little discussion of bad behaviors or bad values in critical race theory. Race crits focus almost entirely on the external aspect of the race problem, which suggests that they believe outsiders contribute nothing of significance to the problem. There seems to be a sentiment among race crits that any serious consideration of internal factors would be tantamount to blaming the victim for his or her subordination. Subordination, then, is seen as an insider's job.[67]

Some prescriptive analysis can, however, be teased out of critical race theory. This fact alone suggests the presence of at least a scintilla of internal diagnosis in critical race theory. One can, for example, view idealists as suggesting that blacks and other outsiders can help to eradicate racial subordination simply by being a participant rather than a bystander in storytelling. Outsiders must be willing to tell their stories and stand up to the master narrative, as unpleasant as that might be. Realists, on the other hand, have in fact argued, albeit relatively recently, that blacks and other outsiders should build political coalitions with progressive whites as well as engage in what for blacks would be "ordinary politics"—protest marches and demonstrations.[68] Delgado and Stefancic give an example of political coalition building: "A globalizing economy removes manufacturing jobs from inner cities. . . . [This] offers opportunities for minorities to form coalitions with American blue-collar workers and unions that face similar issues and have begun to mobilize, as happened in Seattle with the WTO protests."[69] This sounds very reformist. Bell, the racial realist, at times seems to suggest that blacks should forget about effectuating social change through the law. Instead, he suggests that racial progress will require blacks to rely on their collective passion, courage, faith, inspiration, and humility.[70]

Whether idealist or realist, critical race theorists may believe that blacks and other outsiders have a personal obligation to avoid contributing unwittingly to their own subordination. One suspects that they might agree with the critical feminist scholar Marianne LaFrance, who, in speaking of women, opined that by being nice, communal, and agreeable, and by providing emotional labor, women lend support to "a gendered occupational structure."[71] In this way, they sustain their own subordination. The outsider must cease buying into the master narrative. She must, instead, give voice to her own needs and interests.


## C. Summary and Reflections

Critical race theory's central message is complex and potentially transformative, namely, the problem of race in American society is inextricably linked to the problem of power. When one looks at our post–civil rights society, critical race theorists contend, one sees outsiders (the powerless) at the bottom and insiders (the powerful) at the top. Race crits insist that there is something wrong with this black and white picture, that it is unnatural and unfair, that it depicts racial relations constructed out of whole cloth that serve the interest of powerful whites. Given the relationship between race and power in our post–civil rights society, race crits go on to say, our government is not neutral on matters of race when it simply mandates or sanctions color-blind policies. Color blindness does nothing to change the existing racial dynamic and, for that reason, it takes sides ipso facto. It privileges insiders. In the end, white hegemony is the order of the day.

White hegemony is both cause and effect of racial subordination. Race crits believe that their main task, a huge one, is to unpack this relationship for all the world to see. Taking critical race theory one step further, I have tried to show the manner in which critical race theorists might explain how racial subordination sustains disparate resources. Race crits can be understood to argue that there are individual, institutional, and societal filters in our society that sustain disparate resources and, in the process, sustain white hegemony, keeping whites on top and blacks on the bottom. These filters do their job by simultaneously privileging elite white males, or whiteness, and subordinating blacks and other outsiders (people of color, women, and homosexuals). For example, executives in mainstream American institutions have a preference for applicants who "fit in" or, in other words, who look and think like them, meaning white males. Insiders who supervise public works projects find it convenient to place sewage treatment plants and toxic dumps in black or Latino communities. Then there is racial stereotyping, which gives the dominant group the power to create and shape public images in ways that reinforce norms and define other groups. This particular subordinating filter operates through individuals (e.g., the elementary school teacher who believes that black students are lazy and not as smart as whites, or the newspaper editor who believes assigning a black reporter to cover financial news is not a proper "fit") or institutions (e.g., racial profiling by police departments or department stores). Stereotyping functions as a means of understanding difference and determining otherness. The negative racial images stereotyping creates are difficult to erase as they become "the bric-a-bac" carried "around in the attic of our minds." The standard of beauty in our society subordinates black women, filtering the darkest out of contention for many jobs and society's affection. Some critical race theorists see an overarching subordinating filter in society's means of production. Capitalism privileges those with capital, who happen to be mainly white men, and subordinates those without capital, who are disproportionately African American or Latino. (See the racial differentials in the appendix.) With their wealth, the former are able to take advantage of the latter, effectively redistributing wealth downward.

These subordinating filters may or may not be the product of white antipathy toward blacks. Critical race theorists believe they are more likely the result of social cloning by whites, but, in any event, it really does not seem to matter to them because the bottom line is the same: racial subordination. The subordinating filters sustain disparate resources and, thereby, allow whites to retain their power and control in society; in other words, white hegemony continues.

The Marxist debate among race crits is interesting and most enlightening but less important to a basic understanding of critical race theory. This debate concerns the best, most accurate way of describing the social ontology of the subordinating filters. Realists, or materialists, are structuralists in that they believe racial subordination is rooted in the pursuit of profit and power. Accordingly, realists can be understood as suggesting that disparate resources are sustained by the avowed or unconscious desire of insiders to allocate privilege to further their own material interests. Thus, the subordinating filters work at the level of society's structures—economic, educational, political, and so on. In contrast, idealists believe that racial subordination is based in society's superstructure—its ideas or discourse. They take a postmodernist, antiessentialist perspective in that they also believe that racial subordination is manifested in multiple places rather than hardwired to a single place or font of subordination. There is no "white hegemony," only "white hegemonies." Accordingly, idealists can be understood to suggest that disparate resources are sustained by the ideas insiders entertain, by the "master narrative" that plays out in multiple venues. Thus, the subordinating filters work at the cultural level—the attitudes, public images, social information, and stories insiders tell, including the silencing of opposing voices.

I make no attempt to reconcile these fissures in critical race theory because, as I said earlier, I believe they are more complementary than contraposed and, in any event, it is unnecessary to do so. All critical race theorists believe that disparate resources are sustained externally by individual, institutional, or societal filters that privilege whites and subordinate blacks. All believe that the relationship between power and race—whites on top, blacks on the bottom—is ancient history in our country and, like the furniture in Alice's apartment, will not fundamentally change unless something is done externally.

What critical race theorists say should be done is quite remarkable for being unremarkable. No proletariat uprising is prescribed, although that seems to be the only prescription logically responsive to its external diagnosis. Other than prescribing storytelling as a means of changing the national narrative, critical race theory's prescription looks very reformist. It includes "rectifying racism" in the criminal justice system in some unspecified way and more rather than less affirmative action.

Critical race theorists offer little in the way of an internal critique of the American race problem, disparate resources. They lean heavily toward an external critique, and that is what I find most problematic about critical race theory's otherwise powerful message. The absence of real completeness is the same problem I have with traditionalism. Critical race theory and traditionalism take absolutist positions, which tend to foreclose serious consideration of opposing points of view. Race crits argue that extant racial hierarchies are sustained by racialized conditions (realists) or racialized narratives (idealists) established long ago by power elites, all of whom were white men. These mindsets and circumstances privilege insiders, subordinate outsiders, and, hence, sustain disparate resources. Going in the opposite direction, traditionalists argue that bad behaviors and bad values in the black community are what sustain racial hierarchies. Taking a middle position, reformists and limited separatists see both external factors (racism or racial discrimination in the case of reformists, and primarily white self-interest as well as the government's suppression of beneficial forms of racial isolation in the case of limited separatists) and internal factors (black nihilism in the case of both) as contributing agents. Reformists even go so far as to temper their external diagnosis with a rebuttable presumption: they presume, until proven otherwise, that resource disparity is sustained by racism or racial discrimination.[72] In contrast, critical race theory leaves little room for cultural explanations, and traditionalism leaves little room for racial explanations of resource disparities. Neither takes its opposition seriously.

It may be possible to find merit in critical race theory's refusal to accept the rebuttable presumption of racism that we see in reformism. It could be argued that in a post–civil rights America so strongly committed to diversity, it is dangerous to have a racialized society, one with a racially defined top and bottom *for whatever the reason*. At the very least, that would be bad democratic form. Accordingly, it could be argued that it is more productive to spend our limited time, money, and sense of outrage on fixing the problem of disparate resources rather than on attempting to justify a racialized social order. The merit of this position lies less in the possibility that no internal explanation is persuasive than in the desire to concentrate our collective energy on simply fixing the problem. There is precedence for this position in the allied field of critical feminist theory.[73]

The concept of "outsider"—faces at the bottom of the well[74]—is one of the most important yet underdeveloped themes in critical race theory.[75] Obviously, critical race theory is about more than race. Idealists seek to describe a culture composed of interacting identities on the outside of mainstream American culture. Racial identities intersect with nonracial ones, such as gender and sexual orientation, to form complex lives.[76] Similarly, realists see a social order that has historically subordinated people of color, women, and homosexuals. But what about other subordinated identities or subaltern groups in our society, such as the poor (including whites), the elderly (including whites), or even children (including whites)? Why are they not included within the outsider class? What is the basis for deciding who is or is not an "outsider"? Could it be that critical race theorists are trying to limited the term "outsider" to those who are "a permanent member of an unjustly reviled class," groups that have been demonized and persecuted by law and society?[77] That might be a reasonable basis for limiting the outsider class to people of color, women, and homosexuals. The elderly, children, and the poor have no history of being reviled in this society, at least not like the other groups. Also, membership in these groups is not necessarily permanent.

The inclusion of "people of color" in the outsider class also raises conceptual issues. Are some racial groups (such as Asians) outsiders in some contexts (such as housing wherein Asian home ownership is low)[78] but not in other contexts (such as education, wherein Asians have higher college participation rates than even whites)?[79] This suggests that a distinction might be drawn between "permanent outsiders" (outsiders who are always disadvantaged, always at the bottom of the well) and "situational outsiders" (outsiders who are disadvantaged or vulnerable only in a given situation). The issue here has little to do with whether oppression can be quantified (the appendix demonstrates that to a large extent it can)[80] and everything to do with whether the outsider class can be rationally constituted.[81] In articulating the grounds on which the outsider class is to be rationally constructed, critical race theorists must clearly explain how this enterprise differs from the process by which the Supreme Court constructs the "protected classes" under our civil rights laws.[82]

To the extent that critical race theorists' diagnostic and prescriptive analyses privilege the outsider's perspective, they may be vulnerable to an antiessentialist counterargument. This is the charge that critical race theory carries an "essential[ist] claim of epistemic advantage—that the oppressed have not only different ways of knowing but also better ways of knowing, that 'the oppressed may make better biologists, physicists, and philosophers than their oppressors.'"[83] If this were the case, the counterargument continues, "the most disadvantaged groups would produce the best scientists" when "in fact, the oppressed and socially marginalized often have little access to the information and education needed to excel in science, which on the whole puts them at a serious 'epistemic *dis*advantage'" (emphasis in original).[84]

I see merit in certain aspects of the external prescriptions tendered by both the idealists and the realists. Idealists believe changing the master narrative is a necessary precondition to eliminating racial subordination. There must be a change in the ideas Americans have about race, whether these ideas come through the media (such as stories about blacks seen on TV and read in news-papers and magazines), entertainment (such as stories about blacks depicted in films and conveyed on the Internet), educational institutions (such as stories about blacks included or excluded from the literary canon), businesses (such as stories about blacks that Madison Avenue uses to promote products), or other means of disseminating cultural images and information in our society.[85] Realist prescriptive measures, such as "rectifying racism" in the criminal jus-tice system in some unspecified way so that young men of color will have a better chance of going to college than to jail,[86] are to be implemented through interest convergence. Outsiders will show insiders how they (insiders) will benefit materially from the proposed reforms. This is a very pragmatic post–civil rights strategy. Yet the realists do not say what happens when the interests do *not* converge. How are they to change insider minds? It is interesting to note that limited separatists would certainly dismiss as Pollyannaish the notion that whites (or blacks, for that matter) can be convinced to act against their own material interests.

Marxist scholars offer an important observation regarding how subaltern groups come to know and understand what constitutes their best interest. These scholars observe that the subordinated often align their interests with those of the dominant group; in other words, they consent to their own subor-dination. Indeed, this is the seminal contribution to Marxism made by the Italian intellectual Antonio Gramsci in the 1930s. Gramsci contended that he-gemony is achieved not only by physical force or coercion but also, and more important, by the consent (both expressed and tacit) of the dominated them-selves. Hegemony is made possible by consensual submission.[87] Gramsci and those who followed him believed that this consensual feature of hegemony ex-plains why proletarian revolutions never emerged in highly industrialized, capitalistic societies such as England and the United States. This is not to say that subordinated peoples always consent to domination. Certainly, African Americans rose up against racial repression during Jim Crow, and because of this unmistakable rejection of racial domination, a racial revolution took shape in the United States. But it is also true that African Americans today seem to be providing tacit consent to their own racial subordination. The black middle class, which is larger and richer today than at any other time in the history of our country, is not staging protest marches or sit-ins the way it did during the civil rights movement. Middle-class blacks are not alone. There is complacency across the board. Working-class and poor blacks have either gained a level of economic or psychic satisfaction in life, even though they are at or near the bottom (here's to the realists), or imbibed the prevailing cultural ideology, taking it to be natural, neutral, and "an intractable component of common sense"[88] that if they work hard enough they too will be on top one day (here's to the idealists). Discrimination surely bothers blacks, but apparently not subordination.

The job of critical race theorists, it seems to me, is to bring African Americans face-to-face with their own tacit consent to the existing racial hierarchy (as demonstrated in the appendix). Not unlike the marketing challenge that confronts limited separatists,[89] critical race theorists must initiate an internal dialogue among blacks. But I am not sure critical race theorists are capable of providing such guidance. Critical race theorists reject the black/white binary and, consequently, lump blacks in with resource-rich outsiders, such as Asians and homosexuals, each with its own set of civil rights problems.[90] This is like comparing apples with oranges. The race crits' concession that each outsider group suffers its own form of subordination gets lost in their larger commitment to the insider/outsider binary. With this mind-set, they can easily miss civil rights issues unique to blacks, in effect, subjecting blacks to a different form of subordination.

In the end, I believe that critical race theory is the most fascinating and complex civil rights theory articulated during this post–civil rights era. It has tremendous explanatory potential; however, it offers an incomplete answer to the problem of race in our society. There is no theoretical balance—not enough internal critique. In addition, most of its external prescriptions lack the originality and boldness of its external diagnosis. Critical race theory also has no dearth of conceptual and operational flaws, none more serious than its fuzzy conceptualization of the "outsider" class. For these reasons, I view critical race theory as merely one piece of a larger puzzle about race in post–civil rights America. Simply put, post–civil rights theorists—traditionalists, reformists, limited separatists, and race crits—need each other to produce the "best" civil rights theory. Critical race theory cannot stand alone, but the other theories cannot stand without it.

*Epilogue*

# TOWARD THE "BEST" POST–CIVIL RIGHTS THEORY

THIS BOOK SYNTHESIZES the major civil rights theories pertaining to blacks articulated since the early 1970s, the end of the civil rights movement. Four major theoretical positions have emerged during this post–civil rights period—traditionalism, reformism, limited separation, and critical race theory. Informed by the contrasting racial dynamics of the Age of Obama (racial success and racial despair), each theory is built around what I regard to be the central civil rights question of the day, at least as it pertains to African Americans—to wit, what are the major factors that sustain the American race problem, and what should be done to redress these factors? I define the American race problem as resource disparity between black and white America or, in other words, capital deficiencies within black America. Each theory is carefully presented and constructively critiqued based on its completeness (my theory of completeness), that is, based on its external and internal diagnosis of and prescription for the problem of race pertaining to blacks today. The diagnostic analysis proceeds at the empirical level, while the prescriptive analysis proceeds at the normative level. This particular approach reflects my strong view that post–civil rights theory should use the "is" of diagnosis to produce the "ought" of prescription.

Collectively, the post–civil rights theories beg the question, what is the "best" civil rights theory for blacks in this post–civil rights period? More specifically, what is the "best" way to both diagnose and resolve resource deficits in black America? This question can, of course, be raised with respect to nonblack civil rights groups, including Latinos, Asians, and women. But, as I have indicated in the introduction, one would have to begin with a careful definition of the post–civil rights problem facing each group. Resource disparity may or may not be the best way to define the race or gender problem pertaining to these groups. For example, immigration issues may need to be factored into a definition of the post–civil rights problem facing Latinos, and disparate resources may not be the most accurate or complete way to define the civil rights problem facing Asians because they have *greater* resources than whites in some areas of American life (see the appendix). Hence, each civil rights group has its own set of post–civil rights problems that warrant individual attention. My ambition at the moment is to move the discussion forward, toward the discovery of the "best" post–civil rights theory for African Americans.

Proceeding with this discussion, I am guided by two principles. The first is the theory of completeness. Like traditionalism, reformism, limited separation, and critical race theory, the "best" civil rights theory should be complete, meaning it should provide an external and internal diagnosis of (again, an empirical question) and prescription for (a normative question) the American race problem. The second guiding principle governs the prescription's normative stance. In my view, the prescription should be not only logically connected to its antecedent diagnosis but also idealistic yet practical. In other words, it should be responsive to the external or internal diagnosis, and it should be within the reach of morally motivated individuals, men and women with first-rate intellects and first-rate temperaments, men and women of probity and intelligence. This norm of logic and idealism—let us call it "practical idealism"— can help us strive for an effective resolution of the American race problem unhampered by moral doubts and unspoiled by partisan politics. Political details and compromises can be worked out later (in another book), but for now we ought to seek the truth; we ought to try to get it right even if it calls for unprecedented effort by both blacks and the government. Americans should, in short, work to find a coherent, logical, and morally desirable prescription before the political horse trading and ox goring begin.

Defining the "best" post–civil rights theory at this prepolitical stage of the discussion as one that is both complete and imbued with practical idealism means that the "best" theory is likely to be ahead of its time. To that extent, the "best" theory proffered here will be similar to prior "best" theories. Abolitionism was the "best" civil rights theory during slavery, and desegregation/racial integration was the "best" civil rights theory during Jim Crow. Neither was politically feasible, especially in the South, when first articulated. Both theories were articulated well before society could muster the political will to embrace them. In each era, society has had to catch up to the "best" civil rights theory. Americans had to mature morally to be receptive to the "best" civil rights theory. In each era, moral direction was given *before* political feasibility was established.

Thus, it is the job of the civil rights theorist, at least at the initial stage of theory development, to be truthful rather than political. To that extent, I take serious issue with Tommie Shelby, who suggests in *We Who Are Dark: The Philosophical Foundations of Black Solidarity* that civil rights theory, in this instance a "defense of black self determination," "must not be utopian—applicable only in an ideal world—but must be politically viable given the sociohistorical circumstances of contemporary black Americans."[1] Based on that standard, the abolitionist prescription of civil rights theorist and activist Frederick Douglass and the desegregation/integrationist prescription of theorist and activist Martin Luther King were ill conceived. They should have waited for a more favorable political environment before advancing their utopian liberation theories. Atticus Finch be damned.

Guided by the theory of completeness and practical idealism, I have come to the conclusion that there is no "best" post–civil rights theory among the extant theories. True, some theories are more complete than others, but, as I have stressed in previous chapters, even these theories (namely, reformism and limited separation) are not problem-free.[2] I am convinced that the "best" theory begins as an amalgamation of all the extant theories. Together, the four theories offer a wide range of civil rights thought. The initial question then becomes, what is the *proper mix* of traditionalism, reformism, limited separation, and critical race theory? What makes the most sense externally and internally, diagnostically and prescriptively?

One way to answer this threshold question is to look for consensus and conformation among the four theories. Proceeding in this manner makes sense because the theories collectively bring no dearth of wisdom to the table, notwithstanding their individual flaws. Hence, I begin with a kind of town hall meeting among the theories, the kind of discussion one would have at the Black Table.

There is agreement among most of the theories regarding the "best" external diagnosis of the problem. The consensus is that disparate resources are to a significant extent sustained by external factors, specifically, the lingering effects of old-fashioned racism and racial discrimination, more recent patterns of racism and racial discrimination, white self-interest, and white hegemony. It is only the traditionalists who believe race no longer matters. Traditionalists in fact argue that there is no race problem that requires the ministrations of the central government; there is only a class problem. Hence, we are to believe that the capital deficiencies we see in the black community from the end of the civil rights movement to today are sustained by black culture alone. That does not seem empirically valid to me. Race still matters.

Yet race may not matter in the way that most reformists claim. There is, to be sure, motivational racism and racial discrimination today, as reformists contend. Old-fashioned racial antipathy, so prevalent during the civil rights movement, still matters. But that type of racial bias seems to matter less today than self-interested racial bias. Racial bias against blacks in post–civil rights America is motivated less by racial hatred than by white self-interest. Unlike during Jim Crow, the majority of white Americans today do not hate blacks. Much more antiblack bias comes at the hands of whites protecting their own interests (economic, political, educational, and so on). Limited separatists believe blacks would act in a similar fashion if they (blacks) were in power.

But even the limited separatists do not tell the complete story. While some racial bias is motivated by white self-interest, much more (perhaps most) racial bias today is cognitive rather than motivational. Whether racial hatred or naked self-interest, racial bias in post–civil rights America has less to do with motivation than with cognitive mechanisms—one's rational ordering of the world. Racial bias is largely the product of white racial schemas about competency, reasonableness, talent, diligence, beauty, and other human traits. For example, children learn even in preschool that blacks are inferior to whites, without being told so, by simply observing the behavior of adults or older children toward blacks. "When a little freckle-faced white girl tells an ABC News interviewer on national TV that the only thing African Americans do better than whites is 'their hair,'"[3] that is cognitive bias rather than motivational bias. So is the so-called Lincoln factor. President Lincoln abhorred slavery but also believed that the black American "is not my equal in many respects—certainly not in color, perhaps not in moral or intellectual endowment."[4] Like Lincoln, there are white Americans in positions of power today who believe in equal rights in some abstract way but do not believe that blacks on average are the equal of whites in matters of intelligence, morality, and beauty. Their impoverished sense of equality may allow that blacks are better than whites in certain areas, such as sports and entertainment, but not in the things that matter most in life.

Quite often these racial mind-sets, cognitive and motivational, appear together. For example, during the 2008 presidential primary campaign, a former white president, who was once called the first "black" president, played the race card against the first black person to win a major political party's presidential nomination. During the South Carolina Democratic primary, former president Bill Clinton condescendingly compared Senator Barack Obama to controversial civil rights activist Jesse Jackson. When Obama's black supporters expressed disapproval of the comparison, Clinton accused them of "mugging" him.[5] Clinton's statements were not motivated by racial hatred. They were cognitive or, more likely, motivated by self-interest, his desire to help his wife win a political victory against Obama. Similarly, Senator Hillary Clinton, Obama's chief opponent in the 2008 democratic primaries, played to well-entrenched antiblack sentiment among white voters by continuously claiming that Obama did not have the support of "hardworking white Americans."[6] Senator Clinton played the race card not because she hated blacks but because she wanted to win, and she knew she could do so by appealing to white working-class racial hatred, self-interest, or racial stereotyping. A *Washington Post/ABC News* poll taken in June 2008 showed that "30 percent of white voters" were racist, that is, "admitted to harboring racial prejudice."[7] This poll is consistent with an Associated Press/Yahoo news poll taken just two months before the 2008 presidential election, which showed that "one-third [of white Democratic voters polled] harbored negative views toward blacks," finding them, inter alia, "lazy and violent."[8] While these polls reveal racism motivated by either racial antipathy or white self-interest (e.g., the desire to maintain white privilege in America), they may also reflect the voters' cognitive state (e.g., an implicit sense of white privilege or entitlement to political leadership).

Whatever their origin, racial mind-sets are important external factors that cannot be ignored.

In addition to racial mind-sets, racial structures also define the external race problem. Again, each of the post–civil rights theories, with the exception of traditionalism, recognizes the existence of such barriers. There are, to be sure, nuances among the theorists who recognize them. Each of these theorists, however, subscribes to the basic idea that there are deeply rooted, self-sustaining pro-white institutional and social arrangements in this country, what Joe Feagin calls "systemic racism" and what critical race theorists Derrick Bell and Richard Delgado call "racial subordination." The latter concept, in fact, incorporates racial mind-sets as well as racial barriers.

In sum, race still matters in post–civil rights America. It matters less as racial discrimination than as racial subordination, which includes racial mind-sets (racial hatred, self-interest or cognitive schemas such as stereotyping or white privilege) and racial conditions. Manifested as racial subordination, race matters more for some blacks, less for other blacks, and hardly ever for still others. It matters more in some situations, less in others, and hardly at all in still others. Yet, to say that race still matters at all is to say that race still contributes to disparate resources to some degree. Thus, to ignore race, as traditionalists would have us do, is, to borrow from Glenn Loury, "simplistic social ethics and sophomoric social psychology."[9]

There is also a consensus among the theorists regarding the existence of an internal race problem. Here, the traditionalists have been largely correct. Like traditionalists, most theorists believe that blacks contribute to the problem of resource disparity in our post–civil rights society. Again, there are differences around the margins. Some theorists identify the internal race problem as one of despair (a kind of spiritual impoverishment that traditionalist John McWhorter calls victimology and reformist Cornel West calls black nihilism, to which limited separatists subscribe) while others identify it as ghettofabulosity (what reformist Michael Eric Dyson defines as thuggery, misogyny, and instant gratification). As I argued in chapter 3, I would add defiance (racial sensibility) to the mix.[10] These sociopsychological conditions lead to teenage pregnancy, drug use, black-on-black crime, and other manifestations of cultural dysfunction. Another difference among the theorists concerns the exogenous nature of these bad behaviors and bad values. While core traditionalists tend not to connect cultural dysfunction to past or current racism and racial discrimination, reformists and limited separatists do. In addition, limited separatists add society's integrationist impulse as a conditioning factor. Some noncore traditionalists, as well as some reformists, blame a greedy and corrupt American culture writ large (e.g., corporate greed and government corruption) for some of the cultural dysfunction within black society. But all theorists, save the critical race theorists, see a major internal race problem.

In short, the diagnostic consensus among the post–civil rights theorists is that disparate resources are sustained by both external (racial subordination) and internal (despair, ghettofabulosity, and defiance) factors. While there was no internal race problem to speak of during the civil rights movement (the problem was largely external, with overt racism at its center), the race problem today has both external and internal sustaining factors. What to do about this twofold race problem? Here, again, consensus among the theorists, tempered by practical idealism, may provide answers.

The internal prescription is easiest to fashion, so I shall begin there. With the exception of critical race theory, each of the post–civil rights theories relies on some form of black self-help as a prescription for the internal race problem. The only remaining question is what combination of self-help programs (traditionalism's it-takes-the-individual, reformism's it-takes-a-family, or limited separation's it-takes-a-village) is logically connected to a sound understanding of the internal race problem (despair, defiance, and ghettofabulosity) and at the same time within the reach of morally motivated individuals and institutions? My answer is: all the above.

I believe African Americans should be allowed to select the self-help program that works best for the individual, the family, or the community. There is a logical connection between any self-help program and the internal race problem; indeed, the best place to find a helping hand is at the end of one's arm. I say this with two reservations. The first applies to traditionalism's Horatio Alger–style self-help program. As discussed in chapter 2, individual pluck cannot create success on its own. Talented and hardworking individuals (strivers) also need the right social arrangements to succeed. My second reservation, as I argued in chapter 4, is that the professed independence of the limited separatist's it-takes-a-village self-help program is somewhat undercut by the call for government financial assistance. I understand the sense of entitlement here (the government owes blacks), but still it takes away from the desire for racial independence. Also, as I discussed in chapter 4, the material self-interest of middle-class blacks will probably make it difficult for them to accept this self-help program. Some blacks will, however, undoubtedly find its approach appealing. So long as whites are not excluded, I see nothing morally objectionable about the idea of healthy black communities with vibrant black businesses, first-rate black schools, and spiritually uplifting black churches. I applaud the fact that the 2008 valedictorian of Morehouse College, the most prestigious HBCU, was a white male.

With the exception of the core traditionalists, all theorists, including the "compassionate conservatives" (or "comcons"), see the need for an external prescription. There is nothing approaching a consensus here, save for the fact that reformists and critical race theorists are big supporters of race-based affirmative action. So the question is, which prescriptions among the ones proposed or not proposed are most calculated to redress the external race problem, a problem that largely consists of racial subordination, in a morally responsible manner?

The "best" external prescription should respond to each category of resource deficiency in black society: financial, human, and social capital deficiencies (see appendix). Pursuant to that command, I believe that federal loan guarantees and microloans should be made available in a substantial way for black businesses. This prescription speaks to financial capital deficiencies in black America. The Harlem Children's Zone should be greatly expanded with private external financial backing to redress human capital deficiencies. But my preferred prescription for human capital development has two prongs: flood predominantly black schools with good teachers, and turn as many of these schools as possible into KIPP Academies. The first prong is quite simple but revolutionary, and the second one provides a context for maximizing the effectiveness of the first prong. Finally, in response to social capital deficiencies, federal tax credits should be extended to businesses in the entertainment industry that promote positive and truthful images of black Americans. I will discuss these prescriptions in the order of their importance in terms of resource development in the black community.

In my view, education is the key to human capital development, and human capital is the key to financial and social capital development. For that reason I begin with education. One of my educational prescriptions, the Harlem Children's Zone, is discussed in detail in chapter 4. I shall defer to that discussion. As an alternative to expanding the Harlem Children's Zone, I would prescribe and actually prefer something that has never been tried in this country before, but is very simple and effective in resolving the educational problems facing black students in K–12. My preferred prescription is to invest in good teachers and change the "cultural legacy" of black students. That is, in the first instance flood predominantly black schools with good teachers; invest less in educational equipment and facilities and more in educational personnel. In the second instance, turn the schools at which these teachers work into KIPP Academies. Teaching their students to develop the character as well as the academic skills needed to succeed in K–12 and in college, these academies have raised the standardized test scores and overall scholastic achievement of minority students throughout the nation.

Finland sets the precedent for the first prong of my proposal, investing in good teachers. In the 1980s, this country of only 5 million was "by most measures the poorest country in northern Europe." By 2008, Finland had jumped from "an agrarian, timber-based economy into a technological powerhouse." How did it accomplish so much in such a short time? Finnish president Tarja Halonen says she can "sum it up in three words: education, education and education." By investing heavily in education, Finland has created an excellent school system, ranking, for example, number one in the world in standardized test scores in science for fifteen-year-old students. In comparison, the United States ranks twenty-ninth. Finland's teachers are well paid, well trained, and, hence, well respected—just the opposite of teachers in the United States. As one Finnish official has remarked, "You need at least a master's degree to teach in elementary school, and a college degree to teach in kindergarten. Only one of every 10 applicants is admitted to the Finnish universities' teachers colleges." Teachers are willing to work hard for the social esteem, relatively high pay, and two-and-a-half-month vacations they receive. Quality, not quantity, of time teaching is what counts. Teachers are even willing to teach one-on-one sessions. This has helped to "narrow the gap between good students and those lagging behind, which helps explain why Finland does so well in standardized international tests that measure the learning skills of all students, not just the best ones."[11]

To entice good teachers to teach at predominantly black schools in the United States, several specific changes in educational policy will have to take place, following Finland's lead. For example, teachers who teach in predominantly black schools will have to be paid a premium, a starting salary of at least $75,000. They will have to have at least a master's degree from certified master's programs at colleges like Columbia University and San Diego State University. In these programs, they will learn, inter alia, how to teach to the special needs of black students. Classes will be taught by experienced educators like Dr. Shirley Weber at San Diego State University. Salary and social esteem are the key ingredients in attracting good teachers. Law schools and business schools attract the best, brightest, and hardest-working students year after year mainly because of the salaries and social respect these professions afford. We need to redirect these human resources into our public schools, starting with predominantly black schools. Salary and esteem are the best means of accomplishing this. As Ossi Airaskorpi, principal of an elementary school near Helsinki observes: "In the 1980s and 1990s, everybody wanted to go into business. Now, they want to be teachers."[12]

Placing money in the right place is necessary but may not be sufficient to improve the academic performance of underperforming black students. Educational success depends to a large extent on the "cultural legacy" (attitudes and behaviors toward academic achievement) the student brings to school diurnally. KIPP Academies have had remarkable success in giving poor and working-class black students the kind of cultural legacy necessary for academic success. In my view, KIPP Academies should be the rule rather than the exception in K–12 public education.

KIPP stands for "Knowledge Is Power Program." The first KIPP Academy was established by two teachers, David Levin and Michael Feinberg, as an experimental public middle school in the South Bronx in 1994. Today, there are sixty-six KIPP Academies in nineteen states and the District of Columbia, serving over 16,000 students. "Eighty percent of KIPP [students] are low-income, and 90 percent are African American or Latino. Nationally, more than 90 percent of KIPP middle school students have gone on to college-preparatory high schools, and more than 80 percent of KIPP alumni have gone on to college." Student enrollment is based on a lottery system.[13]

This extraordinary record of success is achieved by giving low-income black and brown students the very thing that Asian cultures as well as wealthier American families give to their children: more education. Asian children have a long school year. They spend less time on summer vacation than American children. For example, the school years in Japan and South Korea consist of 243 days and 220 days, respectively. In the United States the school year is on average only 180 days. Although they have longer summer vacations than their Asian counterparts, wealthier American children spend a great deal of their summer vacation being educated. They take classes at summer camps, participate in junior theater, visit museums, read books, and are constantly engaged educationally by their parents. Low-income black families typically have no money to send their children to summer camps or special programs. Nor do parents in these families have the time to keep their children active and interested in education during the summer months. Watching television and going to the mall are the main means of entertainment for children in these families. The consequences are shocking. As Malcolm Gladwell writes:

> The wealthiest kids come back in September, . . . their reading scores have jumped more than 15 points. [When] the poorest kids come back, . . . their scores have *dropped* almost 4 points. Poor kids may out-learn rich kids during the school year. But during the summer, they fall far behind. Virtually all of the advantage that wealthy students have over poor students is the result of differences in the way privileged kids learn while they are *not* in school.[14]

The KIPP antidote is to give its students more education—three extra weeks of schooling in July.

Extending the school year is not the main way KIPP students receive more education. They also spend more time in school during the day and more days at school during the week. School starts at 7:25 A.M. and ends at 5 P.M. Homework, sports, clubs and detention follow. Some students stay at school until 7 P.M. Most students are in a subsidized-lunch program. KIPP students attend school six days a week, Monday through Saturday. On Saturday, students are in school from nine to one.[15]

To succeed in this type of educational program, students must undergo a cultural transformation. They have to jettison the attitude toward education inherited from the community into which they were born (the belief that children "should have time to play and dream and sleep") and imbibe the Asian model of more education. The inherited cultural legacy is no match for a cultural legacy that "uses weekends and summer vacation to push children ahead." American upper-middle-class families are closer to the Asian model than are less fortunate American families. KIPP students seem willing to embrace a new set of beliefs about education in exchange for a chance at a successful life. As Gladwell notes:

> Is this a lot to ask of a child? It is. But think of things from [the KIPP student's] perspective. She has made a bargain with her school. She will get up at five-forty-five in the morning, go in on Saturdays, and do homework until eleven at night. In return, KIPP promises that it will take kids like her who are stuck in poverty and give them a chance to get out.[16]

Educational success, then, is a function of cultural legacy (which may require borrowing from another culture), individual pluck, and opportunities afforded by society, including access to good teachers.

Reformists and a few traditionalists rightfully assert that the entertainment industry has a corrupting influence not only on the black community but also on the nation as a whole. The industry shapes bad behaviors and bad values within the black community and also skews the public's image of blacks, especially that of young black men. It is simply outrageous that, for example, the power elite in the music industry have no qualms about making money from racist and misogynist lyrics, and that television and movie executives push programs and films that present stereotypical images of young black men and women with impunity. These negative images of blacks (e.g., dangerous black men and oversexed black women) come into the homes of young black and white children and teenagers unfiltered. There is no well-informed voice or other mediating force standing between the child or teenager and these harmful messages and images beamed into black and white homes every day. The government should not remain silent in the face of this debasing of African Americans and the American culture. Only it has the power to rectify this problem.

To be sure, socially conscious hip-hop artists have tried but failed to change the tone and content of these racialized messages. Some black artists have complained for years that record companies, which have historically exercised a good amount of control over lyricists, promote and profit from some of the worst behaviors and values in black society. They insist that the music industry forces young rappers to include "commercial elements" in their songs and music videos. Rappers have to use negative images of violence, drugs, sex, and misogyny to sell records. Mos Def, for example, complains about the commercialization of hip-hop in the following song: "Old white men is runnin' this rap shit, / Corporate bosses is runnin' this rap shit… / We poke out our asses for a chance to cash in."[17] Mos Def is one of the few hip-hop artists who have been able to free their music from corporate control. Another is Joy James, who echoes Mos Def, stating, "Commercial rappers aspire to become cyborgs: The thing ($$) becomes human or the human the thing."[18] Some music executives who exploit black stereotypes for financial gain are themselves black. One of the most prominent black record producers was "Suge" Knight, who owned

Death Row Records, which signed the infamous Tupac Shakur. Knight's em-
pire embraced lawlessness, greed, drugs, and the objectification of women. He
was motivated by both profit and conviction.[19]

I do not think the government should legislate racialized images out of existence. I am not a fan of prior restraint. But I do believe the government should
use its taxing power to encourage good behavior, just as it used its spending
power during the civil rights movement to promote equal educational opportunity in Title VI of the 1964 Civil Rights Act.[20] Thus, my proposal is that federal tax credits be given to businesses in the entertainment industry that promote positive racial images. That the industry's resulting good behavior is
financially motivated may bother the purist, but it does not bother me. Good
behavior too often never comes, and so one ought not to reject it merely because of the way it arrives.

Developing financial capital resources in black communities through the
creation of small businesses is always a challenge. As Jonathan Morduch, a
professor of finance at NYU, has noted, banks, credit unions, and other traditional financial institutions have very little presence in black communities,
which tend to be poor or working-class. After family and friends, most blacks
in these communities have to do their business and personal financing with
payday lenders, check cashers, and pawn shops. Using these third-rank financial institutions to provide basic finance is expensive, exploitative, and inefficient. Another problem is regulations and competition. One cannot even set
up a lemonade stand on a street corner without government regulation and
competition from the lemonade stand just across the street. All these issues
need to be addressed if blacks are to develop substantially more resources in
the form of financial capital.

To deal with these issues, I would prescribe federal loan guarantees and the
expansion of microlending for black businesses, which includes managerial assistance for both start-up and expanding businesses. Federal loan guarantees
have been used for a number of years to bail out foreign governments, private
enterprises, and individuals. The rationale for providing loan guarantees for
such diverse entities is that these borrowers would have difficulty obtaining financing at affordable rates without federal assistance and that, consequently,
important socioeconomic interests would go unserved.[21] On this basis, federal
loan guarantees have been given to Chrysler Corporation and New York City.[22]
I do not see why some federal loan guarantees cannot be specifically targeted
for black businesses. Like the traditional recipients of federal loan guarantees,
black businesses have difficulty finding affordable financing, and they serve an
important socioeconomic interest—bringing more financial capital into poor
and working-class black communities. Keeping in mind that we are ultimately
trying to resolve the American race problem as it pertains to blacks, making a
special effort to extend federal loan guarantees to black businesses also serves
the moral interests of this country.

Federal loan guarantees may not be helpful to a large number of black businesses whose financial needs are quite modest. The time and expense of administering small loans makes them unattractive candidates for traditional lenders, even if the loans are guaranteed by the federal government. What is needed for these borrowers is a smaller financing scheme, perhaps microlending. Begun more than forty years ago by community organizers in third world countries in partnership with banks and other traditional financial institutions, microlending provides poor people in Latin America, the Caribbean, Africa, and Asia with small-business loans that help finance their way out of poverty. Microloans are small, as little as $100, and are used to create microbusinesses (e.g., sewing clothes or selling vegetables on the street) as well as expand existing small businesses. Borrowers range from the dirt poor to those with modest assets but without access to mainstream financing. One microlender, ACCION INTERNATIONAL, has partnered with Banco Compartamos in Mexico to serve more than 673,000 poor and low-income entrepreneurs. Worldwide, "ACCION's partner programs increased the number of people served from 13,000 in 1988 to 2.7 million in 2007. While it took twenty years for ACCION's partners to reach their first million clients, it took just three more to reach their second million."[23] Microlending not only extends low-cost financing to microenterprises but also provides managerial support. This ensures the success of the enterprise, whether start-up or expanding. Microlending, in short, has "created an anti-poverty strategy that is permanent and self-sustaining."[24]

Microlending has been brought to the United States, albeit on a very small scale. Perhaps the leading microlender in the United States, Project Enterprise serves only about 400 businesses, even though it has been in existence for more than ten years. Loans can range from as low as $750 to as high as $3,000, just enough to allow a first-time entrepreneur to get started or an existing small business to supplement working capital for expansion. With these loans, a black-owned bakery was able to get started by purchasing small items, such as flour, eggs, and a high-power mixer, and a small publishing company was able to expand by upgrading its computer software. All the while, managerial assistance was provided to each business.

Microlending should be expanded throughout African American communities. It can work in tandem with the internal prescription of black self-help to augment financial capital resources in these resource-deficient communities. Any one of the self-help programs (individual, family, or community) can benefit from microlending. These prescriptions, both external and internal, are well within the reach of morally motivated individuals, institutions, and governments.

A GI Bill for blacks is yet another external prescription that could meet the dictates of practical idealism, but it is one I would not prescribe at the moment. The original GI Bill provided educational and housing benefits to American soldiers returning home from World War II. Many of the reasons for creating this capital-building legislation apply with equal force to blacks.[25] For example, Congress and President Roosevelt feared that millions of returning veterans, whose wartime skills were not well suited to civilian employment, would create a massive drain on the economy. President Roosevelt believed that twelve million returning GIs would flood the job market, and that this would create inflationary pressures and unemployment. Also, the thought of veterans waiting in breadlines or standing on corners selling apples was morally unappealing.

There were political pressures as well. Lawmakers wanted to prevent a recurrence of the Bonus Army, scores of unemployed and disgruntled World War I veterans descending on Washington, D.C. At the end of World War I, GIs received a mere sixty dollars and a train ticket home. In response to widespread dissatisfaction among veterans, Congress in 1924 passed the Adjusted Compensation Act, popularly known as the Bonus Act, which promised bonuses to veterans based on the number of days served in the military. Under the act, however, the veterans would not receive any compensation for twenty years after its passage. Demanding early payment of their benefits, more than 15,000 veterans converged on Washington, D.C., in 1932 in what was called the "Bonus March." The U.S. Army was mobilized to drive the protesters out of town. Loaded rifles and riot control gas were used on American citizens who not only had served their country honorably but now were exercising their civil liberties.

In an attempt to prevent a similar embarrassing display of injustice, members of Congress proposed new legislation to help returning veterans to "reassimilate" into American society. Despite the support of veteran groups, the bill met with strong resistance in both the House and the Senate. Although both chambers of Congress agreed on the proposed educational benefits and home loans, they deadlocked on the unemployment provisions, that is, provisions that gave GIs twenty dollars in unemployment compensation each week for up to one year. Republicans argued that the unemployment benefits were too generous and, thus, would create disincentives for returning troops to search for jobs. Other members of Congress attacked the bill on grounds that it was just another extension of Roosevelt's welfare state. The bill narrowly passed through Congress and was signed into law by President Roosevelt in June 1944.

The last major piece of New Deal legislation, the Serviceman's Readjustment Act of 1944, better known as the GI Bill of Rights, sought to help returning World War II soldiers succeed in postwar America by giving them the financial and human capital they would need to prosper in this new society. Specifically, the act gave male and female veterans up to $500 in college tuition a year,[26] plus living expenses. It also provided federal-guaranteed low-interest home and business loans. Unemployment benefits, mentioned earlier, were given to veterans who could not find jobs.

The GI Bill became far more popular and had a far greater effect on creating resources among the veterans and prosperity in America than anyone had anticipated. It is estimated that more than eight million veterans took advantage of the GI Bill's educational benefits. By the mid-1950s, veterans added to America about a half million new engineers, about a quarter million new teachers, and tens of thousands of doctors, dentists, and scientists. The GI Bill also gave rise to the suburbs, that is, new neighborhoods outside of cities (Levittowns across the nation) created to house the throngs of college-educated veterans climbing the corporate ladder in their gray flannel suits.[27]

Black veterans did not receive the same benefits as their white cohort. The bill was deliberately implemented in a racially discriminatory manner. For example, government-insured loans were not extended to blacks who fought in the war, despite the federal guarantee. Also, the Veterans Administration (VA) often exercised its discretion to reject the medical claims of black GIs.[28]

But for white veterans, the GI Bill was heaven-sent. It enabled them to build financial, human, and social capital from which they and their children and grandchildren continue to benefit today. The bill demonstrated the nation's commitment to the well-being of white veterans. Yet the GI Bill also benefited the nation as a whole. It brought prosperity to many communities and catapulted the United States to leadership on the world stage.

A similar prescription could be written for African Americans. A GI Bill for blacks could give black Americans a wide range of resources, including educational vouchers, college tuition, affirmative action, and federal grants or loans for black businesses. I would concede that all of these resources are responsive to the external race problem, and all are the sort of things morally motivated individuals would want to do to resolve a problem that not only shows no signs of ending on its own but has in fact been in existence, in one form or another, for almost four hundred years. But I am not sure that we need to go this far to resolve the disparate resource problem in black America. My preferred prescriptions—well-paid teachers and KIPP Academies—may be sufficient. We should at least try them. If they fail, we will have a more aggressive prescription waiting in the wings.

When the civil rights debate moves into the political arena, as it inevitably will, the cost of alternative external prescriptions will certainly become a consideration. Moving from a normative discourse to a political one, from discussions about truth and moral judgments to one about horse trading or even ox goring, will generate issues left off the table here. The cost of the external prescription and how to reconcile that problem with the billions of dollars the federal government appropriated for the 9/11 families at a time when the nation supposedly could not afford it are just two of the many issues that will arise in the political arena. We need to have that type of discussion, but not now. In my view, it would be premature and unfair to blacks to move the debate into the political realm at this time. Before partisanship sets in, our nation needs to have a period of prepolitical reflection on the normative issues. This must include an appreciation of the moral enormity of slavery and Jim Crow, especially the shadow they continue to cast over our society. I think African Americans are at least due that.

Politics hangs over the discussion of civil rights, and it seems everything else, these days like the sword of Damocles. I know this, and I also know that, except with human beings like Martin Luther King and the fictional character Atticus Finch, moral precepts are no match for the material needs that negate them. But still I argue that before we bring politics into the discussion, before compromise is placed on the table, we ought to have some vision of the ideal solution. I hope this book moves us in that direction, and does so with the same degree of intellectual integrity and respect for dissenting voices I had the pleasure of seeing at the Black Table.

*Appendix*

# DISPARATE RESOURCES IN AMERICA BY RACE IN THE POST–CIVIL RIGHTS ERA

## Contents

## Introduction

The figures in this appendix provide a statistical profile of resource disparity in the United States based on race during the post–civil rights era (1972–present). They provide an empirical basis for analyzing the American race problem and critiquing the theories presented in this book. Most of the major racial groups are represented, but the emphasis is on black/white disparity for reasons mentioned in chapter 1. Statistical terms and conventions observed in this appendix include the following.

## Coverage

Data for some racial categories are unavailable for some years. For example, the "white, not Hispanic" racial category did not exist before 1972; Hispanics were included in the "white" category. Similarly, there are no data available for "Asians and Pacific Islanders" before 1988. The year 2002 is very important. In that year, the Census Bureau altered the traditional census methodology. Prior to that date, an individual was allowed to pick only one racial category. Since 2002, an individual has been allowed to identify himself or herself as belonging to multiple races. The Census Bureau now tracks races by two categories: (1) "alone" (e.g., "black alone"), which consists of individuals who identify themselves as belonging to only one race; and (2) "in combination" (e.g., "black in combination"), which consists of individuals who identify themselves as belonging to the categorized race and one or more additional races. Because the "alone" numbers most closely follow the system employed prior to 2002, all figures in this appendix use the "alone" data sets for the year 2002 and beyond. For further discussion, see U.S. Census Bureau, *Footnotes for Historical Income Tables from the Current Population Survey (CPS), Annual Social and Economic Supplement (ASEC)*, www.census.gov/hhes/www/income/histinc/ftnotes.html (June 2005).

## Affirmative Action Effect

The figures on college enrollment rates (figures 55–60) show that black and Hispanic college enrollment sharply increased in the years immediately preceding and steadily declined in the years after the Supreme Court's controversial decision in *Regents of the University of California v. Bakke*, 438 U.S. 265 (1978). *Bakke* curtailed the widespread use of affirmative action. Statistical research for this project ended before a similar assessment could be made of the Supreme Court's pro–affirmative action decision in *Grutter v. Bollinger*, 539 U.S. 306 (2003). The figures on occupational status (figures 61–63) indicate that affirmative action has a positive effect on human capital development within the black community but that the development is skewed by gender. Black females have benefited far more than black males from affirmative action, possibly because they are regarded as a "twofer"; they supply both race and gender diversity and, hence, are especially desirable to employers.

## Asian American Housing Conundrum

Although Asians and Pacific Islanders have the highest income levels of all the races (see figures 22–29), they have relatively low home ownership rates (see figure 46). This may be explained, at least in part, by the fact that Asian and Pacific Islander income levels are distributed in an "hourglass" pattern rather than the usual "bell curve." The top 50% of Asians and Pacific Islanders are disproportionately well-off, while the bottom 50% are poor. The strong showing of the top half of Asians and Pacific Islanders brings the median and mean income levels for the group above that for white, not Hispanics. The poor showing of the bottom half is reflected by the fact that Asians and Pacific Islanders have higher poverty rates than white, not Hispanics, as shown in figure 3, and are less homogeneous than white, not Hispanics.

## Definitions

The Census Bureau specifically defines key words and concepts used in this appendix, among which are the following.

*Family* is defined as "a group of two people or more (one of whom is the householder) related by birth, marriage, or adoption and residing together." U.S. Census Bureau, *Current Population Survey (CPS)—Definitions and Explanations,* www.census.gov/population/www/cps/cpsdef.html (June 2005).

*Hate crimes* are defined as crimes in which the perpetrator intentionally selects a victim or damages property based on race, religion, sexual orientation, ethnicity/national origin, or disability. Hate crime offenses include aggravated assault, arson, burglary, destruction or damage to property, intimidation (verbal or physical), larceny, robbery, and simple assault.

*Immigrant flow,* which influences the growth of the Hispanic population, refers to the inflow of foreign-born or first-generation persons, including both legal and unauthorized immigrants. The latter term is used herein to refer to "illegal immigrants" or "undocumented immigrants." The Census Bureau's Current Population Survey does not differentiate between legal and unauthorized immigrants, but it does attempt to include both when surveying the population. Nevertheless, private researchers have attempted to estimate the size of the unauthorized population in the United States by comparing data from the Current Population Survey with data from the Immigration and Naturalization Service (INS) and other sources. The Pew Research Center, a nonprofit and nonpartisan institute, estimates that there were 12 million unauthorized immigrants in the United States in 2005 (referred to by Pew as "unauthorized migrants"). In 2004, when the unauthorized immigrant population was estimated to be 10.5 million, Pew estimated that approximately 1 million were not accounted for in the Current Population Survey, a 10% undercounting of the unauthorized population (see figures 17–20). See also Pew Research Center, *Unauthorized Migrants: Numbers and Characteristics,* pewhispanic.org/files/reports/46.pdf (June 2005).

*Income* means any monetary compensation derived from the following sources: (1) earnings; (2) unemployment compensation; (3) workers' compensation; (4) social security; (5) supplemental security income; (6) public assistance; (7) veterans' payments; (8) survivor benefits; (9) disability benefits; (10) pension or retirement income; (11) interest; (12) dividends; (13) rents, royalties, and estates and trusts; (14) educational assistance; (15) alimony; (16) child support; (17) financial assistance from outside of the household; (16) other income. U.S. Census Bureau, *Current Population Survey (CPS)–Definitions and Explanations*, census.gov/population/www/cps/cpsdef.html (June 2005). In addition, income as used therein refers to *real income*, or *constant income* (in current dollars), meaning that it has been adjusted for inflation and that an increase in real income represents a corresponding increase in purchasing power. When measuring income, the U.S. Census Bureau counts persons fifteen years and older (before 1980, persons fourteen years and older were counted).

*Mean* denotes "average." One calculates the mean income, for example, by counting the total income of all persons in a group and then dividing by the number of persons in that group.

*Median* refers to the "middle point." With respect to income, the median income is the value that an equal number of persons make above and below; thus, if the median income of the nation were $40,000, this would mean that half the nation makes more than $40,000, and half the nation makes less than $40,000.

*Occupational status.* "Managerial and professional" occupations include schoolteachers, lawyers, engineers, legislators, athletes, and entertainers. "Technical, sales, and administrative support" occupations include secretaries, receptionists, hotel clerks, mail carriers, telephone operators, and retail sales workers. "Service" occupations include firefighters, police officers, cooks, waitresses, and janitors. "Precision production, craft, and repair" occupations include mechanics, plumbers, electricians, and dressmakers. "Operators, fabricators, and laborers" include machine operators, construction workers, and garbage collectors. See U.S. Department of Labor, *Occupational Classification System Manual (OCSM)*, www.bls.gov/ncs/ocs/ocsm/commain.htm.

*Poverty* is determined at the family level, based on income thresholds set by family size and composition. Poverty thresholds are adjusted for inflation on an annual basis. The 2003 poverty threshold for a family of four with two children was $18,660. U.S. Census Bureau, *Current Population Survey (CPS)— Definitions and Explanations*, www.census.gov/population/www/cps/cpsdef. html (June 2005).

*Race*, unless otherwise indicated, is merely a group of persons that share similar phenotypical characteristics—facial features, skin color, hair, and so on. The categories of "white, not Hispanic," "black," "Asian and Pacific Islander," and "Hispanic" are derived from the fact that members of these "races" typically share similar physical features. Although such a shallow classification scheme may seem suspect, it is justified because of the human tendency to adhere to it. See chapter 1 for an expanded discussion of the term "race."

*White* refers to all people who identify themselves as belonging to the Caucasian race, including Hispanics who consider themselves Caucasian.

*White, not Hispanic* refers to persons of the Caucasian race, excluding persons of Hispanic origin.

Figure 1: Disparity in Poverty Rate of All Families

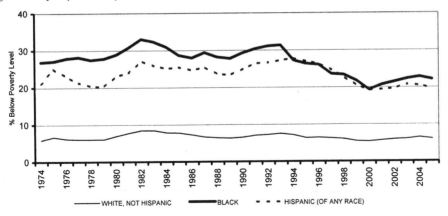

Figure 2: Disparity between Black and White Poverty Rates (Black Rate Minus White, Not Hispanic Rate)

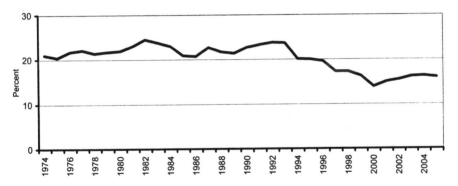

The data shown here, "All Families" (meaning all family structures, e.g., two-parent and single-parent), reveal trends that are very similar to the trends shown elsewhere for all individuals (see figure 3). The level of white, not Hispanic poverty has been fairly constant since 1973, but the percentage of black families below the poverty level has declined some since 1992. As a result, the difference between black and white, not Hispanic poverty rates for families has shrunk slightly since 1992, as seen in figure 2. Family poverty rates are significantly affected by the presence of single-parent-headed families. Compare figures 5 and 7 with figures 11 and 13. In 2005, 54% of black families, 33% of Hispanic families, and 19% of white, not Hispanic families were headed by a single parent. The Hispanic family poverty rate is significantly affected not only by single-parent-headed families but also by immigrant flow (see figures 5 and 7 and the narrative accompanying figures 11 and 13). The above census data are not available for Asians and Pacific Islanders. For other relevant information, see the introduction to the appendix.

*Source:* U.S. Census Bureau, Historical Poverty Tables—Families, table 4, www.census.gov/hhes/www/poverty/histpov/hstpov4.html.

Figure 3: Disparity in Poverty Rate of Individuals

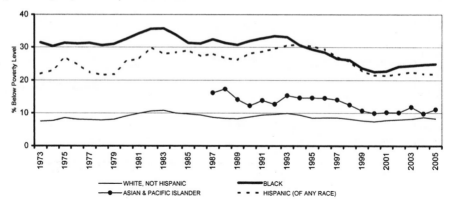

Figure 4: Disparity between Black and White Poverty Rates (Black Rate Minus White, Not Hispanic Rate)

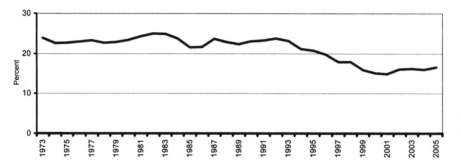

These figures include all individuals living with or without families. The level of white, not Hispanic poverty has been fairly constant since 1973, but the percentage of black Americans below the poverty level has generally declined since 1992. As a result, the difference between black and white, not Hispanic poverty rates has shrunk by 7 percentage points since 1992, as seen in figure 4. Surprisingly, the Asian and Pacific Islander population is erratic and shows a sharp increase in poverty in 2005, which, however, is still below the black and Hispanic rates. The Hispanic rates seem to be affected by immigrant flow (see figures 17 and 18). Although undocumented individuals, who fear deportation, may be reluctant to subject themselves to census counts and surveys, depressing the degree of Hispanic representation, heavy Hispanic immigration nevertheless affects the data. The Immigration Reform and Control Act of 1986 naturalized many previously undocumented Hispanic immigrants, likely increasing their willingness to be counted. In addition, the act may have encouraged the swell of immigration seen in the 1990s. For other relevant information, see the introduction to the appendix.

*Source:* U.S. Census Bureau, Historical Poverty Tables—People, table 2, www.census.gov/hhes/www/poverty/histpov/hstpov2.html.

Figure 5: Disparity in Poverty Rate of All Families Headed by Females

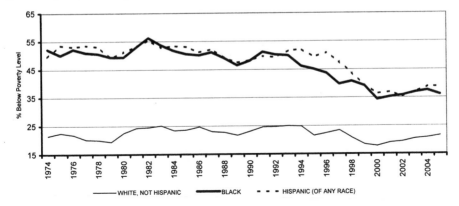

Figure 6: Disparity between Black and White Poverty Rates (Black Rate Minus White, Not Hispanic Rate)

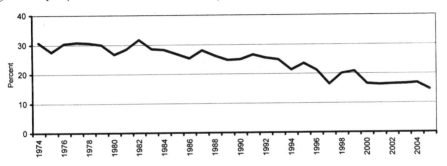

These figures measure female-headed households with and without children. One possible reason why black female-headed households tend to be more impoverished than white, not Hispanic female-headed households is that black female-headed households tend to be larger. As of 2002, 29.2% of black female-headed households had four or more members, compared with only 15.5% of white, not Hispanic female-headed households. Nevertheless, the black rate has been moving closer to the white, not Hispanic rate since the 1980s. One reason the poverty rate of female-headed households is so much greater than that of male-headed households is because female mean and median incomes are significantly lower than those of their male counterparts. The above census data are not available for Asians and Pacific Islanders. For other relevant information, see the introduction to the appendix.

*Source:* U.S. Census Bureau, Historical Poverty Tables—People, table 4, www.census.gov/hhes/www/poverty/histpov/hstpov4.html; U.S. Census Bureau, The Black Population in the United States: March 2002, www.census.gov/prod/2003pubs/p20-541.pdf.

Figure 7: Disparity in Poverty Rate of All Families with Children, Headed by Females

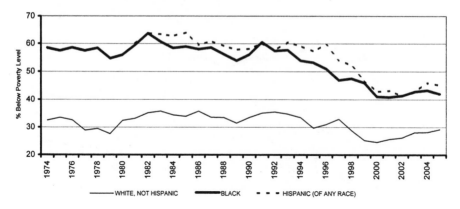

Figure 8: Disparity between Black and White Poverty Rates (Black Rate Minus White, Not Hispanic Rate)

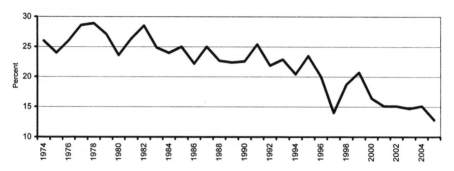

The difference between black and white, not Hispanic poverty rates has narrowed since 1974 for female-headed households with children, declining from a difference of 26% in 1974 to 12.8% in 2005. Black female-headed households tend to be larger than white, not Hispanic female-headed households. See narrative accompanying figures 5 and 6. The above census data are not available for Asians and Pacific Islanders. For other relevant information, see the introduction to the appendix.

*Source:* U.S. Census Bureau, Historical Poverty Tables—People, table 4, www.census.gov/hhes/www/poverty/histpov/hstpov4.html; U.S. Census Bureau, The Black Population in the United States: March 2002, www.census.gov/prod/2003pubs/p20-541.pdf.

Figure 9: Distribution of Total Poor (by Group)

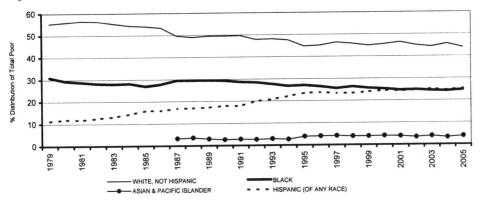

Figure 10: Distribution of Total Population (by Group)

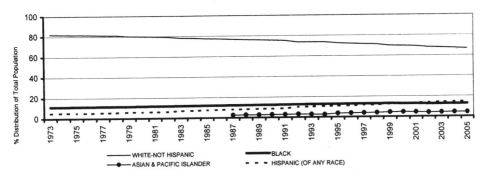

The largest percentage of America's poor are white, not Hispanic. Hispanics continue to make up a larger and larger proportion of America's poor, while the black and the white, not Hispanic proportions are generally falling. The growth rate for the American Hispanic population was 3.3% for the twelve months ending on July 1, 2005. The growth rate for "white alone, not Hispanic or Latino" population was 0.3%, and the growth rate for the "black alone or in combination" population was 1.3%. The Hispanic rate is affected by immigrant flow (see figures 17 and 18). Asians and Pacific Islanders make up the lowest proportion of the poor and the lowest proportion of the total U.S. population. The above data are not available for Asians and Pacific Islanders before 1987. For other relevant information, see the introduction to the appendix.

Source: U.S. Census Bureau, Historical Poverty Tables—People, table 2, www.census.gov/hhes/www/poverty/histpov/hstpov2.html; U.S. Census Bureau, Historical Poverty Tables—People, table 14, www.census.gov/hhes/www/poverty/histpov/hstpov14.html.

Figure 11: Disparity in Poverty Rate of All Married Couples with Children

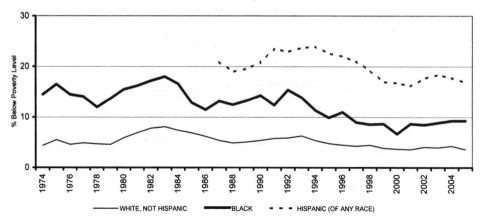

Figure 12: Disparity between Black and White Poverty Rates (Black Rate Minus White, Not Hispanic Rate)

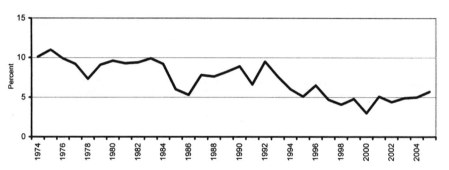

These percentages exclude single-parent-headed households. The difference between the black poverty rate and the white, not Hispanic poverty rate has been cut nearly in half since 1974, as seen in figure 12. Hispanic married couples with children fare much worse than both black and white, not Hispanic married couples with children. Two factors impacting this are (1) "immigrant flow" (see figures 17 and 18) and (2) larger Hispanic families; as of 2005 the Hispanic fertility rate was 49% higher than the fertility rate for the U.S. population as a whole. The above census data are not available for Asians and Pacific Islanders. For other relevant information, see the introduction to the appendix.

*Source:* U.S. Census Bureau, Historical Poverty Tables—Families, table 4. www.census.gov/hhes/www/poverty/histpov/hstpov4.html.

Figure 13: Disparity in Poverty Rate of All Married Couple Families

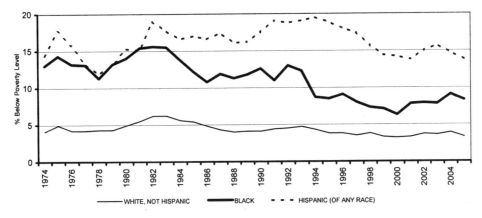

Figure 14: Disparity between Black and White Poverty Rates (Black Rate Minus White, Not Hispanic Rate)

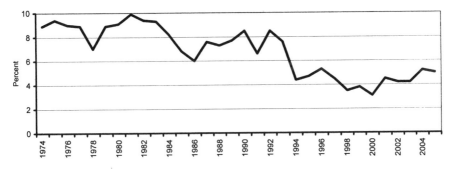

These figures include families with and without children. "Married couple families" can have multiple sources of income, only one source, or none at all. The poverty rate for Hispanic married couples has averaged 16.2% from 1974 to 2005. Again, immigrant flow and Hispanic birthrates cannot be ignored (see figures 17 and 18). Both served to maintain high poverty levels for families consisting of married Hispanic couples. The above census data are not available for Asians and Pacific Islanders. For other relevant information, see the introduction to the appendix.

*Source:* U.S. Census Bureau, Historical Poverty Tables—Families, table 4, www.census.gov/hhes/www/poverty/histpov/hstpov4.html.

Figure 15: Disparity in Poverty Rate of Persons by Sex

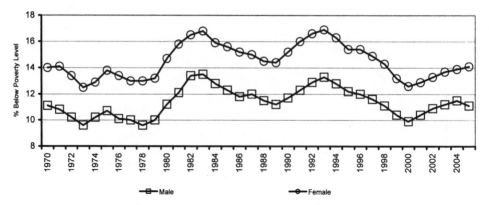

Figure 16: Disparity between Male and Female Poverty Rates (Female Rate Minus Male Rate)

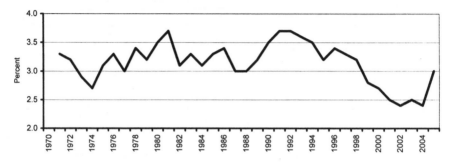

These figures measure the percentages of males and females who are poor. They include married and un-married individuals of both sexes. The difference between the female poverty rate and the male poverty rate increased 0.4 percentage points from 1971 to 1991. From 1991 to 2004, the female rate fell slightly relative to the male rate, with a gap of 2.4% in 2004. In 2005 the gap shot up to 3.0%. For other relevant information, see the introduction to the appendix.

*Source:* U.S. Census Bureau, Historical Poverty Tables—People, table 4, www.census.gov/hhes/www/poverty/histpov/hstpov7.html.

Figure 17: Unauthorized Immigrant Places of Origin in 2005

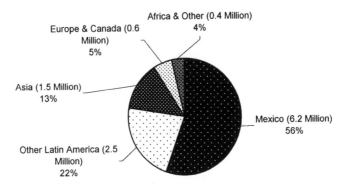

Figure 18: Millions of Unauthorized Immigrants Living in the United States

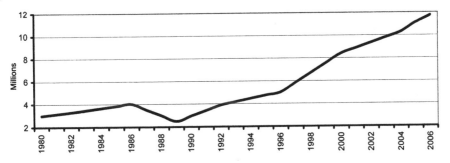

Figures 17 and 18 are evidence of "immigrant flow" (see the introduction to the appendix) from Latin American countries. Figure 17 shows countries of origin for unauthorized immigrants living in the United States. In 2005, 78% of the unauthorized immigrants living in the United States were of Latin American origin. Figure 18 illustrates the estimated growth of the unauthorized population from 1980 to 2005 (regardless of country of origin). Growth of the unauthorized immigrant population was substantial in the 1990s, averaging net inflows of approximately 500,000 per year. Note the decline in the unauthorized population from 1986 to 1989, a result of IRCA legalizations (see narrative accompanying figures 3 and 4). This decline represents persons being legalized, not persons leaving the country. The estimates used in figures 17 and 18 were calculated by the Pew Research Center using a "residual" method: subtracting the total legal foreign-born population (estimated from INS/Department of Homeland Security and other sources) from the total foreign-born population (estimated from Census Bureau data).
*Source:* Pew Research Center, Size and Characteristics of the Unauthorized Migrant Population in the U.S., http://pewhispanic.org/files/reports/61.pdf; Pew Research Center, Unauthorized Migrants: Numbers and Characteristics, http://pewhispanic.org/files/reports/46.pdf;
Pew Research Center, Modes of Entry for the Unauthorized Migrant Population, http://pewhispanic.org/files/factsheets/19.pdf.

Figure 19: 2005 Foreign-Born Population

| Universe: 2005 Household Population | | | | |
|---|---|---|---|---|
| | Total population | Native-born population | Foreign-born population | Percent foreign born |
| Hispanic | 41,926,302 | 25,085,528 | 16,840,774 | 40.2 |
| White alone, not Hispanic | 192,526,952 | 185,083,309 | 7,443,643 | 3.9 |
| Black alone, not Hispanic | 34,410,656 | 31,875,439 | 2,535,217 | 7.4 |
| Asian and Pacific Islander alone, not Hispanic | 12,677,007 | 4,252,962 | 8,424,045 | 66.5 |
| Other, not Hispanic | 6,857,902 | 6,331,978 | 525,924 | 7.7 |
| Total | 288,398,819 | 252,629,216 | 35,769,603 | 12.4 |
| Source: Pew Hispanic Center tabulations of 2005 American Community Survey | | | | |

Figure 20: Hispanic Descent by Country

| Universe: 2005 Hispanic Household Population | | | | |
|---|---|---|---|---|
| | Total | Native Born | Foreign Born | Percent foreign born |
| Mexican | 26,784,268 | 15,928,209 | 10,856,059 | 40.5 |
| Puerto Rican | 3,794,776 | 3,754,043 | 40,733 | 1.1 |
| Cuban | 1,462,593 | 568,691 | 893,902 | 61.1 |
| Dominican | 1,135,756 | 463,374 | 672,382 | 59.2 |
| Costa Rican | 111,978 | 34,801 | 77,177 | 68.9 |
| Guatemalan | 780,191 | 228,767 | 551,424 | 70.7 |
| Honduran | 466,843 | 134,626 | 332,217 | 71.2 |
| Nicaraguan | 275,126 | 85,582 | 189,544 | 68.9 |
| Panamanian | 141,286 | 66,900 | 74,386 | 52.6 |
| Salvadoran | 1,240,031 | 389,051 | 850,980 | 68.6 |
| Other Central American | 99,422 | 33,909 | 65,513 | 65.9 |
| Argentinean | 189,303 | 48,023 | 141,280 | 74.6 |
| Bolivian | 68,649 | 22,530 | 46,119 | 67.2 |
| Chilean | 105,141 | 32,606 | 72,535 | 69.0 |
| Colombian | 723,596 | 217,149 | 506,447 | 70.0 |
| Ecuadorian | 432,068 | 130,926 | 301,142 | 69.7 |
| Paraguayan | 14,204 | 4,242 | 9,962 | 70.1 |
| Peruvian | 415,352 | 105,826 | 309,526 | 74.5 |
| Uruguayan | 51,646 | 8,027 | 43,619 | 84.5 |
| Venezuelan | 162,762 | 40,619 | 122,143 | 75.0 |
| Other South American | 75,239 | 25,734 | 49,505 | 65.8 |
| Spaniard | 362,424 | 303,154 | 59,270 | 16.4 |
| All Other Spanish/Hispanic/Latino | 3,033,648 | 2,458,739 | 574,909 | 19.0 |
| Total | 41,926,302 | 25,085,528 | 16,840,774 | 40.2 |
| Source: Pew Hispanic Center tabulations of 2005 American Community Survey | | | | |

Hispanic immigrant flow has been substantial. In 2005, 17 million out of 42 million Hispanics were foreign born (40%). This includes legal as well as unauthorized immigration. In 2005, 64% of American Hispanics were of Mexican descent.

*Source:* Pew Research Center, A Statistical Portrait of the Foreign-Born Population at Mid-Decade: Table 4, http://pewhispanic.org/files/other/foreignborn/Table-4.pdf; Pew Research Center, A Statistical Portrait of Hispanics at Mid-Decade: Table 4, http://pewhispanic.org/files/other/middecade/Table-4.pdf.

Figure 21: Population Growth Rates: 2004 and 2005

| Race and Hispanic or Latino Origin | July 1, 2005 | July 1, 2004 | Change: July 1, 2004 to July 1, 2005 | |
|---|---|---|---|---|
| | | | Numerical | Percent |
| TOTAL POPULATION | 296,410,404 | 293,655,404 | 2,755,000 | 0.9% |
| | | | | |
| RACE ALONE OR IN COMBINATION | | | | |
| **Black** | **39,724,136** | **39,232,489** | **491,647** | **1.3** |
| American Indian and Alaska Native | 4,453,660 | 4,409,446 | 44,214 | 1.0 |
| Asian | 14,376,658 | 13,956,612 | 420,046 | 3.0 |
| Native Hawaiian and Other Pacific Islander | 989,673 | 976,395 | 13,278 | 1.4 |
| **Hispanic (of any race)** | **42,687,224** | **41,322,070** | **1,365,154** | **3.3** |
| **White alone, not Hispanic or Latino** | **198,366,437** | 197,840,821 | **525,616** | **0.3** |

The growth rate of the Hispanic population has outpaced the growth rates of all other populations shown. The Hispanic growth rate for the twelve months ending July 1, 2005, was 3.3%, compared with 1.3% and 0.3% for the "black alone or in combination" and "white alone, not Hispanic or Latino," populations, respectively. Hispanics accounted for approximately half of all population growth during this period.

*Source:* U.S. Census Bureau, June 9, 2005, press release, www.census.gov/Press-Release/www/releases/archives/natracepop2004_tb1.xls; U.S. Census Bureau, Estimates of the Population by Race Alone or in Combination and Hispanic or Latino Origin for the United States and States: July 1, 2005, www.census.gov/Press-Release/www/2006/cb06-123table1.xls.

Figure 22: Disparity in Family Median Income Levels

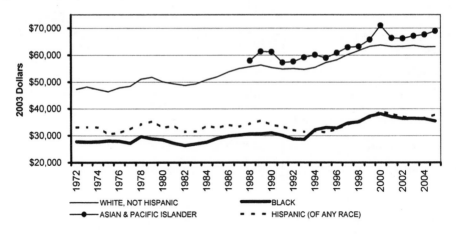

Figure 23: Disparity in Income Levels (Minority Income Divided by White, Not Hispanic Income)

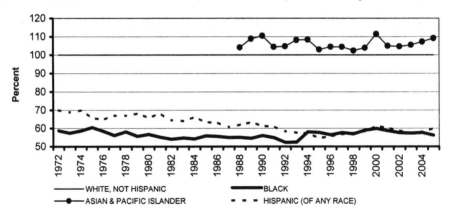

Figure 22 measures family median income levels. Figure 23 measures minority family median income levels as a percentage of white, not Hispanic family median income levels. Notice that since 1972, median income levels have increased for all races. The relatively flat "black" line in figure 23 illustrates that black families have consistently earned around 60% of white, not Hispanic family income since 1972. Black families earned 60.5% of white, not Hispanic family income in 1975; 55.8% in 1985; 57.7% in 1995; and 56.2 % in 2005. Hispanic family income has generally been higher than black family income, even as affected by immigrant flow. See figures 17 and 18 for discussion of immigrant flow. Asian family income has consistently been the highest of all the races. One possible reason for this is that Asians tend to be the most educated of all the races (see figures 49–60). The trends in figures 22 and 23 are generally consistent with the trends shown in figures 24 and 25. The above census data are not available for Asians and Pacific Islanders before 1988. For other relevant information, see the introduction to the appendix.

*Source:* U.S. Census Bureau, Historical Income Tables—Families, table F-05, www.census.gov/hhes/www/income/histinc/f05.html.

Figure 24: Disparity in Family Mean Income Levels

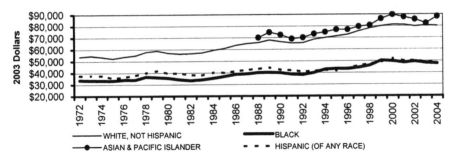

Figure 25: Disparity in Income Levels (Minority Income Divided by White, Not Hispanic Income)

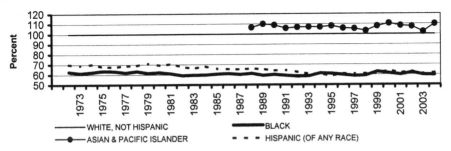

Figure 24 measures family mean income levels. Figure 25 measures minority family mean income levels as a percentage of white, not Hispanic mean income levels. Notice that since 1972, mean income levels have increased for all races. The relatively flat "black" line in figure 25 illustrates that black families have consistently earned around 60% of white, not Hispanic family income since 1972. Black families earned 63.5% of white, not Hispanic family income in 1975; 60.5% in 1985; 60.8% in 1995; and 59.7% in 2005. Hispanic family income has generally been higher than black family income, even as affected by immigrant flow. See figures 17 and 18 for discussion of immigrant flow. Asian family income has consistently been the highest of all the races. One possible reason for this is that Asians tend to be the most educated of all the races (see figures 49–60). The trends in figures 24 and 25 are generally consistent with those shown in figures 22 and 23. The above census data are not available for Asians and Pacific Islanders before 1988. For other relevant information, see the introduction to the appendix.

*Source:* U.S. Census Bureau, Historical Income Tables—Families, table F-05, www.census.gov/hhes/www/income/histinc/f05.html.

Figure 26: Disparity in Female Median Income Levels

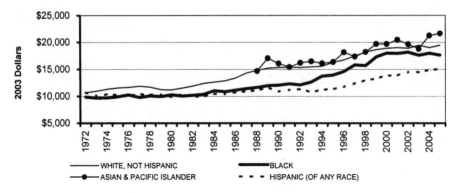

Figure 27: Disparity in Income Levels (Minority Female Income Divided by White, Not Hispanic Female Income)

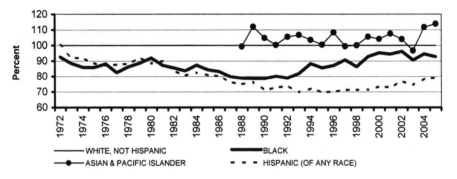

Figure 26 measures female median income levels for females with and without children. Figure 27 measures female median income levels as a percentage of white, not Hispanic female median income levels. Notice that since 1972, median income levels have increased for all races. After starting from a high point, with black females making 92.6% of female white, not Hispanic income in 1972, in the ensuing years a "median income gap" arose between black and white, not Hispanic females. Starting in the 1990s, however, black females dramatically narrowed this gap. Black females earned 85.9% of white, not Hispanic female income in 1975; 84.4% in 1985; 85.6% in 1995; and 92.8 % in 2005. Since 1982, Hispanic females have earned less than black females, possibly as a result of immigrant flow (see figures 17 and 18 for a discussion of immigrant flow). Asians have generally earned more than females of all other races, possibly because Asian females are the most educated (see figures 51, 52, 57, and 58). The above census data are not available for Asians and Pacific Islanders before 1988. For other relevant information, see the introduction to the appendix.

*Source:* U.S. Census Bureau, Historical Income Tables—People, table p54, www.census.gov/hhes/www/income/histinc/p54.html; Table PINC-01, Selected Characteristics of People, by Total Money Income in 2004, Work Experience in 2004, Race, Hispanic Origin, and Sex, http://pubdb3.census.gov/macro/032005/perinc/new01_000.htm; Table PINC-01,Selected Characteristics of People, by Total Money Income in 2005, Work Experience in 2005, Race, Hispanic Origin, and Sex, http://pubdb3.census.gov/macro/032006/perinc/new01_000.htm.

Figure 28: Disparity in Female Mean Income Levels

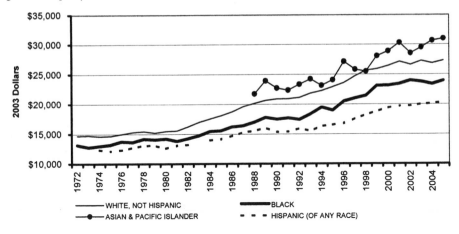

Figure 29: Disparity in Income Levels (Minority Female Income Divided by White, Not Hispanic Female Income)

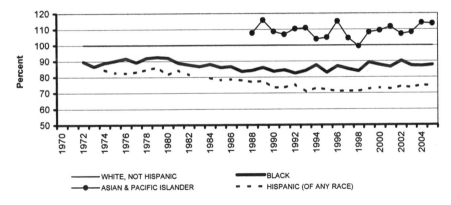

Figure 28 measures female mean income levels, for females with and without children. Figure 29 measures female mean income levels as a percentage of white, not Hispanic female mean income levels. Notice that since 1972, mean income levels have increased for all races. The black female mean income rate, as a percentage of the white, not Hispanic female income rate follows the same general trend as the median rate (see figures 26 and 27), although it is less volatile. Black females earned 90.1% of white, not Hispanic female income in 1975; 86.1% in 1985; 82.7% in 1995; and 87.6% in 2005. Hispanic females have generally earned less than black females, possibly as a result of immigrant flow (see figures 17 and 18 for a discussion of immigrant flow). Asians have generally earned more than females of all other races, possibly because Asian females are the most educated (see figures 51, 52, 57, and 58). The fact that the mean average is higher than the median average for all groups indicates that the difference between top and median incomes is greater than the difference between median and bottom incomes. The above census data are not available for Asians and Pacific Islanders before 1988, and Hispanics in the years 1972, 1973, and 1983. For other relevant information, see the introduction to the appendix.

*Source:* U.S. Census Bureau, Historical Income Tables—People, table p54, www.census.gov/hhes/www/income/histinc/p54.html; Table PINC-01, Selected Characteristics of People, by Total Money Income in 2004, Work Experience in 2004, Race, Hispanic Origin, and Sex, http://pubdb3.census.gov/macro/032005/perinc/new01_000.htm; Table PINC-01, Selected Characteristics of People, by Total Money Income in 2005, Work Experience in 2005, Race, Hispanic Origin, and Sex, http://pubdb3.census.gov/macro/032006/perinc/new01_000.htm.

Figure 30: Disparity in Mean Earnings of Persons Who Failed to Complete High School

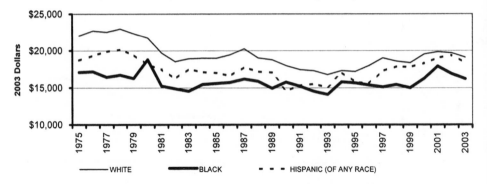

Figure 31: Disparity in Earnings (Minority Earnings Divided by White Earnings)

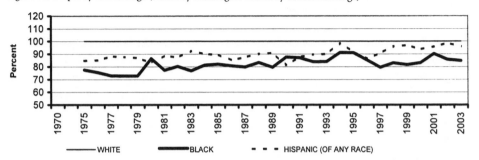

These figures include both male and female persons (but not the institutionalized population) who failed to graduate from high school. Figure 30 shows a sharp decrease in income for all races due to the economic downturn from 1980 to 1982. This holds true for all educational levels (see figures 32–45). Blacks who fail to graduate from high school do not receive the same level of compensation as their white counterparts; however, in the last thirty years, blacks have made substantial progress in closing the income gap in this category. In 1975, blacks who failed to complete high school earned 77.5% of the amount earned by their white counterparts, in 1985, 82.0%; in 1995, 91.0%; and in 2003, 84.8%. Hispanics who failed to complete high school generally earned more than blacks. Notice that for all races the general long-term trend is for the income of persons who failed to complete high school to decrease. The message here is simple: stay in school. Compare figures 30 and 31 with figures 32–45 to see that increased education leads to increased income. The above census data are not available for Asians and Pacific Islanders. For other relevant information, see the introduction to the appendix.

*Source:* U.S. Census Bureau, Mean Earnings of Workers 18 Years and Over, by Educational Attainment, Race, Hispanic Origin, and Sex: 1975 to 2003, table A-3, www.census.gov/population/socdemo/education/tabA-3.xls.

Figure 32: Disparity in Mean Earnings of High School Graduates

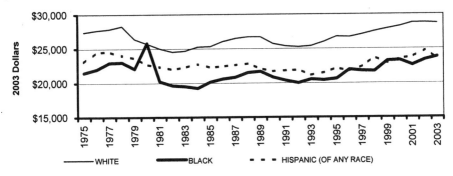

Figure 33: Disparity in Earnings (Minority Earnings Divided by White Earnings)

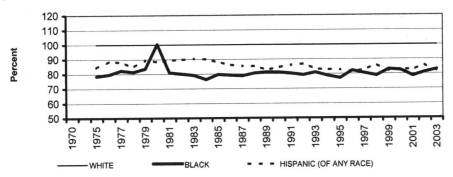

These figures include both male and female persons (but not the institutionalized population) who have graduated from high school. Notice that these figures are affected by the 1980–82 economic downturn (see figures 30 and 31). Black high school graduates do not receive the same level of compensation as their white counterparts. In the last thirty years, black high school graduates have started to close the income gap in this category. In 1975, black high school graduates earned 78.5% of the income earned by their white counterparts, and in 1980, they earned 100.3%. Black income as a percentage of white income has never again reached the 1980 percentage. In 1985, blacks earned 79.6% of the income earned by their white counterparts; in 1995, 77.1%; and in 2003, 82.8%. Hispanics have generally earned more than blacks, with a few exceptions, noticeably in 1980. The above census data are not available for Asians and Pacific Islanders. For other relevant information, see the introduction to the appendix.

Source: U.S. Census Bureau, Mean Earnings of Workers 18 Years and Over, by Educational Attainment, Race, Hispanic Origin, and Sex: 1975 to 2003, table A-3, www.census.gov/population/socdemo/education/tabA-3.xls.

Figure 34: Disparity in Mean Earnings of Persons with a Bachelor's Degree

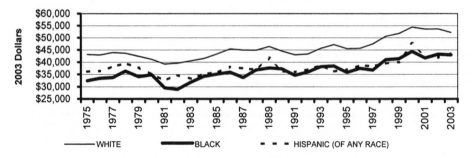

WHITE          BLACK          ▪ ▪ ▪ HISPANIC (OF ANY RACE)

Figure 35: Disparity in Earnings (Minority Earnings Divided by White Earnings)

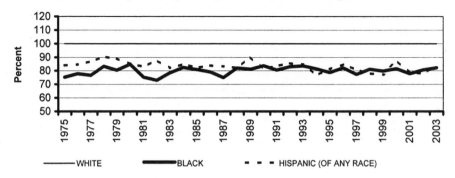

WHITE          BLACK          ▪ ▪ ▪ HISPANIC (OF ANY RACE)

These figures include both male and female persons (but not the institutionalized population) with a bachelor's degree, such as a B.A. or B.S. Notice that these figures are affected by the 1980–82 economic downturn (see figures 30 and 31). Black college graduates do not receive the same level of compensation as their white counterparts; however, in the last thirty years there has been a general trend tending to show black college graduates closing the income gap. In 1975, blacks with college degrees earned 75.2% of the amount earned by their white counterparts; in 1985, 80.9%; in 1995, 78.7%; and in 2003, 82.2%. Hispanics consistently earned more than blacks until the mid-1980s. Since that time, Hispanics and blacks have earned comparable amounts. The above census data are not available for Asians & Pacific Islanders. For other relevant information, see the introduction to the appendix.

*Source:* U.S. Census Bureau, Mean Earnings of Workers 18 Years and Over, by Educational Attainment, Race, Hispanic Origin, and Sex: 1975 to 2003, table A-3, www.census.gov/population/socdemo/education/tabA-3.xls.

Figure 36: Disparity in Mean Earnings of Females with a Bachelor's Degree

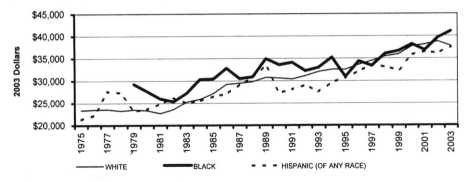

Figure 37: Disparity in Earnings (Minority Female Earnings Divided by White Female Earnings)

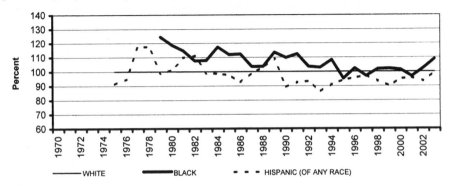

These figures include female persons (but not the institutionalized population) with a bachelor's degree, such as a B.A. or B.S. Notice that these figures are affected by the 1980–82 economic downturn (see figures 30 and 31). Black female college graduates have consistently earned more than their white counterparts, unlike black male college graduates (see figures 38 and 39). One possible explanation may be "twofer" diversity: black women supply both racial and gender diversity. Note, however that the advantage black college-educated women have had over white college-educated women has been in general decline since 1979. In 1979, black women with a bachelor's degree made 125% of the income earned by their white female counterparts; in 1989, 113%; in 1999, 102%; and in 2003, 109%. Hispanic females have consistently earned less than black females. The above census data are not available for Asians and Pacific Islanders, or for blacks before 1979. For other relevant information, see the introduction to the appendix.

*Source:* U.S. Census Bureau, Mean Earnings of Workers 18 Years and Over, by Educational Attainment, Race, Hispanic Origin, and Sex: 1975 to 2003, table A-3, www.census.gov/population/socdemo/education/tabA-3xls.

Figure 38: Disparity in Mean Earnings of Males with a Bachelor's Degree

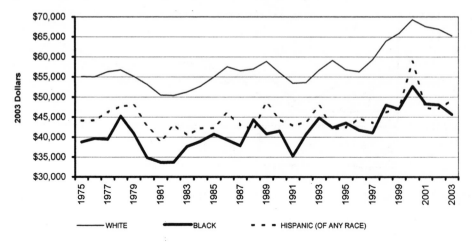

Figure 39: Disparity in Earnings (Minority Male Earnings Divided by White Male Earnings)

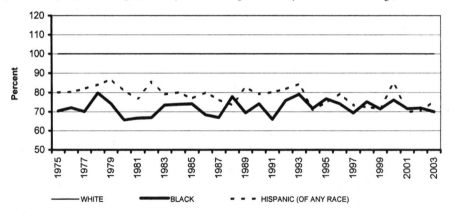

These figures include male persons (not the institutionalized population) with a bachelor's degree, such as a B.A. or B.S. Notice that these figures are affected by the 1980–82 economic downturn (see figures 30 and 31). Black male college graduates have consistently earned less than their white male counterparts, unlike black female college graduates (see figures 36 and 37). Although the trend is fairly volatile, since 1975, black male college graduates have consistently earned around 65 to 75% of the amount earned by white male college graduates. In 1975, blacks in this category earned 70.4% of the amount earned by whites, in 1985, 74.0%; in 1995, 76.6%; and in 2003, 69.9%. Unlike black females, black males have consistently earned less than their Hispanic counterparts (compare figures 38 and 39 with figures 36 and 37). The above census data are not available for Asians and Pacific Islanders. For other relevant information, see the introduction to the appendix.

Source: U.S. Census Bureau, Mean Earnings of Workers 18 Years and Over, by Educational Attainment, Race, Hispanic Origin, and Sex: 1975 to 2003, table A-3, www.census.gov/population/socdemo/education/tabA-3.xls.

Figure 40: Disparity in Mean Earnings of Persons with an Advanced College Degree

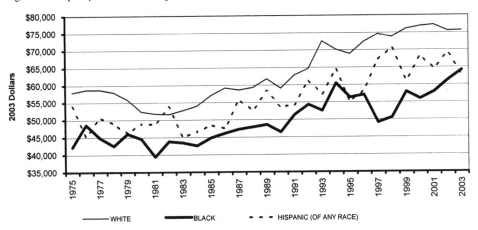

Figure 41: Disparity in Earnings (Minority Earnings Divided by White Earnings)

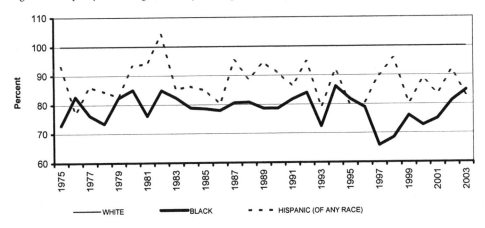

These figures include both male and female persons (but not the institutionalized population) with an advanced college degree, such as a Ph.D., J.D., or M.D. Notice that these figures are not adversely affected by the 1980–82 economic downturn. Even highly educated blacks do not receive the same level of compensation as their white counterparts; however, blacks have narrowed the income gap in the past thirty years. In 1975, blacks with advanced degrees earned 72.9% as much as their white counterparts; in 1985, 78.6%; in 1995, 81.8%; and in 2003, 84.8%. Hispanics have consistently earned more than blacks. The above census data are not available for Asians and Pacific Islanders. For other relevant information, see the introduction to the appendix.

*Source:* U.S. Census Bureau, Mean Earnings of Workers 18 Years and Over, by Educational Attainment, Race, Hispanic Origin, and Sex: 1975 to 2003, table A-3, www.census.gov/population/socdemo/education/tabA-3.xls.

Figure 42: Disparity in Mean Earnings of Females with an Advanced Degree

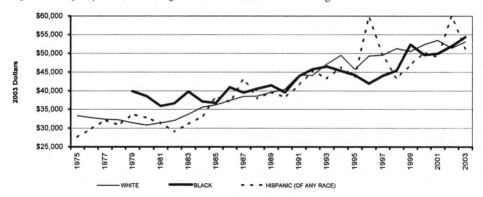

Figure 43: Disparity in Earnings (Minority Female Earnings Divided by White Female Earnings)

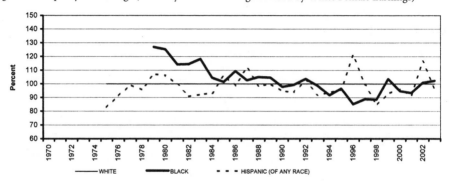

These figures include female persons (but not the institutionalized population) with an advanced college degree, such as a Ph.D., J.D., or M.D. Notice that these figures are not affected by the 1980–82 economic downturn. Black females with advanced degrees have not consistently had the earnings advantage over comparably educated white females (as black females with a bachelor's degree have had) (compare figures 42 and 43 with figures 36 and 37). This may be due to a racialized "glass ceiling" effect, which limits how far a black female executive or professional can advance, or to the employment choices of black and white women at this level. In 1979, black females with advanced degrees earned considerably more than their white female counterparts. Since 1979, whites continually narrowed the earnings gap, actually overtaking black females in this category in the early 1990s before black females reversed this downward trend in the mid-1990s, once again earning more than white females with advanced degrees in the early 2000s. Hispanic females have generally earned less than black females with the noticeable exceptions of 1996 and 2002. These numbers, not seeming to have a simple explanation, could be due to the fact that there was an especially low sampling size in collecting these data; thus, the 1996 and 2002 Hispanic data points might be in error. In 1979, black women with advanced degrees earned 127% as much as their white counterparts; in 1989, 105%; in 1999, 104%; and in 2003, 102%. The above census data are not available for Asians and Pacific Islanders, and for blacks before 1979. For other relevant information, see the introduction to the appendix.

*Source:* U.S. Census Bureau, Mean Earnings of Workers 18 Years and Over, by Educational Attainment, Race, Hispanic Origin, and Sex: 1975 to 2003, table A-3, www.census.gov/population/socdemo/education/tabA-3.xls.

Figure 44: Disparity in Mean Earnings of Males with an Advanced Degree

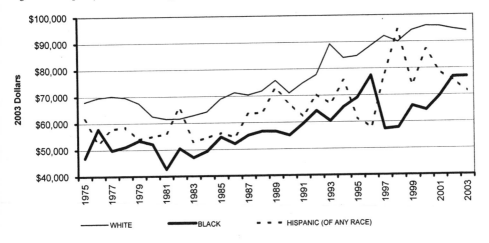

Figure 45: Disparity in Earnings (Minority Male Earnings Divided by White Male Earnings)

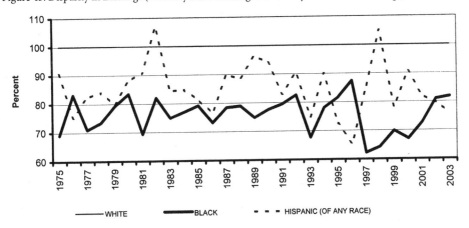

These figures include male persons (but not the institutionalized population) with an advanced college degree, such as a Ph.D., J.D., or M.D. Notice that these figures are not affected by the 1980–82 economic downturn. Black males with an advanced degree have consistently earned less than their white counterparts. In 1975, black males earned 69.1% as much as white males in the same category; in 1985, 79.2%; in 1995, 81.5%; and in 2003, 81.8%. Hispanic males have generally earned more than black males. The above census data are not available for Asians and Pacific Islanders. For other relevant information, see the introduction to the appendix.

*Source:* U.S. Census Bureau, Mean Earnings of Workers 18 Years and Over, by Educational Attainment, Race, Hispanic Origin, and Sex: 1975 to 2003, table A-3, www.census.gov/population/socdemo/education/tabA-3.xls.

Figure 46: Disparity in Home Ownership Rates

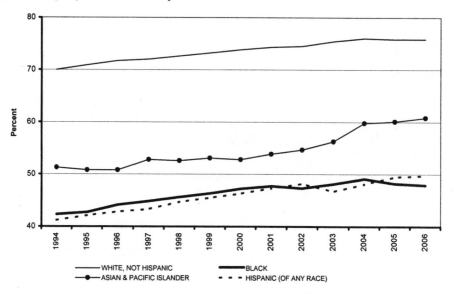

These data include both male and female persons. Although home ownership rates have increased for all races since 1994, there is a wide gap between black and white, not Hispanic home ownership. Interestingly, Asians and Pacific Islanders have much lower home ownership rates than whites, even though they have higher family income levels (see figures 22–29). One possible explanation is that white, not Hispanics are more likely to reside in suburbia, where home ownership rates are high, whereas Asians and Pacific Island-ers may be more likely to rent apartments in large cities, where home ownership rates are relatively low. Nevertheless, the Asian and Pacific Islander home ownership rate is on the rise; in 2006, it stood at 60.8%. There is a wide gap between black and white, not Hispanic home ownership. This gap does not appear to be closing, and unlike the "home ownership gap" between Hispanics and white, not Hispanics, the black/white, not Hispanic gap cannot possibly be explained by immigrant flow. Generally where there is a burst in the "housing bubble" (i.e., a sudden reduction in speculative housing prices), blacks and Hispanics usu-ally fare worse than whites because blacks and Hispanics are the first to lose their jobs ("last hired, first fired") in the economic downturn that usually accompanies a housing downturn. See William Julius Wil-son, *The Truly Disadvantaged: The Inner City, the Underclass, and Public Policy* (Chicago: University of Chicago Press, 1987), 135. Blacks were the only group to experience a declining home ownership rate from 2005 to 2006, as the black rate fell from 48.2% to 47.9%.

*Source:* U.S. Census Bureau, Homeownership Rates by Race and Ethnicity of Householder: 1994 to 2005, Table 20, http://www.census.gov/hhes/www/housing/hvs/annual06/ann06t20.html.

Figure 47: Disparity in Firm Ownership, 2002

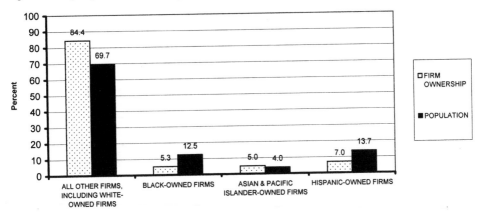

Figure 48: Disparity in Firm Sales and Receipts, 2002

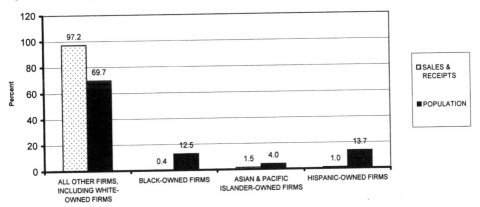

These figures include both males and females, and exclude publicly held companies or corporations. In 2002, black-owned businesses accounted for only 5.3% of all firms, far below their representative population that year of approximately 13%. In addition, black-owned firms accounted for only 0.4% of all sales and receipts. Hispanic-owned businesses fared somewhat better, accounting for 7.0% of all U.S.-owned business, and pulling in 1.0% of all sales and receipts; however, Hispanics still performed below their representative population that year of approximately 14%. Asian and Pacific Islander–owned firms fared much better, accounting for 5.0% of all firms, and 1.5% of all sales and receipts, performing more on a par with their approximate representative population that year of 4%. For other relevant information, see the introduction to the appendix.

*Source:* U.S. Census Bureau, Company Summary: 2002, http://www.census.gov/prod/ec02/sb0200cscosum. pdf; U.S. Census Bureau, Historical Poverty Tables—People, table 2, www.census.gov/hhes/www/poverty/ histpov/hstpov2.html.

Figure 49: Disparity in High School Dropout Rates

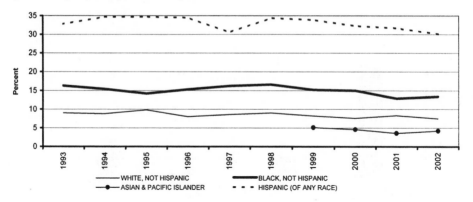

Figure 50: Disparity between Black and White Dropout Rates (Black Rate Minus White Rate)

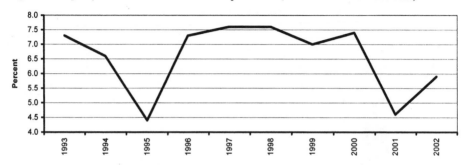

These figures include both males and females. Figure 49 measures high school dropout rates. Figure 50 measures the disparity between white, not Hispanic, and black, not Hispanic high school dropout rates. Notice that high school dropout rates have decreased slightly for all races since 1993. For black, not Hispanics and Hispanics this may be due to the strong showing of females (compare figure 51 with figure 53). The black, not Hispanic dropout rate is significantly higher than the white, not Hispanic rate; however, since 1993 blacks have closed this gap somewhat. Asians and Pacific Islanders have the lowest dropout rate of all the races. This may partially explain why their income is the highest of all the races (see figures 22–29). Interestingly, the Hispanic dropout rate is easily the highest of all the races. According to a 1998 Senate study, a reason for the relatively high Hispanic dropout rate is that the discussions of the dropout problem have too often been "submerged in discussions of dropouts in general, the education of ethnic minorities in general, or politicized debates about immigration, language, and bilingualism." Hence, no specific action has been taken to deal with the unique problem. See "No More Excuses: The Final Report of the Hispanic Dropout Project," bingman.senate.gov/hdprept2.pdf (accessed July 13, 2005), 62. The above census data are not available for Asians and Pacific Islanders before 1999. For other relevant information, see the introduction to the appendix.
Source: U.S. Census Bureau, The Population 14 to 24 Years Old by High School Graduate Status, College Enrollment, Attainment, Sex, Race, and Hispanic Origin, October 1967 to 2002, table A-5, http://www .census.gov/population/socdemo/school/tabA-5.pdf.

Figure 51: Disparity in Female High School Dropout Rates

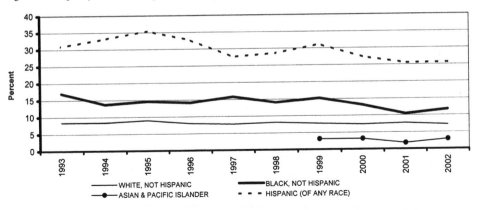

Figure 52: Disparity between Black and White Female Dropout Rates (Black Rate Minus White Rate)

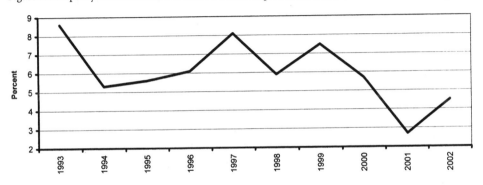

These figures include females with and without children. Figure 51 measures female high school dropout rates. Figure 52 measures the disparity between female white, not Hispanic, and female black, not Hispanic high school dropout rates. Notice that high school dropout rates have decreased slightly for all races since 1993. The black, not Hispanic dropout rate is significantly higher than the white, not Hispanic rate; however, since 1993, black females have significantly closed this gap. Asians and Pacific Islanders have the lowest dropout rate of all the races. This may partially explain why their income is the highest of all the races (see figures 22–29). Interestingly, the Hispanic dropout rate is easily the highest of all the races (see discussion accompanying figures 49 and 50). The above census data are not available for Asians and Pacific Islanders before 1999. For other relevant information, see the introduction to the appendix.

*Source:* U.S. Census Bureau, The Population 14 to 24 Years Old by High School Graduate Status, College Enrollment, Attainment, Sex, Race, and Hispanic Origin, October 1967 to 2002, table A-5, http://www.census.gov/population/socdemo/school/tabA-5.pdf.

Figure 53: Disparity in Male High School Dropout Rates

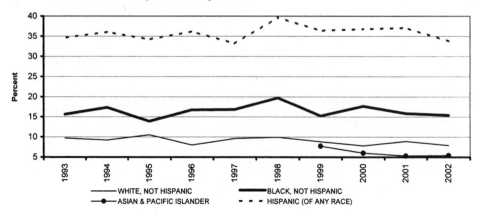

Figure 54: Disparity between Black and White Male Dropout Rates (Black Rate Minus White Rate)

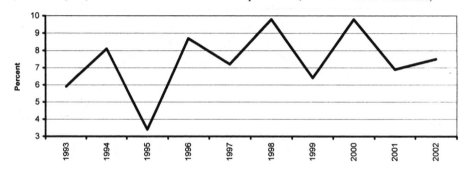

Figure 53 measures male high school dropout rates. Figure 54 measures the disparity between male white, not Hispanic, and male black, not Hispanic high school dropout rates. Notice that high school dropout rates have decreased slightly for all races since 1993. In addition, male high school dropout rates are generally higher for all races (compare figure 53 with figure 51). The black, not Hispanic dropout rate is significantly higher than the white, not Hispanic rate. Moreover, unlike black females, black males have not narrowed this gap. On the contrary, the gap has increased since 1993 (compare figure 54 with figure 52). Asians and Pacific Islanders have the lowest dropout rate of all the races. This may partially explain why their income is the highest of all the races (see figures 22–29). Interestingly, the Hispanic dropout rate is easily the highest of all the races (see discussion accompanying figures 49 and 50). The above census data are not available for Asians and Pacific Islanders before 1999. For other relevant information, see the introduction to the appendix.

*Source:* U.S. Census Bureau, The Population 14 to 24 Years Old by High School Graduate Status, College Enrollment, Attainment, Sex, Race, and Hispanic Origin, October 1967 to 2002, table A-5, http://www.census.gov/population/socdemo/school/tabA-5.pdf.

Figure 55: Disparity in College Participation

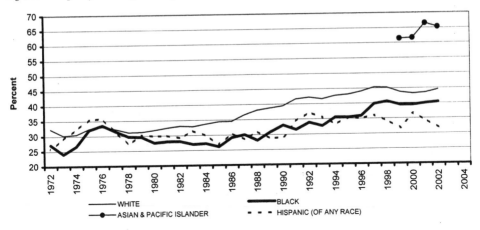

Figure 56: Disparity between Black and White Rates (White Rate Minus Black Rate)

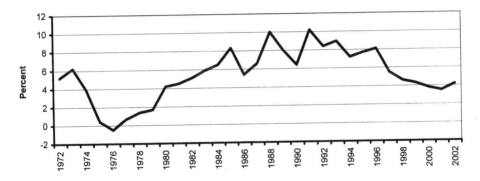

These figures include eighteen- to twenty-four-year-old male and female high school graduates enrolled in college. Since 1972, the percentage of persons enrolled in college has increased for all races. This seems to be primarily due to the strong showing of females (compare figures 55 and 56 with figures 57–60). Blacks and Hispanics have generally had the lowest college enrollment rates, with Asians and Pacific Islanders easily having the highest. The high Asian and Pacific Islander rate may partially explain why Asians and Pacific Islanders earn more income than all the other races (see figures 22–29). The college enrollment gap between blacks and whites has not substantially improved since 1972, with blacks generally having a lower rate. The above census data are not available for Asians and Pacific Islanders before 1999. For a discussion of the "affirmative action effect" and other relevant information, see the introduction to the appendix.

*Source:* U.S. Census Bureau, The Population 14 to 24 Years Old by High School Graduate Status, College Enrollment, Attainment, Sex, Race, and Hispanic Origin: October 1967 to 2002, table A-5, www.census .gov/population/socdemo/school/tabA-5.pdf.

Figure 57: Disparity in Female College Participation

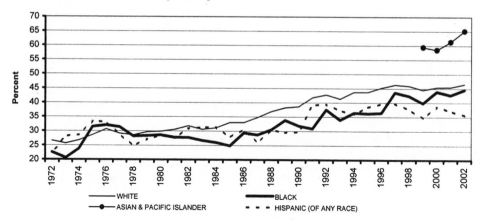

Figure 58: Disparity between Black and White Rates (White Rate Minus Black Rate)

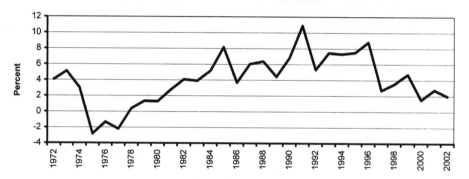

These figures include eighteen- to twenty-four-year-old female high school graduates enrolled in college. Since 1972, the percentage of females enrolled in college has increased for all races. Black and Hispanic females have generally had the lowest college enrollment rates, with Asian and Pacific Islander females easily having the highest. The college enrollment gap between blacks and whites has not substantially improved since 1972, with blacks generally having a lower rate. Note that the "female enrollment gap" is substantially smaller than the "male enrollment gap" (compare figures 57 and 58 with figures 59 and 60). The above census data are not available for Asians and Pacific Islanders before 1999. For a discussion of the "affirmative action effect" and other relevant information, see the introduction to the appendix.

*Source:* U.S. Census Bureau, The Population 14 to 24 Years Old by High School Graduate Status, College Enrollment, Attainment, Sex, Race, and Hispanic Origin: October 1967 to 2002, table A-5, www.census .gov/population/socdemo/school/tabA-5.pdf.

Figure 59: Disparity in Male College Participation Rates

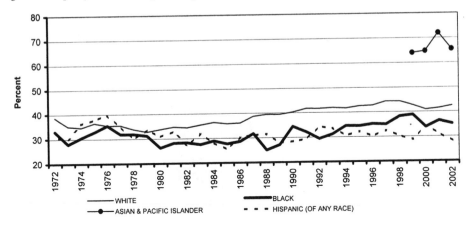

Figure 60: Disparity between Black and White Rates (Black Rate Minus White Rate)

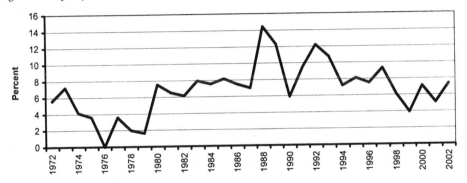

These figures include eighteen- to twenty-four-year-old male high school graduates enrolled in college. Unlike female college enrollment rates, male college enrollment rates have not significantly increased since 1972 (compare figures 57 and 58 with figures 59 and 60). Blacks and Hispanics have generally had the lowest college enrollment rates, with Asians and Pacific Islanders easily having the highest. The college enrollment gap between black and white males has not substantially improved since 1972, with black males consistently having a lower rate. This "black/white male college education gap" is larger than the "black/white female college education gap" (compare figures 57 and 58 with figures 59 and 60). The above census data are not available for Asians and Pacific Islanders before 1999. For a discussion of the "affirmative action effect" and other relevant information, see the introduction to the appendix.

*Source:* U.S. Census Bureau, The Population 14 to 24 Years Old by High School Graduate Status, College Enrollment, Attainment, Sex, Race, and Hispanic Origin: October 1967 to 2002, table A-5, www.census .gov/population/socdemo/school/tabA-5.pdf.

Figure 61: Disparity in Occupational Status

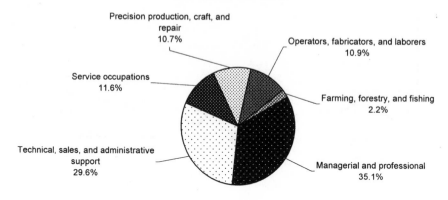

**WHITE, NOT HISPANIC, 2002**

Precision production, craft, and repair
10.7%

Operators, fabricators, and laborers
10.9%

Service occupations
11.6%

Farming, forestry, and fishing
2.2%

Technical, sales, and administrative support
29.6%

Managerial and professional
35.1%

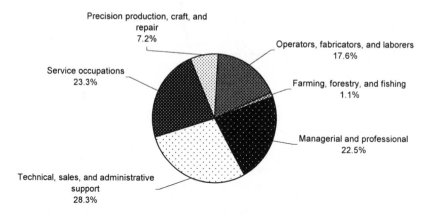

**BLACK, 2002**

Precision production, craft, and repair
7.2%

Operators, fabricators, and laborers
17.6%

Service occupations
23.3%

Farming, forestry, and fishing
1.1%

Managerial and professional
22.5%

Technical, sales, and administrative support
28.3%

These figures portray the occupational status of both males and females. Many more white, not Hispanics are employed in typically higher-paying positions while many more blacks are employed in typically lower-paying positions. For example, 35.1% of white, not Hispanics are employed in "managerial and professional" positions, compared with 22.5% of blacks; 23.3% of blacks are employed in "service occupations," compared with only 11.6% of white, not Hispanics; and 17.6% of blacks are employed as "operators, fabricators, and laborers," compared with only 10.9% of white, not Hispanics. The tendency of white, not Hispanics to be employed in high-paying jobs, and blacks in low-paying jobs, may partially explain the dramatic income disparities between the two races (see figures 22–29). The above census data are not available for Hispanics and Asians and Pacific Islanders. For other relevant information, see the introduction to the appendix.

*Source:* U.S. Census Bureau, Major Occupation Group of the Employed Civilian Population 16 Years and Over by Sex, and Race and Hispanic Origin: March 2002, table 11, www.census.gov/population/socdemo/race/black/ppl-164/tab11.pdf.

Figure 62: Disparity in Female Occupational Status

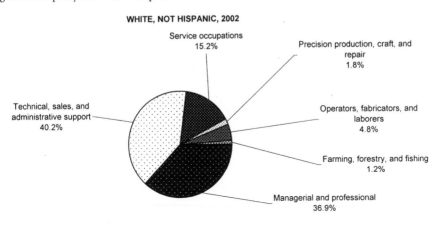

**WHITE, NOT HISPANIC, 2002**

Service occupations
15.2%

Precision production, craft, and
repair
1.8%

Technical, sales, and
administrative support
40.2%

Operators, fabricators, and
laborers
4.8%

Farming, forestry, and fishing
1.2%

Managerial and professional
36.9%

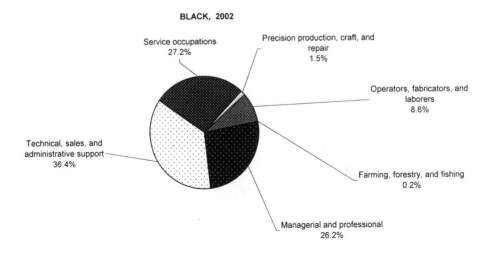

**BLACK, 2002**

Service occupations
27.2%

Precision production, craft, and
repair
1.5%

Operators, fabricators, and
laborers
8.6%

Technical, sales, and
administrative support
36.4%

Farming, forestry, and fishing
0.2%

Managerial and professional
26.2%

These figures portray the occupational status of females with and without children. Many more white, not Hispanic females are employed in typically higher-paying positions while many more black females are employed in typically lower-paying positions. For example, 36.9% of white, not Hispanic females are employed in "managerial and professional" positions, compared with 26.2% of black females; 27.2% of black females are employed in "service occupations," compared with only 15.2% of white, not Hispanic females; and 8.6% of black females are employed as "operators, fabricators, and laborers," compared with only 4.8% of white, not Hispanic females. Interestingly, the percentages of both white, not Hispanic, and black females employed in high-paying "managerial and professional" positions are greater than those of their male counterparts (compare figure 62 with figure 63). This may be due to affirmative action programs. The above census data are not available for Hispanics and Asians and Pacific Islanders. For other relevant information, see the introduction to the appendix.

*Source:* U.S. Census Bureau, Major Occupation Group of the Employed Civilian Population 16 Years and Over by Sex, and Race and Hispanic Origin: March 2002, table 11, www.census.gov/population/socdemo/race/black/ppl-164/tab11.pdf.

Figure 63: Disparity in Male Occupational Status

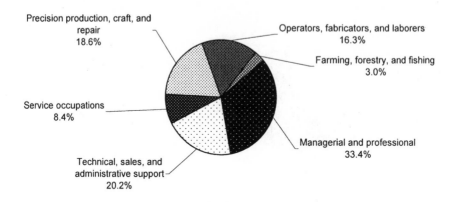

**WHITE, NOT HISPANIC, 2002**

Precision production, craft, and repair
18.6%

Operators, fabricators, and laborers
16.3%

Farming, forestry, and fishing
3.0%

Service occupations
8.4%

Managerial and professional
33.4%

Technical, sales, and administrative support
20.2%

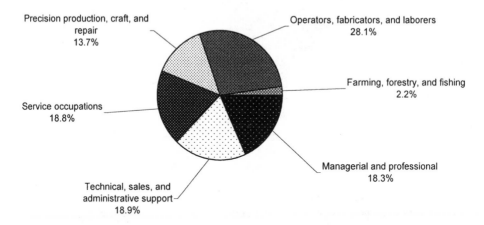

**BLACK, 2002**

Precision production, craft, and repair
13.7%

Operators, fabricators, and laborers
28.1%

Farming, forestry, and fishing
2.2%

Service occupations
18.8%

Managerial and professional
18.3%

Technical, sales, and administrative support
18.9%

These figures portray the occupational status of males. Many more white, not Hispanic males are employed in typically higher-paying positions while many more black males are employed in typically lower-paying positions. For example, 33.4% of white, not Hispanic males are employed in "managerial and professional" positions, compared with 18.3% of black males; 18.8% of black males are employed in "service occupations," compared with only 8.4% of white, not Hispanic males; and 28.1% of black males are employed as "operators, fabricators, and laborers," compared with only 16.3% of white, not Hispanic males. The above census data are not available for Hispanics and Asians and Pacific Islanders. For other relevant information, see the introduction to the appendix.

*Source:* U.S. Census Bureau, Major Occupation Group of the Employed Civilian Population 16 Years and Over by Sex, and Race and Hispanic Origin: March 2002, table 11, www.census.gov/population/socdemo/race/black/ppl-164/tab11.pdf.

Figure 64: Disparity in Percentage of Individuals Living in Families Headed by Females

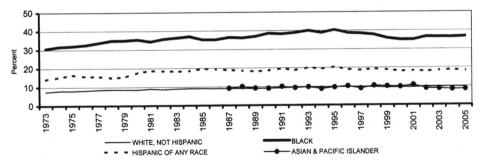

Figure 65: Disparity between Black and White Female-Headed Families (Black Percentage Minus White, Not Hispanic Percentage)

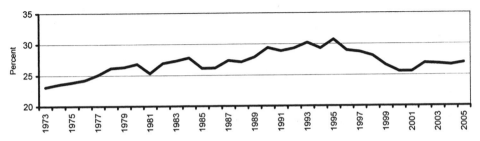

The above data show what percentage of each racial group lives in female-headed families. The Asian and Pacific Islander population tracks very closely with the white, not Hispanic population, averaging slightly below 10%. In 2005, 18.3% of Hispanics and 36.6% of blacks lived in female-headed families. These figures suggest that family structure does not explain the Hispanic high school dropout rate (see figure 49), because the Hispanic female-headed family percentage is approximately half the black percentage, whereas the Hispanic high school dropout rate is approximately double the black rate. The difference between the percentage of blacks and the percentage of white, not Hispanics that live in female-headed families increased from 1979 to 2005, although the gap has narrowed somewhat since 1995. The large percentage of blacks living in female-headed families is partly explained by the large average size of black female-headed families (see figure 66). These data are not available for Asians and Pacific Islanders before 1987. Apparently, no figures for male-headed families are available from this source.

*Source:* U.S. Census Bureau, Historical Poverty Tables—People, table 2, www.census.gov/hhes/www/poverty/histpov/hstpov2.html.

Figure 66: Disparity In Size of Female-Headed Families

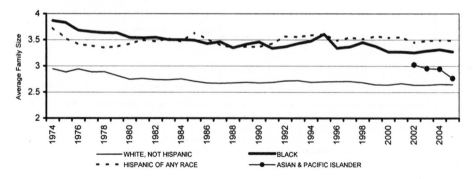

Figure 67: Disparity between Black and White Female-Headed Family Size (Black Family Size Minus White, Not Hispanic Family Size)

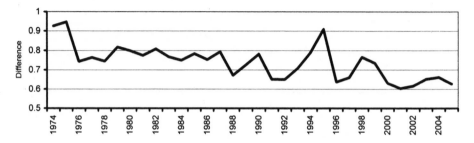

These figures show the average size of families headed by females. Female-headed white, not Hispanic families are smaller than corresponding families from other races. Overall, the average size of female-headed families has declined since 1974. The difference between the average size of a female-headed black family and a female-headed white family was 0.63 persons in 2005. These data are not available for Asians and Pacific Islanders before 2002. Apparently, no figures for male-headed families are available from this source. For other relevant information, see the introduction to the appendix.

*Source:* U.S. Census Bureau, Historical Poverty Tables—People, table 2, www.census.gov/hhes/www/poverty/histpov/hstpov2.html; U.S. Census Bureau, Historical Poverty Tables—People, table 4, www.census.gov/hhes/www/poverty/histpov/hstpov4.html.

Figure 68: Disparity in Average Family Size (All Families)

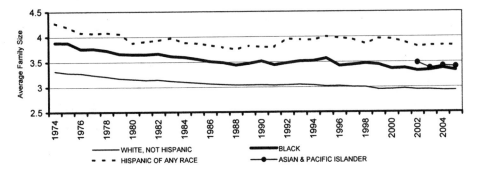

Figure 69: Disparity between Black and White Family Size (Black Family Size Minus White, Not Hispanic Family Size)

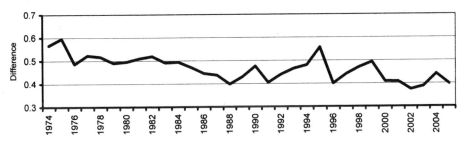

These figures show the average size of all families, regardless of family structure, by race. Hispanics have the largest families, averaging 3.8 persons per family in 2005. Although few data are available for Asians and Pacific Islanders, as of 2005, Asian and Pacific Islander families were close in size to African American families. Across all groups, family size has declined since 1974. Black and white, not Hispanic families have become closer in size. In 1974, the average black family had 0.57 more members than the average white, not Hispanic family. By 2005, this difference had dropped to 0.40 persons. These data are not available for Asians and Pacific Islanders before 2002. For other relevant information, see the introduction to the appendix.

*Source:* U.S. Census Bureau, Historical Poverty Tables—People, table 2, www.census.gov/hhes/www/poverty/histpov/hstpov2.html; U.S. Census Bureau, Historical Poverty Tables—People, table 4, www.census.gov/hhes/www/poverty/histpov/hstpov4.html.

Figure 70: Disparity in Marital Status of Men Age Fifteen and Older

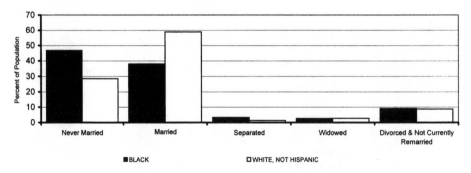

Figure 71: Disparity between Black and White Marital Status (Black Percentage Minus White, Not Hispanic Percentage)

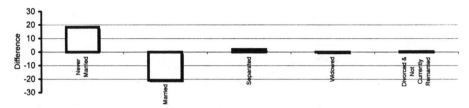

The above data compare the marital status of African American men with that of white, not Hispanic men as of 2004. Figure 70 shows that a larger percentage of black men (47%) have never been married, compared with white, not Hispanic men (29%). The converse of this statistic is that a smaller percentage of black men than white, not Hispanic men have been married. No doubt, the high incarceration rate for black men (4.7% as of 2005) reduces the number of black men available for marriage. Yet similar proportions of black and white, not Hispanic male populations are divorced, hinting at a higher divorce rate for black men compared with white, not Hispanic men. For other relevant information, see the introduction to the appendix.

*Source:* U.S. Census Bureau, The Black Population in the United States: March 2004, http://www.census
.gov/population/socdemo/race/black/ppl-186/tab2.csv; U.S. Department of Justice, Prison and Jail Inmates
at Midyear 2005. http://www.ojp.usdoj.gov/bjs/pub/pdf/pjim05.pdf.

Figure 72: Disparity in Marital Status of Women Age Fifteen and Older

Figure 73: Disparity between Black and White Marital Status (Black Percentage Minus White, Not Hispanic Percentage)

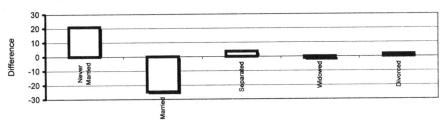

The above data compare the marital status of African American women with that of white, not Hispanic women as of 2004. The patterns seen here are very similar to those shown for men in figures 70 and 71. Nevertheless, women in both black and white, not Hispanic populations are more likely to be widowed or divorced than are the men in those populations. Females show greater disparity in marital behavior between the races than do men. For women, the disparity between the percentage of blacks and the percentage of whites who are married is 25%. For men, this disparity is 21%. The incarceration rate of black males (4.7% as of 2005) directly impacts marital status in that the former effectively decreases the number of marriageable males (see figure 84). For other relevant information, see the introduction to the appendix.

*Source:* U.S. Census Bureau, The Black Population in the United States: March 2004, http://www.census .gov/population/socdemo/race/black/ppl-186/tab2.csv; U.S. Department of Justice, Prison and Jail Inmates at Midyear 2005. http://www.ojp.usdoj.gov/bjs/pub/pdf/pjim05.pdf.

Figure 74: Disparity in Total Unemployment Rate

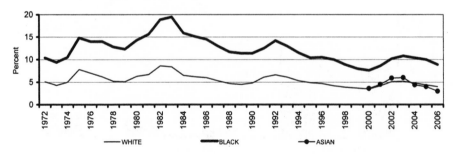

Figure 75: Disparity between Black and White Unemployment Rates (Black Rate Minus White Rate)

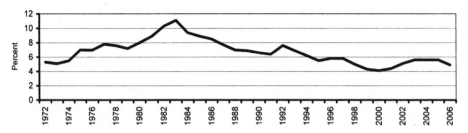

The above data show the unemployment rates for whites, blacks, and Asians. The Department of Labor uses the term "white" instead of "white, not Hispanic" and "black" instead of "black, not Hispanic." Consequently, these racial designations do not exclude persons of Hispanic ethnicity. The black unemployment rate continues to exceed the white unemployment rate. From 1972 to 1982, when the economy was undergoing a structural change from smokestack to high-tech industries, the black and white unemployment rates nearly doubled. From 1972 to 2006, the black rate has consistently been approximately double the white rate. In 2006, the difference between the black unemployment rate and the white unemployment rate was 4.9%, close to the difference in 1972 of 5.3%. See the introduction to the appendix for other relevant information.

*Source:* U.S. Department of Labor, Table A2. Employment Status of the Civilian Population by Race, Sex, and Age, http://www.bls.gov/webapps/legacy/cpsatab2.htm.

Figure 76: Disparity in Unemployment Rate for Men Age Twenty or Older

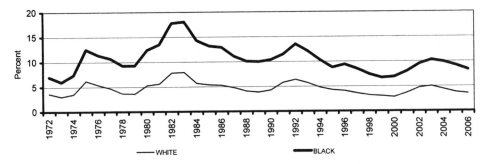

Figure 77: Disparity between Black and White Unemployment Rates (Black Rate Minus White Rate)

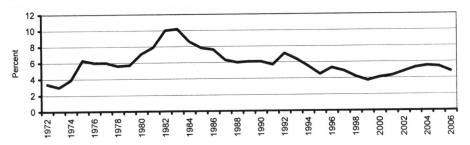

These figures show that the rate of black unemployment has consistently been double the white unemployment rate. The black-white unemployment disparity for men age twenty or older has widened since 1972. By 1972, black and white unemployment rates differed by 3.4%. In 2006, the difference had widened to 4.8%. While white men age twenty or older displayed an unemployment rate of 3.5% in 2006, the corresponding rate for black men age twenty or older was more than double, at 8.3%. See the introduction to the appendix for other relevant information.

*Source:* U.S. Department of Labor, Table A2. Employment Status of the Civilian Population by Race, Sex, and Age, http://www.bls.gov/webapps/legacy/cpsatab2.htm.

Figure 78: Disparity in Unemployment Rate for Women Age Twenty or Older

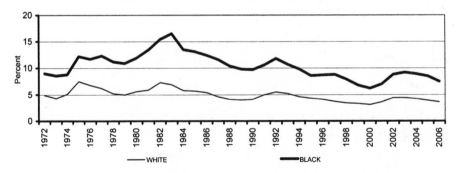

Figure 79: Disparity between Black and White Unemployment Rates (Black Rate Minus White Rate)

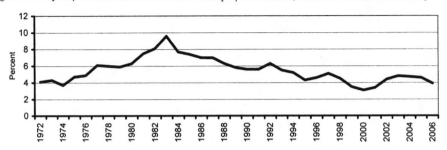

These figures show that black-white unemployment for women essentially mirrors that for men. Overall, women have lower unemployment rates than men, for both blacks and whites. The disparity in unemployment rates between blacks and whites has not improved since 1972. The difference between the black and white unemployment rates for women over the age of twenty in 1972 was 4.1%. In 2006, the difference was 3.9%. See the narrative accompanying figures 74 and 75 and the introduction to the appendix for other relevant information.

*Source:* U.S. Department of Labor, Table A2. Employment Status of the Civilian Population by Race, Sex, and Age, http://www.bls.gov/webapps/legacy/cpsatab2.htm.

Figure 80: Disparity in Unemployment Rate for Persons Age Sixteen to Nineteen

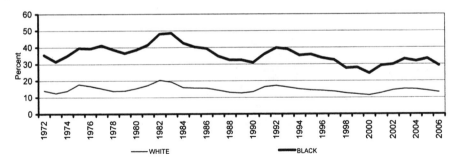

Figure 81: Disparity between Black and White Unemployment Rates (Black Rate Minus White Rate)

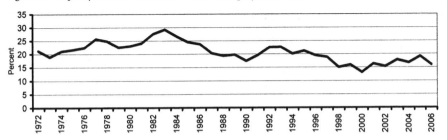

For the population as a whole, teen unemployment rates exceed the overall unemployment rate. But when teen unemployment dynamics are compounded by racial disparity, the result is a staggering 29.1% unemployment rate for blacks between the ages of sixteen and nineteen, more than twice the rate for the white teen population. Nearly one-third of African American teens who want to work cannot find work. For other relevant information, see the introduction to the appendix.

*Source:* U.S. Department of Labor, Table A2. Employment Status of the Civilian Population by Race, Sex, and Age, http://www.bls.gov/webapps/legacy/cpsatab2.htm.

Figure 82: Disparity in Population of Local Jails

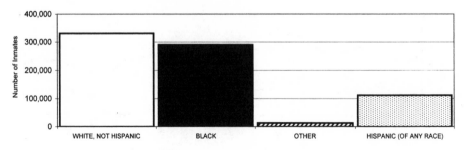

Figure 83: Disparity in Local Jail Incarceration Rates

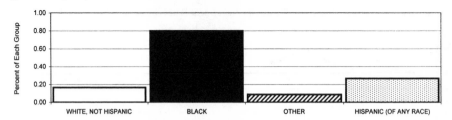

Data shown are as of July 1, 2005. Although the white, not Hispanic population is the largest segment of the population in local jails, blacks have a disproportionately large incarceration rate. In addition, whereas blacks represent 13% of the U.S. population, they represent 39% of the local jail population; whites constitute 67% of the U.S. population and 44% of the local jail population; Hispanics constitute 15% of the U.S. population and 15% of the local jail population. The black local jail incarceration rate of 0.800% is almost five times the corresponding rate for the white, not Hispanic population and is almost three times the corresponding rate for the Hispanic population. For other relevant information, see the introduction to the appendix.

*Source:* U.S. Department of Justice, Prison and Jail Inmates at Midyear 2005, http://www.ojp.usdoj.gov/bjs/ pub/pdf/pjim05.pdf; U.S. Census Bureau, Historical Poverty Tables—People, table 2, www.census.gov/ hhes/www/poverty/histpov2.html

Figure 84: Disparity in Male Incarceration for All Jails and Prisons

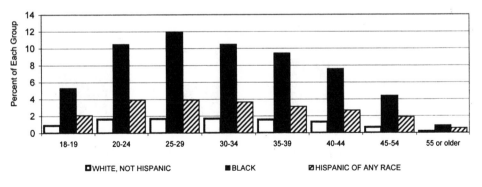

Figure 85: Disparity between Black and White Male Incarceration Rates (Black Rate Minus White, Not Hispanic Rate)

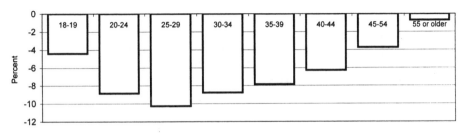

The above incarceration rates include local jails, federal prisons, and state prisons. The incarceration rates for blacks between the ages of twenty-five and twenty-nine is a shocking 12.0%. This is compared with 1.6% for whites, a difference of nearly eightfold, and is compared with 3.9% for Hispanics, a difference of more than threefold. For other relevant information, see the introduction to the appendix.

*Source:* U.S. Department of Justice, Prison and Jail Inmates at Midyear 2005, http://www.ojp.usdoj.gov/bjs/pub/pdf/pjim05.pdf.

Figure 86: Disparity in Life Events: Incarceration, Bachelor's Degree, or Military Service

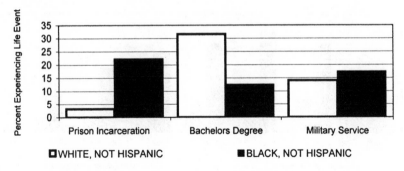

Figure 87: Disparity between Black and White Life Events (Black, Not Hispanic Percentage Minus White, Not Hispanic Percentage)

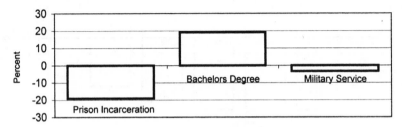

The above data reflect a study of men born between 1965 and 1969 who survived until 1999. Black men in this group were almost twice as likely to experience incarceration than to obtain a bachelor's degree or serve in the military. Comparatively, the men in the white, not Hispanic population were ten times more likely to earn a bachelors degree than they were to go to prison. Black men were seven times more likely to go to prison than white men and less than half as likely to earn a bachelor's degree. The probability of entering military service was similar between the two groups. These figures were not available for Hispanics in this source. For other relevant information, see the introduction to the appendix.

*Source:* Becky Pettit and Bruce Western, *Mass Imprisonment and the Life Course: Race and Class Inequality in U.S. Incarceration*, http://www.princeton.edu/~western/ASRv69n2p.pdf.

Figure 88: Disparity in Racial Profiling: Driving While Black (DWB)

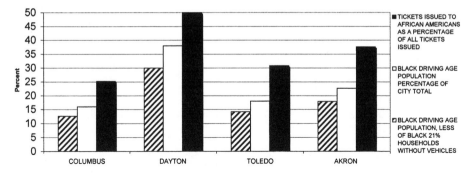

Figure 89: Disparity in the Likelihood of Being Pulled Over: The Social Cost of DWB

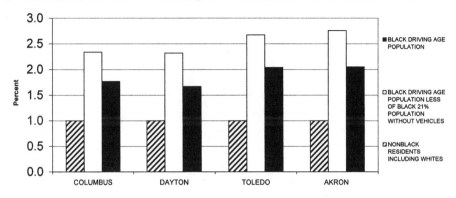

These figures are derived from a study in Ohio conducted by David A. Harris, professor of law at the University of Toledo College of Law in the years 1996, 1997, and 1998. Figure 88 measures the tickets issued to African Americans as a percentage of all tickets issued. Figure 89 measures how being black increases the likelihood of being pulled over. For example, in Akron, simply being black makes an individual 2.1 times more likely to be pulled over for the same driving behavior as exhibited by whites. Analyzing these numbers makes it clear that in Ohio, at least, the police engage in "racial profiling." Driving while black is a problem that exists nationwide, and even black celebrities are not immune. Wesley Snipes, Will Smith, Johnnie Cochrane, and Marcus Allen are among the many black celebrities who have been pulled over for the "crime" of being black. Unfortunately, no nationwide data are available, although other statewide studies have produced similar results. Harris explains: "Data on this problem are not easy to come by. This is, in part, because the problem has only recently been recognized beyond the black community. It may also be because records concerning police conduct are either irregular or nonexistent. But it may also be because there is active hostility in the law enforcement community to the idea of keeping comprehensive records of traffic stops. In 1997, Representative John Conyers of Michigan introduced H.R. 118, the Traffic Stops Statistics Act, which would require the Department of Justice to collect and analyze data on all traffic stops around the country—including the race of the driver, whether a search took place, and the legal justification for the search. When the bill passed the House with unanimous, bipartisan support, the National Association of Police Organizations (NAPO), an umbrella group representing more than 4,000 police interest groups across the country, announced its strong opposition to the bill. Officers would 'resent' having to collect the data, a spokesman for the group said. Moreover, there is 'no pressing need or justification'

*Continued on page 176*

Figure 90: Disparity in Victims of Racial Hate Crimes, 2005

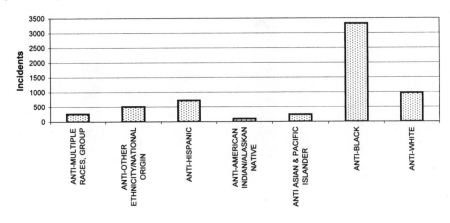

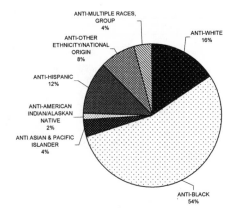

These graphs include the number of known hate crime incidents committed in 2005. The bar graph depicts the total number of race/ethnicity hate crimes by the type of racial bias motivation. The corresponding pie graph depicts the racial bias motivation as a percentage of the total number of race/ethnicity hate crimes. More than half of all race/ethnicity hate crimes were committed against blacks in 2005, despite the fact that blacks constitute only 13% of the total population. Note that most of these antiblack crimes are committed by white offenders (see figure 91). For other relevant information, see the introduction to the appendix. *Source:* Federal Bureau of Investigation, Hate Crime Statistics, 2005, http://www.fbi.gov/ucr/hc2005/table1 .htm.

---

*Continued from page 175*
for collecting the data. In other words, there is no problem, so there is no need to collect data. NAPO's opposition was enough to kill the bill in the Senate in the 105th Congress." David A. Harris, "The Stories, the Statistics, and the Law: Why 'Driving While Black' Matters," *Minnesota Law Review* 84 (1999): 265, 276. For a discussion of "shopping while black" (SWB) and "dining out while black" (DOWB), see, e.g., Bruce Graham, "The Crime of Shopping While Black," *Point Reyes Light*, May 27, 1999, www.ptreyeslight.com/ stories/may27_99/graham.html, and Pete Kotz, Dining While Black, May 11, 2005, www.clevescene.com/ Issues/2005-05-11/news/kotz.html. For other relevant information, see the introduction to the appendix.

Figure 91: Disparity in Perpetrators of Antiblack Hate Crimes, 2005

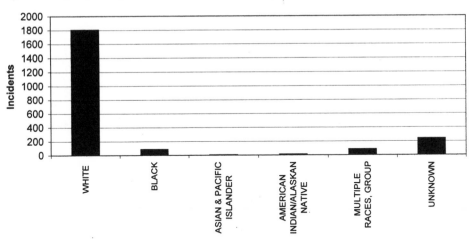

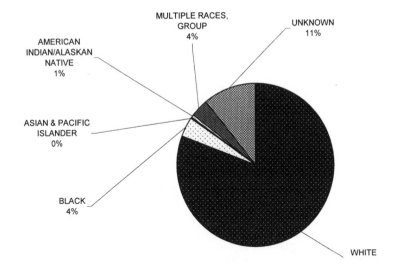

These figures depict all antiblack hate crimes with a known offender committed in 2005. In that year, 80% of the antiblack hate crime perpetrators were white, while 11% were of an "unknown race." Hispanics are not represented as a separate group in these figures because they are considered an "ethnicity," not a "race," and may be included within the racial groups shown. For other relevant information, see the introduction to the appendix.

*Source:* Federal Bureau of Investigation, Hate Crime Statistics, 2005, http://www.fbi.gov/ucr/hc2005/table5 .htm.

Figure 92: Disparity in Hate Crimes, 2005

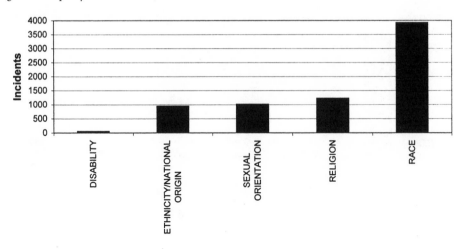

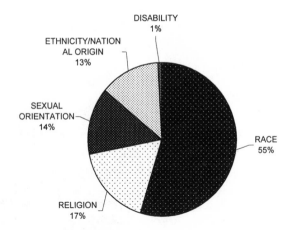

These figures include the number of known hate crime incidents committed in 2005. More than half of the hate crimes committed in 2005 were antirace acts. In addition, 13% of hate crimes were anti–ethnicity/ national origin motivated, a category that includes anti-Hispanic crimes. "Anti–ethnicity/national origin" crimes combined with "anti-race" crimes therefore accounted for 68% of all hate crimes in 2005. For other relevant information, see figures 90 and 91 and the introduction to the appendix.

*Source:* Federal Bureau of Investigation, Hate Crime Statistics, 2005, http://www.fbi.gov/ucr/hc2005/table1. htm.

Figure 93: Disparity in Percentage of Citizens Age Eighteen or Older Who Voted

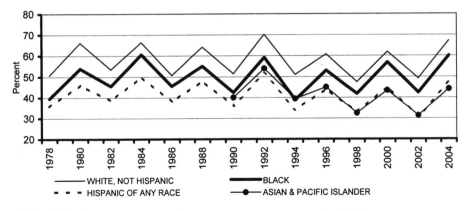

Figure 94: Disparity between Black and White Voting Rate (Black Rate Minus White, Not Hispanic Rate)

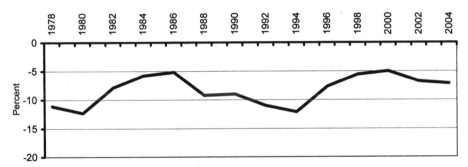

The above data show the percentage of people eighteen and older who voted. The data show a "zigzag" formation created by greater turnout during presidential election years. Consistently, the percentage of white, not Hispanics who show up at the polls is greater than that of any other group. Blacks exercise their right at a greater rate than Asians and Hispanics. Blacks saw the greatest turnout in 1984, the year of Jesse Jackson's first presidential campaign. The gap between white, not Hispanic and black voter participation narrowed from 1978 to 2004, from –11.1% to –7.2%. These data are not available for Asians and Pacific Islanders before 1990. For other relevant information, see the introduction to the appendix.

*Source:* U.S. Census Bureau, Voting and Registration—Historical Time Series Tables, table A-1, www.census .gov/population/www/socdemo/voting.html.

Figure 95: Disparity in Percentage of Population Age Eighteen or Older Who Voted

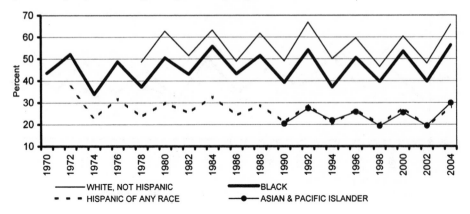

Figure 96: Disparity between Black and White Voting Rate (Black Rate Minus White, Not Hispanic Rate)

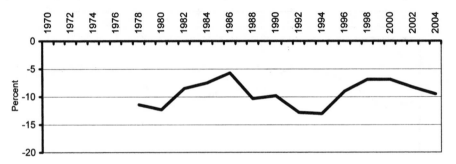

The above data show the percentage of people eighteen and older (citizen or otherwise) that voted. Asians and Hispanics have much lower voter representation than blacks and white, not Hispanics. This is due in part to a significant number of noncitizens within the Hispanic and Asian populations (for more information, see figures 17 and 18). The gap between the black and the white, not Hispanic rate did not improve much from 1978 to 2004, moving from –11.4 to –9.5. These data are not available for Asians and Pacific Islanders before 1990, not available for white, not Hispanics before 1978, and not available for Hispanics before 1972. For other relevant information, see the introduction to the appendix.

*Source:* U.S. Census Bureau, Voting and Registration—Historical Time Series Tables, table A-1, www.census .gov/population/www/socdemo/voting.html.

Figure 97: Disparity in Percentage of Citizens Age Eighteen or Older Who Registered to Vote

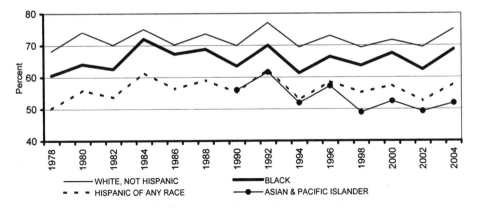

Figure 98: Disparity between Black and White Registration Rate (Black Rate Minus White, Not Hispanic Rate)

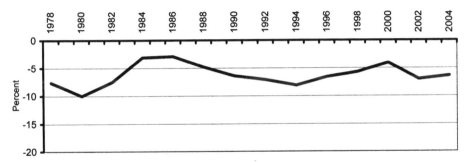

The above data show what percentage of eligible citizens (age eighteen and older) registered to vote. A record 72% of eligible black citizens were registered to vote in the 1984 presidential election, the year of Jesse Jackson's first presidential campaign. The Asian and Pacific Islander citizen-registration rate continues to fall while other groups remain relatively flat. Moreover, Asians and Pacific Islanders show the greatest apathy, with only 51.8% of eligible citizens registering to vote in 2004, the lowest of all groups. The gap between black and white, not Hispanic citizen-registration rates changed little from 1978 (–7.6%) to 2004 (–6.4%). These data are not available for Asians and Pacific Islanders before 1990. For other relevant information, see the introduction to the appendix.

*Source:* U.S. Census Bureau, Voting and Registration—Historical Time Series Tables, table A-1, www.census .gov/population/www/socdemo/voting.html.

Figure 99: Disparity in Percentage of Population Age Eighteen or Older Who Registered to Vote

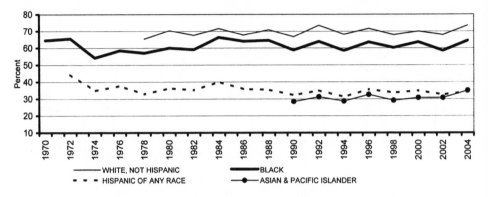

WHITE, NOT HISPANIC    BLACK
HISPANIC OF ANY RACE    ASIAN & PACIFIC ISLANDER

Figure 100: Disparity between Black and White Voter Registration Rate (Black Rate Minus White, Not Hispanic Rate)

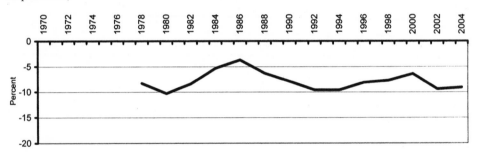

The above data show what percentage of the age eighteen and older population (citizen or otherwise) registered to vote. As of 2004, less than half of Hispanics (34.3%) and Asian or Pacific Islanders (34.9%) over the age of eighteen were registered to vote, driven both by voter apathy and by low citizenship rates. The gap between black and white population-registration rates did not improve from 1978 (−8.3%) to 2004 (−9.1%). These data are not available for Asians and Pacific Islanders before 1990, not available for white, not Hispanics before 1978, and not available for Hispanics before 1972. For other relevant information, see the introduction to the appendix.

*Source:* U.S. Census Bureau, Voting and Registration—Historical Time Series Tables, table A-1, www.census .gov/population/www/socdemo/voting.html.

# NOTES

PREFACE. THE AGE OF OBAMA

1. *Dred Scott v. Sandford*, 60 U.S. (19 How.) 393, 408 (1857).

2. 163 U.S. at 558 (Harlan, J., dissenting). See *Fullilove v. Klutznick*, 448 U.S. 448, 522–23 (1980) (Stewart, J., dissenting).

3. 163 U.S. at 558 (Harlan, J., dissenting).

4. Gene Roberts and Hank Klibanoff, *The Race Beat: The Press, the Civil Rights Struggle, and the Awakening of a Nation* (New York: Vintage Books, 2006), 5.

5. Ibid.

6. Arnold Rampersad, *Ralph Ellison: A Biography* (New York: Knopf, 2007), 184 (Wright reporting on Ralph Ellison's fear).

7. In addition to *Brown v. Board of Education*, 347 U.S. 483 (1954), which overturned state school segregation statutes, Congress passed several important pieces of civil rights legislation that ended Jim Crow in numerous venues, mainly, the Civil Rights Act of 1964 (42 U.S.C. §§ 2000e to 2000e-15), the Voting Rights Act of 1965 (42 U.S.C. §§ 1971 to 1973aa-6), the Fair Housing Act of 1968 (42 U.S.C. §§ 3601–19), and the Equal Opportunity Act of 1972 (42 U.S.C. §§ 2000e to 2000e-17).

8. See the appendix for a more detailed discussion of these and other racial disparities.

9. National Urban League, "National Urban League's State of Black America 2006," press release, Wednesday, March 29, 2006.

10. "For Financing Higher Education, the Racial Wealth Gap Remains Huge," *Journal of Blacks in Higher Education, Weekly Bulletin*, March 1, 2007. See generally Melvin L. Oliver and Thomas Shapiro, *Black Wealth, White Wealth: A New Perspective on Racial Inequality*, 2nd ed. (New York: Routledge, 2006).

11. Orlando Patterson, "A Poverty of the Mind," *New York Times*, March 26, 2006, sec. 4, p. 13. Patterson argues that some civil rights theorists are reluctant to recognize cultural explanations because they fear that to do so would blame the victim (which Patterson says is "bogus" because the external factors remain viable explanations); because they assume internal explanations are "wholly deterministic, leaving no room for human agency" (which Patterson says is "nonsense" because "while it [culture] partly determines behavior, it also enables people to change behavior"); and because they often assume that "cultural patterns cannot change" (which Patterson calls "nonsense" because internal patterns are often easier to change than external conditions, taking as an example southern whites' ability to change their racists views toward blacks while at the same time economic inequality "has hardened in the South, like the rest of America"). Ibid.

12. For a discussion of DuBois's intellectual journey, see Roy L. Brooks, *Integration or Separation? A Strategy for Racial Equality* (Cambridge, Mass.: Harvard University Press, 1996), 125–31. For a discussion of Glenn Loury's conversion from traditionalist to re-

formist, see Adam Shatz, "About Face," *New York Times Magazine*, January 20, 2002, 18.

13. For further discussion, see chapter 2, section B1.


1. INTRODUCTION

1. Much of the data on Asians, for example, were not collected until after 1993 or 1999. See, e.g., appendix, figures 49, 51, 53, 55, 57, and 59.

2. Lena Williams, *It's the Little Things: Everyday Interactions That Anger, Annoy, and Divide the Races* (San Diego: Harcourt, 2000), 244, quoting the former president.

3. James Q. Wilson, "American Dilemma: Problems of Race Still Cry to Be Solved," *National Review*, December 19, 2005, 62.

4. See the appendix. Also, the principle of practical idealism, discussed in the epilogue, and the theory of completeness certainly apply to nonblack civil rights groups.

5. Perhaps the most memorable part of the Declaration states: "We hold these truths to be self-evident, that all Men are created equal, that they are endowed by their Creator with certain unalienable Rights, that among these are Life, Liberty, and the Pursuit of Happiness." See Joseph Tussman and Jacobus tenBroek, "The Equal Protection of the Laws," *California Law Review* 37 (1949): 341, 341 ("The doctrine of equality is, of course, embodied in the Declaration of Independence").

6. Ibid.

7. Treating similarly situated individuals differently is usually actionable only when the different treatment is based upon the victim's membership in a "protected class," which term is discussed later in this chapter. See *Anup Engquist v. Oregon Department of Agriculture*, 128 S. Ct. 2146 (2008).

8. U.S. Const. amend. XIV, sec. 1.

9. See, e.g., 42 U.S.C. § 2000a (public accommodations); 42 U.S.C. §§ 2000e to 2000e-15 (employment); 42 U.S.C. §§ 1971 to 1973aa-6m (voting); 42 U.S.C. §§ 3601–19 (housing); 42 U.S.C. §§ 12101–12213 (disability).

10. 347 U.S. 483 (1954).

11. For affirmative action, see, e.g., *Grutter v. Bollinger*, 539 U.S. 306 (2003); *Adarand Constructors, Inc. v. Peña*, 515 U.S. 200 (1995); *Regents of California v. Bakke*, 438 U.S. 265 (1978). In *Plyler v. Doe*, 457 U.S. 202 (1982), the Supreme Court invalidated a Texas law under the Equal Protection Clause that required children of illegal aliens to pay for their public education whereas children of citizens and documented aliens received a free public education. The Court held that, unlike their parents, the children of undocumented aliens were blameless; they were not responsible for creating their status, and the state "could not abandon the innocent."

12. See, e.g., Title II of the Civil Rights Act of 1964, 42 U.S. C. §§ 2000a to 2000a-6. See S. Rep. No. 88-872, at 2366 (1964). See *Heart of Atlanta Motel, Inc. v. United States*, 379 U.S. 241 (1964).

13. See, e.g., Title VI of the Civil Rights Act of 1964, 42 U.S. C. §§ 2000d to 2000d-7. See *Alexander v. Sandoval*, 532 U.S. 275 (2001).

14. See, e.g., 42 U.S. C. § 1983. See *Monell v. Department of Social Services of the City of New York*, 436 U.S. (1978).

15. See, e.g., 42 U.S.C. §§ 2000e to 2000e-15. (employment); 42 U.S.C. §§ 1971 to 1973aa-6m (voting); 42 U.S.C. §§ 3601–19 (housing).

16. An unusual example of procedural rights involves the Terri Schiavo right-to-die case. President George Walker Bush signed into law a private bill in the controversial right-to-die case involving Terri Schiavo that came to be called the "Palm Sunday Compromise." Overwhelmingly passed by Republicans and Democrats in Congress, the bill's official title is the Act for the Relief of the Parents of Theresa Marie Schiavo. Ruling against Mrs. Schiavo's parents, the Schindlers, the Florida state courts permitted doctors to remove the comatose Schiavo from a life-support system as her husband had requested. The bill President Bush signed into law on March 21, 2005, after flying to Washington, D.C., from his vacation in Texas, transferred jurisdiction of the Schiavo case from state to federal courts. But, as in the state courts, all of the Schindlers' federal petitions and appeals were denied. The U.S. Supreme Court declined to grant certiorari in the case, which effectively ending the Schindlers' legal options. The private bill President Bush signed seems to go against civil rights tradition. Individuals have civil rights to the extent that they are affiliated with a protected class or raise an issue of government neutrality with respect to a protected class. The latter point is discussed in greater detail later in this section. Neither requirement was met in the Schiavo case. The civil rights provided in the bill were in personam rather than group-based. For background in the Terri Schiavo case, see, e.g., David Gibbs and Bob DeMoss, *Fighting for Dear Life: Inside the Terri Schiavo Story and What It Means for All of Us* (Minneapolis, Minn.: Bethany House, 2006); Arthur Caplan, James J. McCartney, and Dominic Sisti, eds., *The Case of Terri Schiavo: Ethics at the End of Life* (Amherst, N.Y.: Prometheus Books, 2006).

17. U.S. Const. art. II, sec. 1, clause 5.

18. For a discussion of formal equal opportunity, see, e.g., Roy L. Brooks, Gilbert Paul Carrasco, and Michael Selmi, *Civil Rights Litigation: Cases and Perspectives*, 3rd ed. (Durham, N.C.: Carolina Academic Press, 2005), 11–12.

19. *Dred Scott v. Sandford*, 60 U.S. (19 How.) 393, 408 (1857).

20. The equality ideal in the Declaration of Independence was undercut by the widely held notion that blacks were subhuman. Given this notion of racial inferiority, the equality ideal was deemed to be inapplicable to blacks. As the Supreme Court observed in *Dred Scott v. Sandford*, 60 U.S. (19 How.) 393 (1856), blacks were "regarded as beings of an inferior order...unfit to associate with the white race" and, as such, "they had no rights which the white man was bound to respect." Ibid., 408.

21. U. S. Const. amend. XIII, sec. 1.

22. U. S. Const. amend. XIV, sec. 1.

23. U. S. Const. amend. XV, sec. 1.

24. Ira Katznelson, *When Affirmative Action Was White: An Untold History of Racial Inequality in America* (New York: Norton, 2005).

25. Ira Katznelson, "When Affirmative Action Was White," *Poverty and Race Research Action Council* 15, no. 2 (March/April 2006): 1, 1. See also Katznelson, *When Affirmative Action Was White*, 140.

26. Katznelson, "When Affirmative Action Was White," 1. See Katznelson, *When Affirmative Action Was White*, 22, 27, 32, 36–38, 50–53, 114, 143, 163.

27. *United States v. Carolene Products Co.*, 304 U.S. 144, 152 n. 4 (1938).

28. *Tennessee v. Lane*, 541 U.S. 509, 516 (2004).

29. *Carolene Products Co.*, 304 U.S. 144, 152 n. 4. "In some sense, the rationale for this form of heightened [or special] judicial scrutiny was procedural: Failures in the political process provided the explanation for why laws targeting these groups are sub-

ject to more searching judicial review than laws that focus on what other groups receive. But ultimately the courts' response is substantive: A reviewing court…would strike down the offending law, rather than seeking to revamp the political process that produced it." Pamela S. Karlan, "John Hart Ely and the Problem of Gerrymandering: The Lion in Winter," *Yale Law Journal* 114 (2005):1329, 1335. There are several levels of heightened scrutiny. See *City of Richmond v. J. A. Croson*, 488 U.S. 469 (1989); *Adarand Constructors, Inc. v. Peña*, 515 U.S. 200 (1995). See also Brooks, Carrasco, and Selmi, *Civil Rights Litigation*, 1197–1318; Kathleen M. Sullivan and Gerald Gunther, *Constitutional Law*, 15th ed. (New York: Foundation Press, 2004), 667–769.

30. Pamela Karlan correctly notes: "For [John Hart] Ely, as for the Warren Court, the 'core case' of a group deserving such special judicial solicitude was blacks." Karlan, "John Hart Ely and the Problem of Gerrymandering," 1335.

31. For a further discussion, see, e.g., Erwin Chermerinsky, *Constitutional Law: Principles and Policies* (New York: Aspen Law and Business Publishers, 1997), 414–17; Daniel A. Farber and Philip P. Frickey, "Is Carolene Products Dead? Reflections on Affirmative Action and the Dynamics of Civil Rights Legislation," *California Law Review* 79 (1991): 685; Bruce A. Ackerman, "Beyond Carolene Products," *Harvard Law Review* 98 (1971): 713.

32. 42 U.S.C. § 12101(a)(7).

33. *Hazen Paper Co. v. Biggins*, 507 U.S. 604, 610 (1993). See Age Discrimination in Employment Act of 1975, 42 U.S.C. §§ 6101–7.

34. See, e.g., *Lawrence v. Texas*, 539 U.S. 558 (2003) (overturning a Texas statute that made it a crime for two persons of the same sex to engage in intimate sexual conduct); *Romer v. Evans*, 517 U.S. 620 (1996) (overturning a state statute that excluded homosexuals from state civil rights protections). However, Congress still limits the definition of marriage to opposite-sex couples. See U.S.C. § 7. As of this writing, sexual orientation is deemed to be a "suspect classification" in California, which is the highest of civil rights protections. See *In re Marriage Cases*, 43. Cal. 4th 757 (2008). See generally Gilbert Paul Carrasco, *Sexuality and Discrimination: A Rights and Liberties Perspective* (Durham, N.C.: Carolina Academic Press, 2005).

35. 509 U.S. 630 (1993).

36. Ibid., 633.

37. Karlan, "John Hart Ely and the Problem of Gerrymandering," 1341. Karlan also notes, "On its face, *Shaw* seemed to embrace a previously rejected notion of citizen standing: Any individual who objected to the state's use of race in the redistricting process could bring an equal protection lawsuit. And while the Court backed off somewhat from this position in *United States v. Hays* [515 U.S. 737, 739 (1995)], requiring plaintiffs actually to live in the districts they challenged, it remained circumspect about what precisely the constitutionally cognizable injury was in a *Shaw* lawsuit. Ibid. See *Shaw*, 509 U.S. 636–37 (describing the plaintiffs' characteristics).

38. See, e.g., *McDonald v. Santa Fe Trial Transportation Co.*, 427 U.S. 273 (1976) (Title VII protects white employees).

39. Jeremy Waldron, "Autonomy and Perfectionism in Raz's Morality of Freedom," *California Law Review* 62 (1989): 1097, 1102. See generally George Sher, *Beyond Neutrality: Perfectionism and Politics* (New York: Cambridge University Press, 1997); Kimberly A. Yuracko, "Private Nurses and Playboy Bunnies: Explaining Permissible Sex Discrimination," *California Law Review* 92 (2004): 147, 191–95.

40. Orlando Patterson, *The Ordeal of Integration: Progress and Resentment in America's "Racial" Crisis* (New York: Basic Books, 1997), xi.

41. Ibid.

42. Ibid.

43. See, e.g., The Civil Rights Act of 1964 (42 U.S.C. §§ 2000e to 2000e-15), the Voting Rights Act of 1965 (42 U.S.C. §§ 1971 to 1973aa-6), the Fair Housing Act of 1968 (42 U.S.C. §§ 3601–19), and the 1972 amendments to Title VII of the 1964 Civil Rights Act (42 U.S.C. §§ 2000e to 2000e-17).

44. For further discussion, see Derrick A. Bell, *Race, Racism, and American Law*, 5th ed. (New York: Aspen, 2004), 2–4. For further discussion of biological, sociological, and political concepts of race see, e.g., Roy L. Brooks, "Race as an Under-inclusive and Over-inclusive Concept," *African-American Law & Policy Report* 1 (Fall 1994): 9.

45. Roy L. Brooks, *Integration or Separation? A Strategy for Racial Equality* (Cambridge, Mass.: Harvard University Press, 1996), ix.

46. For a more detailed discussion of the concept of capital deficiencies, see Roy L. Brooks, *Atonement and Forgiveness: A New Model for Black Reparations* (Berkeley: University of California Press, 2004), 21 (sources cited therein).

47. See, e.g., Walter Benn Michaels, *The Trouble with Diversity: How We Learned to Love Identity and Ignore Inequality* (New York: Metropolitan Books/Henry Holt, 2006) (arguing that capitalism [wealth distribution], or "neoliberalism," is all that matters when discussing racial inequality).

48. See chapters 2–5. I would disagree with critical race theorists who assert that the distribution of community resources along racial lines necessarily constitutes "racism." Some of this maldistribution is internally generated. See in particular chapters 2, 3, and 4.

49. See, e.g., John Hope Franklin and Alfred A. Moss Jr., *From Slavery to Freedom: A History of Negro Americans*, 6th ed. (New York: Knopf, 1988), 174–75.

50. For a discussion, see, e.g., ibid., 277–323; Brooks, *Atonement and Forgiveness*, chap. 3.

51. Roy L. Brooks, "Affirmative Action in Law Teaching," *Columbia Human Rights Law Review* 14 (1982): 15, 43 (sources cited therein).

52. As I indicated in an earlier note, I would not automatically label racialized resources as "racist" as critical race theorists do in chapter 5. Racism is not responsible for all racial disparities, for the whole of the race problem.

53. See Gunnar Myrdal, *An American Dilemma: The Negro Problem and Modern Democracy* (New York: Harper and Brothers, 1944).

54. National Urban League, "National Urban League's State of Black America 2006," press release, March 29, 2006. The racial gap even exists within socioeconomic strata: "white middle-class families had on average 113 times more financial assets than black middle-class families." "For Financing Higher Education, the Racial Wealth Gap Remains Huge," *Journal of Blacks in Higher Education, Weekly Bulletin*, March 1, 2007. See generally Melvin L. Oliver and Thomas Shapiro, *Black Wealth, White Wealth: A New Perspective on Racial Inequality*, 2nd ed. (New York: Routledge, 2006).

55. For a discussion of the distinction between discrimination and subordination, see chapter 5. I do not wish to suggest that the contours of civil rights theory should be determined by civil rights law, but it is instructive to note that expressed racism by itself does not trigger a violation of civil rights law. An employer who says, "I am an equal

opportunity employer; I treat whites and N——s the same" is racist, but he has not committed an actionable civil rights wrong so long as he accords similar treatment to his black and white employees in all aspects of the business. In our society, we go after the prejudiced or nonprejudiced discriminator and leave the prejudiced nondiscriminator alone. See Brooks, Carrasco, and Selmi, *Civil Rights Litigation*, 417–19. Cf. *Ash v. Tyson Foods, Inc.*, 126 S. Ct. 1195 (2006) (the use of the word "boy" by a plant manager in reference to a black employee can be evidence of racial animus depending on the context in which the word was used, including the manager's inflection, tone of voice, local custom, and historical usage). Some civil rights theorists would argue that racial attitudes constitute a major part of the race problem and, consequently, should be actionable under antidiscrimination law. See Catharine A. MacKinnon, *Only Words* (Cambridge, Mass.: Harvard University Press, 1993) (current approach to free speech "silences" women and subordinates them in political arena); Richard Delgado, "Words That Wound: A Tort Action for Racial Insults, Epithets, and Name Calling," *Harvard Civil Rights–Civil Liberties Law Review* 17 (1982): 133, 178 (attacking First Amendment protection of racial insults as "contributing to a stratified society in which political power is possessed by some and denied to others"); Charles Lawrence, "If He Hollers Let Him Go: Regulating Racist Speech on Campus," *Duke Law Journal* 1990 (1990): 431, 471 (arguing that protection of racist speech leads to "exclusion of nonwhites from full participation in the body politic"). See generally Mari J. Matsuda, Charles R. Lawrence, Richard Delgado, and Kimberlé Williams Crenshaw, eds., *Words That Wound: Critical Race Theory, Assaultive Speech, and the First Amendment* (Boulder, Colo.: Westview Press, 1993).

56. See appendix, figures 22–29, 51, 53, 55, 57, 59. Asians do, however, experience resource disparity in other areas of American life, such as home ownership. See appendix, figure 46.

57. John Hart Ely, *Democracy and Distrust: A Theory of Judicial Review* (Cambridge, Mass.: Harvard University Press, 1980), 170. See Skelly Wright, "Professor Bickel, the Scholarly Tradition, and the Supreme Court," *Harvard Law Review* 84 (1971): 769.

58. See the appendix.

59. Compare, e.g., appendix, figure 11 with figures 19 and 5–10.

60. Clarence Page, "Black Immigrants: A 'Model Minority,'" *San Diego Union-Tribune*, March 20, 2007, B6.

## 2. TRADITIONALISM

1. For a discussion of the van Gogh murder and its aftermath, see Ian Buruma, *Murder in Amsterdam: The Death of Theo van Gogh and the Limits of Tolerance* (New York: Penguin Press, 2006). See also International Helsinki Federation for Human Rights, "Intolerance and Discrimination against Muslims in the EU: Developments since September 11," March 2005, http://www.ihf-hr.org. For a discussion of Ayaan Hirsi Ali and her break from Islam, see her memoir, *Infidel* (New York: Free Press, 2007). See also Christopher Caldwell, "Daughter of the Enlightenment," *New York Times Magazine*, April 3, 2005, 26–31.

2. Clarence Page, "To the Rescue of the Party of Lincoln," *San Diego Union Tribune*, June 20, 2006, B7.

3. Norman Podhoretz and Irving Kristol are perhaps the chief architects of neocon-

servatism. William Kristol and David Horowitz are more recent converts. See, e.g., Norman Podhoretz, *My Love Affair with America: The Cautionary Tale of a Cheerful Conservative* (New York: Free Press, 2000); Irving Kristol, *Neoconservatism: The Autobiography of an Idea* (New York: Free Press, 1995); William Kristol, *Neoconservative Imagination: Essays in Honor of Irving Kristol*, ed. Christopher DeMuth and William Kristol (Washington, D.C.: AEI Press, 1995); David Horowitz, *Hating Whitey* (Dallas, Tex.: Spence, 1999).

4. See, e.g., Roy L. Brooks, *Integration or Separation? A Strategy for Racial Equality* (Cambridge, Mass.: Harvard University Press, 1996), 125–31.

5. Thomas Sowell, *Race, Culture, and Equality* (Stanford, Calif.: Hoover Institution on War, Revolution and Peace, 1998), 8.

6. Ibid. Sowell says that "cultural, social, economic, and other factors" interact to cause and explain disparity. Ibid., p. 11.

7. Bill O'Reilly, *Who's Looking Out for You?* (New York: Broadway Books, 2003), 170–71.

8. Ibid., 170.

9. Ibid., 171.

10. See Dinesh D'Souza, *What's So Great about America* (Washington, D.C.: Regnery, 2002), 101–2.

11. Ibid., 118.

12. Ibid., 119.

13. George F. Will, "Why Civil Rights No Longer Are Rights," *San Diego Union-Tribune*, March 10, 2005, B12.

14. Ibid.

15. Thomas Sowell, *Cosmic Justice* (New York: Free Press, 1999), 163.

16. Shelby Steele, *The Content of Our Character: A New Vision of Race in America* (New York: St. Martin's Press, 1990), 119.

17. See Stephan Thernstrom and Abigail Thernstrom, *America in Black and White: One Nation, Indivisible* (New York: Simon and Schuster, 1997), 539–40.

18. See ibid.

19. *Adarand Constructors, Inc. v. Peña*, 515 U.S. 200, 240–41 (1995) (Thomas, J., concurring).

20. Ibid., 241.

21. Thernstrom and Thernstrom, *America in Black and White*, 360.

22. See Stephan Thernstrom, "Diversity and Meritocracy in Legal Education: A Critical Evaluation of Linda F. Wightman's 'The Threat to Diversity in Legal Education,'" *Constitutional Commentary* 15 (1998): 11, 23–24. See also Steele, *The Content of Our Character*, 112–21.

23. See Jesse Rothstein and Albert Yoon, "Mismatch in Law School" (February 1, 2006), Northwestern Law and Econ Research Paper No. 881110, http://ssrn.com/abstract=881110 (no mismatch in elite law schools); William G. Bowen and Derek Bok, *The Shape of the River: Long-Term Consequences of Considering Race in College and University Admissions* (Princeton, N.J.: Princeton University Press, 1998), 59–68 (no mismatch in elite colleges).

24. Steele, *The Content of Our Character*, 48, 60, 80, 89–90, 115, 118.

25. Shelby Steele, *White Guilt: How Blacks and Whites Together Destroyed the Promise of the Civil Rights Era* (New York: HarperCollins, 2006), 24.

26. Ibid., 100.

27. Robert J. Samuelson, "Must CEOs Be Multimillionaires?" *San Diego Union-Tribune*, July 12, 2006, B8.

28. O'Reilly, *Who's Looking Out for You?* 170.

29. Ibid., 156–66.

30. Ibid., 71–84, 137–43, 178–85.

31. Ibid., 77.

32. Ibid.

33. See Sowell, *Cosmic Justice*, 5, 8, 14, 72. See also Robert Bork, *Slouching toward Gomorrah: Modern Liberalism and American Decline* (New York: Regan Books, 1996) (arguing that the quest for egalitarianism has corrupted American society).

34. Thomas Sowell, "Is Yankee Stadium a 'Level Playing Field'?" *Wall Street Journal*, October 27, 1999, A18.

35. Sowell, *Cosmic Justice*, 91, 152.

36. Ward Connerly, "Why I'm Still Fighting Preferences in Florida," *Wall Street Journal*, November 18, 1999, A26.

37. Thernstrom and Thernstrom, *America in Black and White*, 541.

38. "The Limits of Compassionate Conservatism," *Economist*, June 17, 2006, 64.

39. Sowell, *Race, Culture, and Equality*, 12.

40. Steele, *The Content of Our Character*, 91.

41. Ibid., 120.

42. Thernstrom, "Diversity and Meritocracy in Legal Education, 43.

43. Sowell, *Race, Culture, and Equality*, 11. See also ibid., 2–3.

44. Sowell, *Race, Culture, and Equality*, 11.

45. George F. Will, "The Real Flaw of No Child Left Behind," *San Diego Union-Tribune*, June 23, 2005, B10.

46. Sowell, *Race, Culture, and Equality*, 2–3, 11.

47. O'Reilly, *Who's Looking Out for You?* 58.

48. See Bill O'Reilly, *Culture Warrior* (New York: Broadway Books, 2006).

49. O'Reilly, *Who's Looking Out for You?* 119. See also 113–125.

50. Ibid., 120.

51. Ibid., 123–24.

52. See, e.g., Myron Magnet, "What Is Compassionate Conservatism?" *Wall Street Journal*, February 5, 1999, A14. See also William J. Bennett, *Our Children and Our Country: Improving America's Schools and Affirming the Common Culture* (New York: Simon and Schuster, 1988); "The Gun Windmills," *Wall Street Journal*, December 13, 1999, A34 (editorial).

53. Magnet, "What Is Compassionate Conservatism?" A14.

54. Steele, *White Guilt*, 180.

55. See Will, "Why Civil Rights No Longer Are Rights," B12.

56. Ibid.

57. See Horowitz, *Hating Whitey*.

58. Steele, *The Content of Our Character*, 15.

59. McWhorter, *Losing the Race*, 43. See also John H. McWhorter, *Winning the Race: Beyond the Crisis in Black America* (New York: Gotham Books, 2006).

60. Steele, *The Content of Our Character*, 14.

61. Ibid., 15.

62. Ibid., 14–16, 34–35, 68–69.

63. Thomas Sowell, *Black Rednecks and White Liberals* (San Francisco: Encounter Books, 2005), 1–2.

64. Ibid, 3–4.

65. Steele, *The Content of Our Character*, 49.

66. Ibid.

67. Ibid., 48.

68. Ibid., 49.

69. Ibid., 43.

70. Ibid., 26.

71. Ibid., 24. See also 26.

72. Ibid., 24, 26, 27, 49–51.

73. O'Reilly, *Who's Looking Out for You?* 7.

74. Ibid.

75. Ibid., 8.

76. Ibid., 169–70.

77. Ibid., 19–20.

78. *Hudson v. McMillian*, 503 U.S. 1, 28 (1992) (Thomas, J., with whom Scalia, J., joins, dissenting).

79. Steele, *White Guilt*, 109–10. See also 45, 58–60.

80. See, e.g., Thernstrom and Thernstrom, *America in Black and White*, 186, 189, 194–98, 233–45, 253–57, 534; Sniderman and Carmines, *Reaching beyond Race*, 142; Will, "Why Civil Rights No Longer Are Rights," B12. See also Brooks, *Rethinking the American Race Problem*, 110–11 (discussing the structuralism versus behavioralism [or "culture of poverty"] debate between Edward Banfield and William Ryan).

81. "The Gun Windmills," A34. See Rob Nelson, "The Word 'Nigga' Is Only for Slaves and Sambos," *Journal of Blacks in Higher Education* 21 (Autumn 1998):117 (African American student editor argues that "blacks [must] wake up and realize what an incredibly damaging step backwards using the word nigger really is").

82. O'Reilly, *Who's Looking Out for You?* 10, 14–16. In particular, O'Reilly notes the deleterious effects of excessive drinking and doing drugs. Ibid., 3.

83. Ibid., 21, 22.

84. Brent Staples, "Why Slave-Era Barriers to Black Literacy Still Matter," *New York Times*, January 1, 2006, sec. 4, p. 7.

85. Michael Eric Dyson, *Come Hell or High Water* (New York: Basic Civitas Books, 2006), 164. See also "Black People Loot, White People Find?" *Boingboing: A Directory of Wonderful Things*, August 30, 2005, http://www.boingboing.net/2005/08/30/black_people_loot_wh.html.

86. Dyson, *Come Hell or High Water*, 164.

87. See ibid., 164–65.

88. Ibid., 165.

89. See ibid., 174.

90. O'Reilly, *Culture Warrior*, 196.

91. Ibid., 197.

92. The poverty rates for families headed by single females appear in figures 5–8 in the appendix.

93. Elisabeth Bumiller, *Condoleezza Rice: An American Life* (New York: Random House, 2007), 45.

94. U.S. Department of Justice, Office of Justice Programs, Bureau of Justice Statistics, *Criminal Victimization in the United States, 2002 Statistical Tables*, table 42: Personal Crimes of Violence, 2002.

95. O'Reilly, *Who's Looking Out for You?* 177.

96. Malcolm Gladwell, *Outliers: The Story of Success* (New York: Little Brown, 2008), 18, 19, 267.

## 3. REFORMISM

1. Paul M. Barrett, *The Good Black: A True Story of Race in America* (New York: Dutton, 1999), 42–43. See also Dorothy A. Brown, *Critical Race Theory: Cases, Materials, and Problems* (St. Paul, Minn.: Thomson/West, 2003), 40–53.

2. He lost the case. See *Mungin v. Katten Muchin & Zavis*, 116 F. 3d 1549 (D.C. Cir. 1997).

3. Cornel West, *Race Matters* (New York: Vintage Press, 2001), 3.

4. Joe R. Feagin, *Racist America: Roots, Current Realities, and Future Reparations* (New York: Routledge, 2000), 6, 16, 204.

5. Glenn C. Loury, *The Anatomy of Racial Inequality* (Cambridge, Mass.: Harvard University Press, 2002), 144.

6. See Michael Eric Dyson, *The Michael Eric Dyson Reader* (New York: Basic Civitas Books, 2004); Ellis Cose, *The Rage of a Privileged Class* (New York: HarperCollins, 1993); *The Covenant with Black America*, introduction by Tavis Smiley (Chicago: Third World Press, 2006); Joe Feagin and Eileen O'Brien, *White Men on Race: Power, Privilege, and the Shaping of Cultural Consciousness* (Boston: Beacon Press Books, 2003); Joe R. Feagin and Hernan Vera, *White Racism* (New York: Routledge,1995); Joe R. Feagin and Melvin Sikes, *Living with Racism: The Black Middle-Class Experience* (Boston: Beacon Press, 1994); David Stokes, "Racial Lawsuits Filed against Waffle House," *Atlanta Inquirer*, January 29, 2005, 1; J. Zamgba Browne, "Black Bikers Bring Suit," *New York Amsterdam News*, May 29, 2003, 3; Timothy Brezina and Kenisha Winder, "Economic Disadvantage, Status Generalization, and Negative Racial Stereotyping by White Americans," *Social Psychology Quarterly* 66 (2003): 402; "Florida Black Colleges Receive Settlement from Hotel Bias Case," *Black Issues in Higher Education*, April 11, 2002, 15; Andrew Hacker, *Two Nations: Black and White, Separate, Hostile, Unequal* (New York: Ballantine Books, 1992); Michael Hughes and Melvin E. Thomas, "The Continuing Significance of Race Revisited: A Study of Race, Class, and Quality of Life in America, 1972 to 1996," *American Sociological Review* 63 (1998): 785; Joe R. Feagin, "The Continuing Significance of Race: Antiblack Discrimination in Public Places," *American Sociological Review* 56 (1991): 101.

7. West, *Race Matters*, 6.

8. Roy L. Brooks, *Rethinking the American Race Problem* (Berkeley: University of California Press, 1990), 150. See Joe R. Feagin, "Heeding Black Voices: The Court, Brown, and Challenges in Building a Multiracial Democracy," *University of Pittsburgh Law Review* 66 (Fall 2004): 57.

9. Dinesh D'Souza, *What's So Great about America* (Washington, D.C.: Regnery, 2002), 101–2.

10. Juan Williams, *Enough: The Phony Leaders, Dead End Movements, and Culture of*

*Failure That Are Undermining Black America—And What We Can Do about It* (New York: Crown, 2006), 220.

11. U.S. Census Bureau, *Current Population Reports: Income in the United States: 2002,* Series P-60, no. 221, table A-1, www.census.gov/prod/2003pubs/p60-221.pdf.

12. Brooks, *Rethinking the American Race Problem,* 177.

13. U.S. Census Bureau, Historical Poverty Tables—People, table 2. www.census.gov/hhes/www/poverty/histpov/hstpov2.html. See also figures1 and 3 in the appendix.

14. For further discussion, see section B1b, infra.

15. For a comparison between the concept of discrimination and the concept of subordination, see chapter 5, section B1.

16. *United States v. Leviner,* 31 F. Supp. 2d 23, 33 (D. Mass. 1998); Department of Justice, Office of Justice Programs, Press Release, April 29, 2007, http://www.ojp.usdoj .gov. The report, "Contacts between Police and the Public, 2005 (NCJ-215243)," is based on statistical data gathered during 2005, is written by BJS statisticians Matthew R. Durose, Erica L. Smith, and Patrick A. Langan, and is available at http://www.ojp.usdoj .gov/bjs/abstract/cpp05.htm. Eugene Robinson provides a good analysis of the report, "Another Peril for Black or Brown Drivers," *San Diego Union-Tribune,* May 2, 2007, B7. The RAND report is discussed at *U.S. News & World Report,* Desk News Blog, May 3, 2007, and can be found on the RAND Corporation's Web site. See *Commonwealth v. Gonsalves,* 429 Mass. 658 (1999) (discussing racial profiling, or "DWB"); Sean Hecker, "Race and Pretextual Traffic Stops: An Expanded Role for Civilian Review Board," *Columbia Human Rights Law Review* 28 (1997): 551 (discussing several studies showing the use of racial profiling in such places as New Jersey and Maryland); Carl T. Rowan, "The Hidden Costs of Racial Profiling," *San Diego Union-Tribune,* June 4, 1999, B13 (discussing racial profiling in four Ohio metropolitan areas). See generally Robert Gooding-Williams, ed., *Reading Rodney King/Reading Urban Uprising* (New York: Routledge, 1993). For a general discussion of race in the criminal justice system, see, e.g., Randall Kennedy, *Race, Crime, and the Law* (New York: Pantheon Books, 1997); Tracey Maclin, "Terry v. Ohio's Fourth Amendment Legacy: Black Men and Police Discretion," *St. John's Law Review* 72 (1998): 1271.

17. See, e.g., Timothy Williams, "N.Y. Cabbies Have a Fare Day," *San Diego Union-Tribune,* November 13, 1999, A2.

18. Barrett, *The Good Black,* 42–43.

19. See Gabriella Glaser, "Study Questions Blacks' Treatment in Emergency Room," *San Diego Union-Tribune,* December 28, 1999, A10.

20. Ibid.

21. See Federal Bureau of Investigation, U.S. Department of Justice, "Hate Crime Statistics (2003)", http://www.fbi.gov/ucr/03hc.pdf..

22. Ruben Navarrette Jr., "Race: The Elephant in the Room," *San Diego Union-Tribune,* August 6, 2008, B5.

23. Ibid.

24. Leslie Houts Picca and Joe R. Feagin, *Two-Faced Racism: Whites in the Backstage and Frontstage* (New York: Routledge, 2007), x.

25. Ibid.

26. Ibid., xi.

27. Ibid. (emphasis in original).

28. Ibid., viii, 91.

29. Levitt and Dubner, *Freakonomics*, 78.

30. The ABC News Web site reported the incident, which caused Senator Lott to lose his leadership in the Senate, as follows:

> At Thurmond's 100th birthday party last Thursday [December 5, 2002], Lott boasted that his state of Mississippi backed Thurmond for president 54 years ago. "When Strom Thurmond ran for president, we voted for him," Lott told those gathered at the Capitol Hill celebration. "We are proud of it." To that, the jovial invitation-only crowd of Republican supporters applauded and laughed. Then Lott continued, "If the rest of the country followed our lead we wouldn't have had all these problems." The room went virtually silent and some in the audience gasped. In 1948, Thurmond ran as a self-described "Dixiecrat" on a segregationist platform. In his campaign, Thurmond vowed that "all the laws of Washington and the bayonets of the Army cannot force the Negro into our homes, our schools, our churches...." Thurmond garnered the 39 electoral votes of South Carolina, Alabama, Louisiana, and Mississippi. He later recanted his segregationist views....[L]ast week was not the first time Lott has spoken out in favor of Thurmond's 1948 campaign in just those words. In November 1980, the [*New York*] *Times* reported, Lott said virtually the same thing at a campaign rally for Ronald Reagan in Jackson, Miss. After a speech by Thurmond at the rally, Lott said: "You know, if we had elected this man 30 years ago, we wouldn't be in the mess we are in today.

"Whole Lott of Trouble," AbcNews.com, December 11, 2002.

31. For the traditionalist view, see chapter 2, section B1.

32. See West, *Race Matters*, 5–7.

33. See *Raytheon Co. v. Hernandez*, 540 U.S. 44, 52–53 (2003) (cases cited therein).

34. See section B2 infra.

35. *Miller-El v. Dretke*, 125 S. Ct. 2317, 2323 (2005).

36. To successfully claim a peremptory challenge is being used in a racially discriminatory manner, one must navigate through the three-step test established in *Batson v. Kentucky*, 476 U.S. 79 (1986), by first establishing a prima facie case of discrimination, then asking prosecutors to provide a race-neutral explanation for their use of the peremptory, and finally proving that the explanation offered is pretextual. Difficult to prove or not, as Justice Breyer points out in his concurrence in *Miller-El*, drawing racial lines in jury selection not only is common but is considered good practice. Jury selection manuals and tools currently marketed to attorneys encourage the use of "demographic profiling" in jury selection, using age, gender, and ethnic-background (including racial) stereotypes to ensure a jury sympathetic to the client's cause. Justice Breyer suggests that the only way to eliminate racial discrimination in jury selection is to eliminate the peremptory challenge altogether. *Miller-El v. Dretke* at 2342–44.

37. See, e.g., Roy L. Brooks, Gilbert Paul Carrasco, and Michael Selmi, *Civil Rights Litigation: Cases and Perspectives*, 2nd ed. (Durham, N.C.: Carolina Academic Press, 2005), 415–69.

38. See, e.g., *Raytheon Co. v. Hernandez*, 540 U.S. 44, 52–53 (2003), citing *Teamsters v. United States*, 431 U.S. 324, 335 n. 15 (1977) (describing "disparate impact discrimination").

39. See, e.g., *Hazelwood School District v. United States*, 433 U.S. 299 (1977); *International Brotherhood of Teamsters v. United States*, 431 U.S. 324 (1977).

40. See, e.g., Michael Selmi, "Remedying Societal Discrimination through the Spending Power," *North Carolina Law Review* 80 (2002): 1575, 1604 (sources cited therein).

41. Roy L. Brooks, *Atonement and Forgiveness: A New Model for Black Reparations* (Berkeley: University of California Press, 2004), 82 (internal citations omitted).

42. *Wygant v. Jackson Board of Education*, 476 U.S. 267, 288 (1986) (O'Connor, J., concurring). See *Regents of the University of California v. Bakke*, 438 U.S. 912 (1978) (opinion of Powell, J.).

43. Selmi, "Remedying Societal Discrimination," 1604.

44. Ibid., 1603–4 (citations omitted).

45. For example, the cumulative effects of bad schools and poor-paying jobs (societal discrimination) can have a deleterious impact on black SAT performance (institutional discrimination).

46. *Wygant v. Jackson Board of Education*, 476 U. S. 267, 276 (1986) (plurality opinion).

47. For a comparison between the concept of discrimination and the concept of subordination, see chapter 5, section B1.

48. Feagin, *Racist America*, 26.

49. Ibid., 16.

50. Ibid.

51. Baynes, "Racial Justice in the New Millennium," 245–46 (citations omitted).

52. Thomas M. Shapiro, *The Hidden Cost of Being African American: How Wealth Perpetuates Inequality* (New York: Oxford University Press, 2004), 36–41.

53. Ibid., 38–39.

54. "For Financing Higher Education, the Racial Wealth Gap Remains Huge," *Journal of Blacks in Higher Education, Weekly Bulletin*, March 1, 2007. See also National Urban League, "National Urban League's State of Black America 2006," press release, Wednesday, March 29, 2006; Thomas M. Shapiro, "The Racial Wealth Gap," www.atsweb.neu .edu/jkenty/j.kenty/The%20Black-White%20Wealth%20Gap_Chapter_072803.doc (accessed July 7, 2005). 49; see generally Melvin L. Oliver and Thomas Shapiro, *Black Wealth, White Wealth: A New Perspective on Racial Inequality*, 2nd ed. (New York: Routledge, 2006).

55. Baynes, "Racial Justice in the New Millennium," 244, citing Gary Orfield and Susan B. Eaton, *The Harvard Project on School Desegregation, Dismantling Desegregation: The Quiet Reversal of* Brown v. Board of Education (New York: New Press, 1996), 60.

56. See, e.g., *Raytheon Co. v. Hernandez*, 540 U.S. 44, 52–53 (2003), citing *Teamsters v. United States*, 431 U.S. 324, 335 n. 15 (1977).

57. See, e.g., the examples involving Larry Mungrin, section A, supra, and Pat Washington, section B2, infra; Brooks, *Rethinking the American Race Problem*, 43–45.

58. See, e.g., "Departments: Race Relations on Campus," *Journal of Blacks in Higher Education* 47 (Spring 2005): 106.

59. See, e.g., Brooks, *Rethinking the American Race Problem*, 39–51 (middle class), 69–83 (working class), 109–16 (poverty class).

60. For a more detailed discussion see ibid., 69–116.

61. See Brent Staples, "A Short History of Class Antagonism in the Black Community," *New York Times*, May 29, 2005, sec. 4, p. 9.

62. See section C1, infra, for further discussion.

63. Loury, *The Anatomy of Racial Inequality*, 126.

64. Ibid.

65. Ibid., 125–26.

66. See section B2, infra.

67. *The Covenant with Black America*, introduction by Tavis Smiley (New York: Third World Press, 2006).

68. Michael K. Brown, Martin Carnoy, Elliott Currie, Troy Duster, David B. Oppenheimer, Marjorie M. Schultz, and David Wellman, eds., *Whitewashing Race: The Myth of a Color-Blind Society* (Berkeley: University of California Press, 2003).

69. This redistribution could be structured as a negative income tax program or take the form of a controversial proposal put forth by libertarian Charles A. Murray in his provocative book, *In Our Hands: A Plan to Replace the Welfare State* (Washington, D.C.: AEI Press, 2006). In a seemingly nonlibertarian move, Murray proposes scrapping the entire welfare system in favor of a system that gives $10,000 in tax-free money annually to every adult over twenty-one years of age (regardless of color or gender or wealth) provided that $3,000 of it is paid into a health care program and $2,000 of it is invested in a pension system of some sort. All transfers are done electronically, so the money never reaches the individual's hands. This program may make sense if one believes that governments can handle complex human needs in a competent manner. Here, it behooves us to think about Hurricane Katrina. See relevant discussion in chapter 2, section D, supra.

70. See West, *Race Matters*, 3, 4, 6; Feagin, *Racist America*, 248, 253–54, 255.

71. Joel J. Kupperman, "Relations between the Sexes: Timely and Timeless Principles," *San Diego Law Review* 25 (1988): 1027.

72. See Loury, *The Anatomy of Racial Inequality*, 166, 122.

73. Ibid., 166.

74. Ibid., 166–68. See also Feagin, *Racist America*, 249; West, *Race Matters*, 96–97; Baynes, "Racial Justice in the New Millennium," 245–46; Goodwin Liu, "Methods to Achieve Non-discrimination and Comparable Racial Equality: Race, Class, Diversity, Complexity," *Notre Dame Law Review* 80 (November 2004): 292, 299–302.

75. For a response to this concern, see section D, infra.

76. West, *Race Matters*, 95.

77. Pat Washington, "Does an EEOC Finding in Favor of the Plaintiff in an Academic Discrimination Case Mean Anything?" e-mail message to author, May 2005.

78. For a more detailed discussion, see, e.g., Brooks, *Rethinking the American Race Problem*, 55–57.

79. See, e.g., *Saylor v. Lindsley*, 456 F.2d 896 (2d Cir. 1972).

80. See section C2, infra.

81. Brooks, *Rethinking the American Race Problem*, 167.

82. West, *Race Matters*, 12.

83. Feagin, *Racist America*, 258–60.

84. See ibid., 258–60, 265–66; Joe R. Feagin, "Documenting the Costs of Slavery, Segregation, and Contemporary Racism: Are Reparations in Order for African Americans?" *Harvard Black Letter Law Journal* 20 (Spring 2004): 49, 73–81.

85. Loury, *The Anatomy of Racial Inequality*, 126.

86. Staples, "A Short History of Class Antagonism in the Black Community," 9.

87. See Michael Eric Dyson, *Is Bill Cosby Right? Or Has the Black Middle Class Lost Its Mind?* (New York: Basic Civitas Books, 2005).

88. Loury, *The Anatomy of Racial Inequality*, 124.

89. See Liu, "Methods to Achieve Non-discrimination and Comparable Racial Equality," 297.

90. See William Julius Wilson, *The Truly Disadvantaged: The Inner City, the Underclass, and Public Policy* (Chicago: University of Chicago Press, 1987).

91. West, *Race Matters*, 23, 28, 41.

92. Ibid., 19–20.

93. Ibid., 5–7, 27.

94. Ibid., 48. See also ibid., 4, 25–27.

95. Ibid., 68.

96. Ibid., 58.

97. Ibid., 93.

98. See section B2, supra.

99. See Feagin, *Racist America*, 240.

100. See discussion of Thomas Sowell and Shelby Steele in chapter 2, section B.

101. West, *Race Matters*, 30–31.

102. Ibid., 30–31, 38–42.

103. See Brooks, *Rethinking the American Race Problem*, 128, 133, 141, 143–44.

104. Ibid., 132.

105. "State, ACLU Settlement Affords Little Funding for Shoddy Schools," *San Diego Union-Tribune*, August 11, 2004, A5.

106. Brooks, *Rethinking the American Race Problem*, 14.

107. Ibid., 143–44.

108. See Feagin, *Racist America*, 240.

109. Ibid., 267–72. See West, *Race Matters*, 70.

110. Brooks, *Rethinking the American Race Problem*, 131–49.

111. *Hazelwood School District v. United States*, 433 U.S. 299, 307 (1977) (citing *International Brotherhood of Teamsters v. United States*, 431 U.S. 324, 340 note 20 (1977)).

112. Ibid.

113. For a more detailed discussion of the effectiveness of class-based affirmative action, see Brooks, Carrasco, and Selmi, *Civil Rights Litigation*, 1316–18.

114. See Michael Eric Dyson, *Holler If You Hear Me: Searching for Tupac Shakur* (New York: Basic Civitas Books, 2001), 144. Rap artist Tupac Shakur, who died a violent death at the age of twenty-five in September 1996, coined the expression "thug life" in an attempt to rescue the hip-hop term "nigga," or "nigger," "by redefining it" to stand for an "underdog" who is "never ignorant [and] get[s] goals accomplished." Ibid. Yet the absurdity of this misadventure is irrefutably demonstrated by the fact that "historically astute and racially sensitive whites have rarely attempted to use the term, even with black friends. When these whites stepped out of bounds, black friends or colleagues readily set them straight." Ibid., 145. If the revisionism were successful, blacks rappers would feel pride rather than pain when their savvy white friends used their invention. The hip-hop generation is not the first generation of blacks to use the derogatory "N" word as a form of civil rights protest. Black comedian Dick Gregory, for example, used the term in this manner in the 1960s. See Dick Gregory, *Nigger: An Autobiography* (New

York: Dutton, 1964). See generally Randall Kennedy, *Nigger: The Strange Career of a Troublesome Word* (New York: Pantheon Books, 2002).

115. Dyson, *Holler If You Hear Me*, 153, quoting the rap artist Tupac Shakur.

116. Brooks, Carrasco, and Selmi, *Civil Rights Litigation*, 684.

117. Erin Aubry Kaplan, "These People," *Los Angeles Times Magazine*, July 24, 2005, 30–31.

118. Michael Eric Dyson, *The Michael Eric Dyson Reader* (New York: Basic Civitas Books, 2004), 439.

119. For a discussion of this heritage, see, e.g., Roy L. Brooks, "Re-packaging Noblesse Oblige," *American Visions* 2 (June 1987): 12.

## 4. LIMITED SEPARATION

1. Henry Louis Gates Jr., *Colored People: A Memoir* (New York: Knopf, 1994).

2. See, e.g., *Brown v. Board of Education*, 347 U.S. 483 (1954); *Bolling v. Sharpe*, 347 U.S. 497 (1954); *Cooper v. Aaron*, 358 U.S. 1 (1958); *Green County School Board of New Kent County, Virginia*, 391 U.S. 430 (1968).

3. Gates, *Colored People*, 213.

4. Ibid., 8.

5. Ibid., 64–65. See also ibid., 167, 184, 186, 211.

6. Elisabeth Bumiller, *Condoleezza Rice: An American Life* (New York: Random House, 2007), 44–45.

7. Steven Barboza, ed., *The African American Book of Values* (New York: Doubleday, 1998).

8. On Garvey, see, e.g., Robert A. Hill, ed., *The Marcus Garvey and Universal Negro Improvement Association Papers* (Berkeley: University of California Press, 1983); Tony Martin, *Marcus Garvey, Hero: A First Biography* (Dover, Mass.: Majority Press, 1983). On the Nation of Islam, see, e.g., Eugene V. Wolfenstein, *The Victims of Democracy: Malcolm X and the Black Revolution* (Berkeley: University of California Press, 1981); Elijah Muhammad, "Separation of the So-Called Negroes from Their Slavemasters' Children Is a Must," in *Black Nationalism in America*, ed. John H. Bracey Jr., August Meier, and Elliott Rudwick (New York: Bobbs-Merrill, 1970); C. Eric Lincoln, *The Black Muslims in America* (Boston: Beacon Press, 1961). On Native Americans, see, e.g., Roy L. Brooks, ed., *When Sorry Isn't Enough: The Controversy over Apologies and Reparations for Human Injustice* (New York: New York University Press, 1999) (sources cited therein). On the Amish, see, e.g., Charles George, *Amish* (Farmington Hills, Mich.: Kid-Haven Press, 2006); Carol M. Highsmith and Ted Landphair, *The Amish* (New York: Crescent Books, 1999).

9. *Parents Involved in Community Schools v. Seattle School District No. 1*, 127 S. Ct. 2738, 2768 (2007) (Thomas, J., concurring).

10. Roy L. Brooks, *Integration or Separation? A Strategy for Racial Equality* (Cambridge, Mass.: Harvard University Press, 1996), 189.

11. Ibid., 258.

12. Ibid.

13. See, e.g., ibid., 247–57; Albert L. Samuels, *Is Separate Unequal? Black Colleges and the Challenge to Desegregation* (Lawrence: University Press of Kansas, 2004); Lloyd Gite,

"The New Agenda of the Black Church: Economic Development for Black America," *Black Enterprise*, December 1993, 56; Maureen M. Smith, "Church Combines Activism, Spiritual Guidance," *Minnesota Daily*, April 15, 1991, 1.

14. Interview with Rev. James H. Cone on National Public Radio, March 31, 2005, http://www.npr.org/templates/story/story.php?storyId=89236116. See, e.g., James H. Cone, *Black Theology and Black Power* (Maryknoll, N.Y.: Orbis Books, 1997); Rev., James H. Cone and Gayraud S. Wilmore, eds., *Black Theology: A Documentary History*, 2nd ed. (Maryknoll, N.Y.: Orbis Books, 1993).

15. Tommie Shelby distinguishes between what he terms "strong black nationalism" and "weak black nationalism." Both terms are defined politically and are discussed in section D, infra. See Brooks, *Integration or Separation?* pt. 2 (discussing total separation) and pt. 3 (discussing limited separation). See also Harold Cruse, *The Crisis of the Negro Intellectual* (New York: Morrow, 1967); Theodore Draper, *The Rediscovery of Black Nationalism* (New York: Viking Press, 1969); Michael Wilson, "A Legacy of Freedom Is Teetering with Age," *New York Times*, July 3, 2005, sec. 1, p. 12; Tommie Shelby, *We Who Are Dark: The Philosophical Foundations of Black Solidarity* (Cambridge, Mass.: Harvard University Press, 2005).

16. Brooks, *Integration or Separation?* 205.

17. See, e.g., Barbara Ehrenreich, "A Soldier in the Army of the Lord," *New York Times Book Review*, April 17, 2005, 17 (commenting on how textbooks have portrayed John Brown over the years); James M. McPherson, "Days of Wrath," *New York Review of Books*, May 12, 2005, 14.

18. David S. Reynolds, *John Brown, Abolitionist* (New York: Knopf, 2005).

19. McPherson, "Days of Wrath," 14.

20. See, e.g., Ehrenreich, "A Soldier in the Army of the Lord," 17.

21. *Grutter v. Bollinger*, 539 U.S. 306, 345 (2003) (Ginsburg, J., concurring) (citing Erica Frankenberg et al., *A Multiracial Society with Segregated Schools: Are We Losing the Dream?* 4, 11, http://www.civilrightsproject.harvard.edu/research/reseg03/AreWeLosingtheDream.pdf (available in clerk of court's case file).

22. Sheryll Cashin, *The Failures of Integration* (New York: Public Affairs, 2004).

23. Ibid., 10.

24. Ibid.

25. Ibid., 102, 103, 110–13.

26. Roy L. Brooks, *Rethinking the American Race Problem* (Berkeley: University of California Press, 1990), 40.

27. See chapter 3, section A.

28. Ellis Cose, *The Rage of a Privileged Class: Why Are Middle-Class Blacks Angry? Why Should America Care?* (New York: HarperCollins, 1993).

29. Joe R. Feagin and Melvin Sikes, *Living with Racism: The Black Middle-Class Experience* (Boston: Beacon Press, 1994).

30. Ibid., 135.

31. Constance Johnson, "The Sad Ways Kids Look at Integration," *U.S. News & World Report*, May 23, 1994, 33.

32. Derrick Bell, *Silent Covenants: Brown v. Board of Education and the Unfulfilled Hopes for Racial Reform* (New York: Oxford University Press, 2004), 161.

33. Brooks, *Integration or Separation?* 110 (sources cited therein).

34. Ibid., 112 (sources cited therein).

35. Ibid., 110–11.

36. Ibid., 114.

37. Ibid., 190.

38. Samuels, *Is Separate Unequal?*

39. See, e.g., *Adarand Constructors, Inc. v. Peña*, 515 U.S. 200 (1995); *City of Richmond v. Croson*, 488 U.S. 469 (1989). The Equal Protection Clause grants all persons within the jurisdiction of any state the equal protection of the laws. See U.S. Const., amend. XIV, clause 1.

40. Brooks, *Integration or Separation?*207. See ibid., 206–13 (discussing Supreme Court cases that arguably support the nonsubordination principle).

41. See section A, supra.

42. The histories of Greenwood and Durham are told in a handful of excellent books, most notably, Alfred Brophy, *Reconstructing the Dreamland: The Tulsa Riot of 1921* (New York: Oxford University Press, 2002); Brooks, *Integration or Separation?* 270–73; John Sibley Butler, *Entrepreneurship and Self-Help among Black Americans* (Albany: State University of New York Press, 1991); Scott Ellsworth, *Death in a Promised Land: The Tulsa Race Riot of 1921* (Baton Rouge: Louisiana State University Press, 1982); Jimmie Lewis Franklin, *The Blacks in Oklahoma* (Norman: University of Oklahoma Press, 1980); R. Halliburton Jr., *The Tulsa Race War of 1921* (San Francisco: R and E Research Associates, 1975). See also *Alexander v. Governor of Oklahoma*, 2004 U.S. Dist. LEXIS 5131 (March 19, 2004), aff'd 382 F.3d 1206 (10th Cir. 2004), rehearing denied 391 F.3d 1155 (10th Cir. 2004), cert. denied, 125 S.Ct. 2257 (2005). For the story of Durham, see William Kenneth Boyd, *The Story of Durham, City of the New South* (Durham, N.C.: Duke University Press, 1925); Christina Greene, *Our Separate Ways: Women and the Black Freedom Movement in Durham, North Carolina* (Chapel Hill: University of North Carolina Press, 2005); Jim Wise, *Durham: A Bull City Story* (Charleston, S.C.: Arcadia, 2002).

43. Timothy Bates, *Banking on Black Enterprise: The Potential of Emerging Firms for Revitalizing Urban Economics* (Washington, D.C.: Joint Center for Political and Economic Studies, 1993), xix.

44. *Grutter v. Bollinger*, 345–46 (citing Erica Frankenberg et al., *A Multiracial Society with Segregated Schools: Are We Losing the Dream?* 4, 11).

45. See Bell, *Silent Covenants*, 165–70.

46. Brooks, *Integration or Separation?* 222.

47. Ibid., 227.

48. Ibid., 229. See also ibid., 222–27.

49. See Marva Collins and Civia Tamarkin, *Marva Collins' Way* (Los Angeles: Tarcher, 1982), 54; Marva Collins Preparatory School, "Frequently Asked Questions," http://www.marvacollinspreparatory.com/faq.html.

50. Professor Carlton Waterhouse takes this position in his dissertation. See Carlton Waterhouse, "The Full Price of Freedom: African Americans' Shared Responsibility to Repair the Harms of Slavery and Segregation" (Ph.D. diss., Emory University, 2006). See also "Detroit School Board Push for Black Curriculum," *Jet*, March 18, 1991, 38.

51. African American Academy "Mission & Vision," http://www.seattleschools.org/schools/aaa/mission.htm.

52. African American Academy "Mission & Vision," http://www.seattleschools.org/schools/aaa/nguzosaba.htm.

53. *Parents Involved in Community Schools v. Seattle School District No. 1*, 127 S. Ct. 2738, 2777–78 (2007) (Thomas, J., concurring)..

54. Cornel West, *Race Matters* (Boston: Beacon Press, 1993), 12–13.

55. Brooks, *Integration or Separation?* 205.

56. As was noted in chapter 2, section C1, Shelby Steele similarly writes, "If conditions have worsened for most of us as racism has receded, then much of the problem must be of our own making."

57. Bell, *Silent Covenants*, 187 (quoting Dr. Gail Foster, a leading black educator).

58. Brooks, *Integration or Separation?* 205.

59. Ibid., 105.

60. John Edgar Wideman, *Fatheralong: A Meditation on Fathers and Sons, Race and Society* (New York: Pantheon Books, 1994), xxiv.

61. Gates, *Colored People*, 73, 85, 102, 186, 199.

62. Brooks, *Integration or Separation?* 199.

63. Wendy Brown-Scott, "Race Consciousness in Higher Education: Does 'Sound Educational Policy' Support the Continued Existence of Historically Black Colleges?" *Emory Law Journal* 43 (1994): 1, 48.

64. Lloyd Gite, "The New Agenda of the Black Church: Economic Development for Black America," *Black Enterprise*, December, 1993, 54 (citing Emmett D. Carson, *A Hand Up: Black Philanthropy and Self-Help in America* [Washington, D.C.: Joint Center for Political and Economic Studies Press, 1993]).

65. Ibid., 56

66. See ibid., 54–59; Bates, *Banking on Black Enterprise*, 6; Smith, "Church Combines Activism, Spiritual Guidance," 1.

67. Kenneth B. Clark, "Separate Is Still Unequal," *Nation*, July 7, 1979, 7.

68. On the funding problems HBCUs face, see Gil Kujovich, "Public Black Colleges: The Long History of Unequal Instruction," *Journal of Blacks in Higher Education* 3 (Spring 1994): 65. For excellent discussions of HBCUs, see, e.g., Samuels, *Is Separate Unequal?*; Frank Adams Jr., "Why *Brown v. Board of Education* and Affirmative Action Can Save Historically Black Colleges and Universities," *Alabama Law Review* 47 (1996): 481; Wendy Brown-Scott, "Race Consciousness in Higher Education," *Emory Law Journal* 43 (1994): 1; Alex M. Johnson Jr., "Bid Whist, Tank, and *United States v. Fordice*: Why Integrationism Fails African-Americans Again," *California Law Review* 81 (1993): 1401; Gil Kujovich, "Equal Opportunity in Higher Education and the Black Public Colleges: The Era of Separate but Equal," *Minnesota Law Review* 72 (1987): 29.

69. Carnegie Commission on Higher Education, *From Isolation to Mainstream: Problems of the Colleges Founded for Negroes: A Report and Recommendations by the Carnegie Commission on Higher Education* (New York: McGraw-Hill, 1971), 11.

70. Brooks, *Integration or Separation?* 280–81.

71. Ibid., 281.

72. See ibid., 200.

73. See ibid., 201.

74. Ibid.

75. See, e.g., *UAW v. Johnson Controls, Inc.*, 499 U.S. 187 (1991); Suzanne V. Samuels, "The Fetal Protection Debate Revisited: The Impact of *U.A.W. v. Johnson Controls* on Federal and State Courts," *Women's Rights Law Reporter* 17 (1996): 209.

76. See Brooks, *Integration or Separation?* 201.

77. Ibid., 203.

78. See Erin Aubry Kaplan, "These People," *Los Angeles Times Magazine*, July 24, 2005, 14.

79. For a detailed discussion, see Samuels, *Is Separate Unequal?*

80. "Congress shall make no law respecting an establishment of religion...." U.S. Const. amend. I.

81. Some estimate that about "25%" of blacks fall into this category. See Kaplan, "These People," 14.

82. See chapter 3, section C2.

83. See chapter 2, section B2.

84. CBSNews.com (accessed May 15, 2006).

85. Ibid.

86. Ibid.

87. Ibid.

88. Eric Anderson and Alfred A. Moss Jr., *Dangerous Donations: Northern Philanthropy and Southern Black Education, 1902–1930* (Columbia: University of Missouri Press, 1999), ix, x, 45.

89. Perhaps I should note here that limited separatists would probably not prescribe reparations, which is a reformist external prescriptive measure; see chapter 3, section B2. Many reparations programs seek disgorgement of unjust white enrichment. These programs are too preoccupied with white Americans to suit the taste of limited separatists. Indeed, one of the criticisms limited separatists have lodged against critical race theorists, to which we shall turn next, is that they are too obsessed with obtaining white approval. Garnering white approval is one of the sins limited separatists associate with the integrationist impulse in black America. Limited separatists would simply permit whites to retain their unjust gains from slavery and Jim Crow. The focus of limited separatists is on black self-determination and nothing else. Interestingly, one scholar has argued that limited separation should be viewed as a form of reparations—a shared responsibility on the part of African Americans themselves to repair the harms wrought by slavery and Jim Crow. See Carlton Waterhouse, "The Full Price of Freedom: African Americans' Shared Responsibility to Repair the Harms of Slavery and Segregation" (Ph.D. diss., Emory University, 2006). For a general discussion of reparations, see Roy L. Brooks, *Atonement and Forgiveness: A New Model for Black Reparations* (Berkeley: University of California Press, 2004).

90. Shelby states, "It is imperative that more-affluent blacks extend special concern to the least advantaged." Shelby, *We Who Are Dark*, 246.

91. Ibid., 9–10.

92. Ibid., 105. See section A, supra.

93. See Shelby, *We Who Are Dark*, 28–27. See also section A, supra.

94. Shelby, *We Who Are Dark*, 10–11.

95. Ibid., 10.

96. Ibid., 11.

97. Ibid., 3.

98. Ibid., 136–37.

99. Ibid., 113.

100. Ibid., 3–4, 9–13, 113, 136–38.

101. Ibid., 28.

102. Ibid., 137.

103. Ibid.

104. Ibid., 136. Thus, Shelby "urges a joint commitment to defeating racism, to eliminating unjust racial inequalities, and to improving the material life prospects of those racialized as 'black,' especially the most disadvantaged." Ibid., 4

105. Ibid., 137.

106. Ibid., 137–38.

107. Ibid., 138.

108. Ibid., 113.

109. Ibid., 137.

110. Ibid., 141.

111. Ibid., 246.

112. Ibid., 11. Shelby defines black identity as a "shared racial identity and culture of African Americans." Ibid., 1.

113. See section C2, supra; chapter 3, section C2.

114. See, e.g., Brooks, *Integration or Separation?* 244–57.

115. See chapter 2, section C1.

116. For further discussion, see David Berreby, *Us and Them: Understanding Your Tribal Mind* (New York: Little, Brown, 2005).

117. See Cashin, *The Failures of Integration*, 138–41, 147, 153–60.

118. See Mary Patillo McCoy, *Black Picket Fences* (Chicago: University of Chicago Press, 1999).

119. Brooks, *Integration or Separation?* 190.

120. For example, in 2007, the Cherokee Nation voted to revoke the tribal citizenship of an estimated 2,800 descendants of freed blacks who the Cherokees once owned as slaves. "Nation Update: Cherokees Vote to Eject Black Members," *San Diego Union-Tribune*, March 4, 2007, A5.

## 5. CRITICAL RACE THEORY

1. Among the hundreds of pieces of scholarship written on some aspect of critical race theory or the broader category of critical theory, see, e.g., in addition to sources cited in this chapter, Francisco Valdes, Jerome McCristal Culp, and Angela P. Harris, eds., *Crossroads, Directions and a New Critical Race Theory* (Philadelphia: Temple University Press, 2002); Richard Delgado and Jean Stefancic, *Critical Race Theory: An Introduction* (New York: New York University Press, 2001); David Kairys, ed., *The Politics of Law: A Progressive Critique*, 3rd ed. (New York: Basic Books, 1998); Frances E. Olsen, ed., *Feminist Legal Theory II: Positioning Feminist Theory within the Law*, vol. 2 (New York: New York University Press, 1995); Richard Delgado and Jean Stefancic, eds., *Critical Race Theory: The Cutting Edge*, 2nd ed. (Philadelphia: Temple University Press, 2000); Mary E. Williams, ed., *Homosexuality: Opposing Viewpoints* (San Diego: Greenhaven Press, 1999); William N. Eskridge Jr., *Gaylaw: Challenging the Apartheid of the Closet* (Cambridge, Mass.: Harvard University Press, 1999); Richard Delgado and Jean Stefancic, eds., *Critical White Studies: Looking behind the Mirror* (Philadelphia: Temple University Press, 1997); Richard Delgado and Jean Stefancic, eds., *The Latino/a Condition: A Critical Reader* (New York: New York University Press, 1998);

Adrien Katherine Wing, ed., *Critical Race Feminism: A Reader* (New York: New York University Press, 1997); Kimberlé Williams Crenshaw, Neil Gotanda, Garry Peller, and Kendall Thomas, eds., *Critical Race Theory: The Key Writings That Formed the Movement* (New York: New Press, 1995); Mari J. Matsuda, Charles R. Lawrence III, Richard Delgado, and Kimberlé Williams Crenshaw, eds., *Words That Wound: Critical Race Theory, Assaultive Speech, and the First Amendment: New Perspectives on Law, Culture and Society* (Boulder, Colo.: West View Press, 1993); Symposium—"The Future of Intersectionality and Critical Race Feminism," *Journal of Contemporary Legal Issues* 11 (2001): 667–936.

2. Jerome M. Culp Jr., Angela P. Harris, and Francisco Valdes, "Subject Unrest," *Stanford Law Review* 55 (2003): 2435, 2448. For further discussion of the distinction between discrimination and subordination, see section B1, infra.

3. See generally sources cited in note 1, supra.

4. See Derrick A. Bell Jr., *And We Are Not Saved: The Elusive Quest for Racial Justice* (New York: Basic Books, 1987), 156. See also Derrick A. Bell Jr., *Faces from the Bottom of the Well: The Permanence of Racism* (New York: Basic Books, 1992); Kimberlé Crenshaw, "Race, Reform and Retrenchment: Transformation and Legitimation in Antidiscrimination Law," *Harvard Law Review* 101 (1988): 1331.

5. John Hayakawa Torok, "Freedom Now!—Race Consciousness and the Work of De-colonization Today," *Howard Law Journal* 48 (2004): 351, 357 (sources cited therein). I first called attention to the lack of prescription in critical race theory in a law review article I coauthored long ago. See Roy L. Brooks and Mary Jo Newborn, "Critical Race Theory and Classical-Liberal Civil Rights Scholarship: A Distinction without a Difference?" *California Law Review* 82 (1994): 787.

6. See Roy L. Brooks, *Critical Procedure* (Durham, N.C.: Carolina Academic Press, 1998), 5–6. See generally Stephanie M. Wildman, *Privilege Revealed-How Invisible Preference Undermines America* (New York: New York University Press, 1996).

7. Delgado and Stefancic, *Critical Race Theory: An Introduction*, 145. Compare this definition with the Supreme Court's less-than-favorable-treatment definition of discrimination discussed in chapter 3, section B1.

8. See chapter 3, section B1.

9. See ibid.

10. Delgado and Stefancic, *Critical Race Theory: An Introduction*, 156.

11. See Richard Delgado and Daniel A. Farber, Krinock Lecture Series: "Is American Law Inherently Racist?" *Thomas M. Cooley Law Review* 15 (1998): 361, 385.

12. Ibid.

13. See, e.g., John Shelton Reed, "A Flag's Many Meanings," *Wall Street Journal*, January 20, 2000, A22; Glenn C. Loury, "Some Truths about the Confederate Flag," *San Diego Union Tribune*, January 18, 2000, B7.

14. Loury, "Some Truths about the Confederate Flag," B7.

15. Stokely Carmichael and Charles Hamilton, *Black Power: The Politics of Liberation in America* (New York: Random House,1967), 3–4. Stokely Carmichael became known later as Kwame Ture.

16. Delgado and Farber, "Is American Law Inherently Racist?" 384.

17. Ibid.

18. See Roy L. Brooks, *Structures of Judicial Decision Making from Legal Formalism to Critical Theory*, 2nd ed. (Durham, N.C.: Carolina Academic Press, 2005), 239–40.

19. Richard Delgado, "When a Story Is Just a Story: Does Voice Really Matter?" *Virginia Law Review* 76 (1990): 95, 106.

20. See the appendix for details on this differential.

21. Derrick A. Bell Jr., "Racial Realism," *Connecticut Law Review* 24 (1992): 363, 373. See Bell, *Faces from the Bottom of the Well.*

22. See, e.g., Robert W. Gordon, "New Developments in Legal Theory," in *The Politics of Law: A Progressive Critique,* ed. David Kairys (New York: Pantheon Books, 1982), 281; Robert W. Gordon, "Unfreezing Legal Reality: Critical Approaches to Law," *Florida State University Law Review* 15 (1987): 195.

23. See Douglas Litowitz, "Gramsci, Hegemony, and the Law," *Brigham Young University Law Review* 2000 (2000): 534, 534. See also Michel Foucault, *Madness and Civilization: A History of Insanity in the Age of Reason,* trans. Richard Howard (New York: Vintage Books, 1973); Jean François Lyotard, *Postmodern Condition: A Report on Knowledge,* trans. Geoff Bennington and Brian Massumi (Minneapolis: University of Minnesota Press, 1984); Alan Hunt, "The Big Fear: Law Confronts Postmodernism," *McGill Law Journal* 35 (1990): 507, 523.

24. See discussion of Antonio Gramsci in section C, infra.

25. Litowitz, "Gramsci, Hegemony, and the Law," 533–34.

26. Ibid., 536.

27. See Kimberlé W. Crenshaw, "Demarginalizing the Intersection of Race and Sex: A Black Feminist Critique of Antidiscrimination Doctrine, Feminist Theory, and Antiracist Politics," *University of Chicago Legal Forum* 1989 (1989): 139; Paulette M. Caldwell, "A Hair Piece: Perspectives on the Intersection of Race and Gender," *Duke Law Journal* 1991 (1991): 365.

28. Roy L. Brooks, *Critical Procedure* (Durham, N.C.: Carolina Academic Press, 1998), 29 (citing Patricia Williams, *Alchemy of Race and Rights* [Cambridge: Harvard University Press, 1991]).

29. See Angela P. Harris, "Race and Essentialism in Feminist Legal Theory," *Stanford Law Review* 42 (1990): 581.

30. Richard Delgado, "Crossroads and Blind Alleys: A Critical Examination of Recent Writing about Race," *Texas Law Review* 82 (2003): 121, 124.

31. Richard Delgado, "Two Ways to Think about Race: Reflections on the Id, the Ego, and Other Reformist Theories of Equal Protection," *Georgetown Law Journal* 89 (2001): 2279, 2282 (sources cited therein).

32. Delgado, "Crossroads and Blind Alleys," 121, 123. For a response to Delgado's charge, see Kevin Johnson, "Roll Over Beethoven: 'A Critical Examination of Recent Writing about Race,'" *Texas Law Review* 82 (2004): 717.

33. Andrew Hacker, "Andrew Hacker on George Fredrickson's *Racism,*" *Journal of Blacks in Higher Education* 38 (Winter 2002/2003): 100.

34. Charles McGrath, "Mapping the Unconscious," *New York Times Book Review,* March 6, 2005, 1.

35. Charles Lawrence, "The Id, the Ego, and Equal Protection: Reckoning with Unconscious Racism," *Stanford Law Review* 39 (1987): 317, 323.

36. See Michael Pickering, *Stereotyping: The Politics of Representation* (New York: Palgrave, 2001), 5; Ediberto Roman, "What Exactly Is Living La Vida Loca? The Legal and Political Consequences of Latino-Latina Ethnic and Racial Stereotypes in Film and Other Media," *Gender, Race and Justice* 4 (2000): 37, 41.

37. Delgado, "Crossroads and Blind Alleys," 121, 134–135.

38. Delgado and Stefancic, *Critical Race Theory: An Introduction*, 108–9, 111–13.

39. Again, racism "is much more than having an unfavorable impression of members of other groups." Ibid., 17 (referring to realists).

40. Derrick Bell writes: "[Racial realism] requires us to acknowledge the permanence of our subordinate status. That acknowledgment enables us to avoid despair and frees us to imagine and implement racial strategies that can bring fulfillment and even triumph." Derrick A. Bell Jr. "Racial Realism," in *Critical Race Theory: The Key Writings That Formed the Movement*, ed. Kimberlé Crenshaw, Neil Gotanda, Garry Peller, and Kendall Thomas (New York: New Press, 1995), 306.

41. Derrick A. Bell Jr., *Race, Racism, and American Law*, 2nd ed. (Boston: Little, Brown, 1980), 39. See also Derrick A. Bell Jr., "*Brown v. Board of Education* and the Interest-Convergence Dilemma," *Harvard Law Review* 93 (1980): 518.

42. Malcolm X, "The Ballot or the Bullet" (April 3, 1964), in *Malcolm X Speaks: Selected Speeches and Statements*, ed. George Breitman (New York: Grove Weidenfeld, 1990), 23, 40.

43. Derrick A. Bell, *Race, Racism, and American Law*, 4th ed. (New York: Aspen Law and Business, 2000), 28.

44. Ibid., 29 (emphasis in original). See *Abraham Lincoln: Speeches and Writings 1859–1865: Speeches, Letters, and Miscellaneous Writings, Presidential Messages and Proclamations*, ed. Don E. Fehrenbacher (New York: Literary Classics of the United States, 1989), 358.

45. James M. McPherson, *For Cause and Comrades: Why Men Fought in the Civil War* (New York: Oxford University Press, 1997), 128–29.

46. See Philip A. Klinkner and Roger M. Smith, *The Unsteady March: The Rise and Decline of Racial Equality in America* (Chicago: University of Chicago Press, 1999), 3–4.

47. Brooks, *Critical Procedure*, 4–5 (discussing the "realist" scholarship of Robin Barnes, Robin West, and Derrick Bell).

48. Delgado and Stefancic, *Critical Race Theory: An Introduction*, 17.

49. For another important aspect of this story, see the discussion of Gramsci in section D, infra.

50. For a collection of original works written by Karl Marx (1818–93) and Friedrich Engels (1820–95), see the Marxists Internet Archive, <http://www.marxists.org/archive/marx/txindex.htm> (accessed March 2005).

51. "Hegel thought that the life of reason proceeded by a continuing sequence of ideas, in which the opposition between two positions might eventually be resolved by moving the debate to a new level. First, someone develops a systematic theory—which Hegel's predecessor, Fichte, called a 'thesis.' Then it is challenged, Fichte said, by those who support the antithesis; finally, a new view develops that takes what is best of each to produce a new synthesis. Hegel's suggestion is that the new idea can be said to 'transcend' the old debate, moving it to a higher level." Kwame Anthony Appiah, *Thinking It Through: An Introduction to Contemporary Philosophy* (New York: Oxford University Press, 2003), 378.

52. Litowitz, "Gramsci, Hegemony, and the Law," 528 (Marxists had "espoused a deterministic causality from the base [relations of production] to the superstructure [law, morality, and ideology])."

53. See *The Communist Manifesto: New Interpretations*, ed. Mark Cowling (New York:

New York University Press, 1998) (includes, in full, *The Manifesto of the Communist Party*, written by Karl Marx and Frederick Engels, trans. Terrell Carver, first published in 1848).

54. My excellent research assistant, Timothy S. Carey, USD Law class of 2005, believes there is evidence that Marx expressed the answer (hegemony) himself in his earlier "humanistic" essays. Mr. Carey thus asserts that "Marx had, arguably, two phases of socialist theory and it is his 'scientific' phase that most directly lends itself to the deterministic reading." Only a fool would disagree with a research assistant of Mr. Carey's caliber.

55. Litowitz, "Gramsci, Hegemony, and the Law," 519.

56. See section D, infra.

57. Bell, *And We Are Not Saved*, 156 (quoting Manning Marable).

58. Derrick Bell, *Silent Covenants:* Brown v. Board of Education *and the Unfulfilled Hopes for Racial Reform* (New York: Oxford University Press, 2004), 9. See also p. 200.

59. See Delgado and Stefancic, *Critical Race Theory: The Cutting Edge*, 2nd ed., xiii–xvii.

60. See further discussion of the idealists in section C, infra.

61. Delgado, "Crossroads and Blind Alleys," 123.

62. See Kimberlé Crenshaw, "Race, Reform, and Retrenchment: Transformation and Legitimation in Anti-discrimination Law," in *Critical Race Theory: The Key Writings That Formed the Movement*, 119.

63. Delgado and Stefancic, *Critical Race Theory: An Introduction*, 92.

64. See, e.g., Daniel Farber and Suzanna Sherry, *Beyond All Reason: The Radical Assault on Truth in American Law* (New York: Oxford University Press, 1997).

65. See, e.g., Delgado and Stefancic, *Critical Race Theory: An Introduction*, 103–7; Charles R. Lawrence III and Mari J. Matsuda, *We Won't Go Back: Making the Case for Affirmative Action* (Boston: Houghton Mifflin, 1997).

66. See, e.g., Delgado and Stefancic, *Critical Race Theory: An Introduction*, 113–14.

67. See, e.g., ibid.; Bell, *And We Are Not Saved*; Bell, *Faces from the Bottom of the Well*; Crenshaw, "Race, Reform, and Retrenchment." See also Richard Delgado, "Alternative Dispute Resolution Conflict as Pathology: An Essay for Trina Grillo," *Minnesota Law Review* 81 (1997): 1391.

68. See, e.g., Johnson, "Roll Over Beethoven," 726; Girardeau Spann, "Pure Politics," in Delgado and Stefancic, *Critical Race Theory: The Cutting Edge*, 2nd ed., 124; Julie Su and Eric Yamamoto, "Critical Coalitions: Theory and Praxis," in *Crossroads, Directions and a New Critical Race Theory*, ed. Francisco Valdes, Jerome McCristal Culp, and Angela P. Harris (Philadelphia: Temple University Press, 2002), 379, 385–87, 390.

69. Delgado and Jean Stefancic, *Critical Race Theory: An Introduction*, 111.

70. See Derrick Bell, *Ethical Ambition: Living a Life of Meaning and Worth* (London: Bloomsbury, 2002), cited with approval in Delgado, "Crossroads and Blind Alleys," 146–50

71. Marianne LaFrance, "The Schemas and Schemes in Sex Discrimination," *Brooklyn Law Review* 65 (1999): 1063, 1071.

72. A rebuttable presumption in favor of racism or racial discrimination is established based on the theory that, in the absence of discrimination, resources should be more proportionally distributed because blacks have the same desires and abilities as whites. See chapter 3, section B1.

73. The critical feminist theory notion of "equality as acceptance" "asserts that eliminating the unequal consequences of sex differences is more important than debating whether such differences are 'real,' or even trying to eliminate them altogether." Roy L. Brooks, *Critical Procedure* (Durham, N.C.: Carolina Academic Press, 1998), 19 (quoting Christine Littleton). The focus here is "on disparate impact—the bottom line." Ibid., 20.

74. See Bell, *Faces from the Bottom of the Well.*

75. For a collection of the many scholars who have questioned the soundness of the "outsider" concept, see, e.g., Devon W. Carbado, "Critical Race Studies: Race to the Bottom," *UCLA Law Review* 49 (2002): 1283, 1284 n. 1.

76. See Devon W. Carbado, "Black Rights, Gay Rights, Civil Rights," *UCLA Law Review* 47 (2000): 1467; Darren Lenard Hutchinson, "Ignoring the Sexualization of Race," *Buffalo Law Review* 47 (1999): 1.

77. Harvard Law Association, "Exclusionary Zoning and Equal Protection," *Harvard Law Review* 84 (1971): 1645, 1660.

78. See figure 46. For a more detailed discussion, see, e.g., Sumayyah Waheed, "Limiting Ourselves: A Response to Elbert Lin's 'Identifying,'" *Asian Law Journal* 12 (2005): 187.

79. See figures 55, 57, and 59 in the appendix. Thus, some have argued that Asians should not be entitled to affirmative action in college admissions. See Paul Brest and Miranda Oshige, "Affirmative Action for Whom?" *Stanford Law Review* 47 (1995): 890, 896–97. This suggestion has been criticized; see Marty B. Lorenzo, "Race-Conscious Diversity Admissions Programs: Furthering a Compelling Interest," *Michigan Journal of Race and Law* 2 (1997): 361, 413–14. As Robert Chang asserts, "There is no 'essential' Asian ethnic identity." Adrien Katherine Wing, Book Survey—USA 2050: "Identity, Critical Race Theory, and the Asian Century," *Michigan Law Review* 99 (2001): 1390, 1395 (citing Robert S. Chang, *Disoriented: Asian Americans, Law and the Nation-State* [New York: New York University Press, 1999], 5.) Some Asian scholars view "Asian as a Panethnic identity," whereas others "define[] it to include people from China, Japan, Korea, the Philippines, India, Vietnam, Laos, and Cambodia." Ibid. (sources cited therein). Adrian Wing, an African American, "would add Pakistan and Bangladesh, as well as Thailand." Ibid.

80. Carbado, "Critical Race Studies," 1290.

81. See ibid., 1284–1306, for a more detailed discussion.

82. As discussed in the introduction, the Supreme Court in *United States v. Carolene Products Co.*, 304 U.S. 144, 152 n. 4 (1938), declared that although legislative enactments carry a presumption of constitutionality, "a correspondingly more searching judicial inquiry" is to be applied in such cases requiring the protection of "discrete and insular minorities" or the trashing of the Bill of Rights. The Court, thereby, introduced the concepts of "protected classes" and levels of judicial scrutiny. For further discussion, see chapter 1, section A, supra; Abner S. Greene, "Is There a First Amendment Defense for Bush v. Gore?" *Notre Dame Law Review* 80 (2005): 1643, 1679; L. A. Powe Jr., "Does Footnote 4 Describe?" *Constitutional Commentary*, January 1, 1994, 11; Donald A. Dripps, "Criminal Procedure, Footnote Four, and the Theory of Public Choice; or, Why Don't Legislatures Give a Damn about the Rights of the Accused?" *Syracuse Law Review* 44 (1993): 1079, 1081. See generally John Hart Ely, *Democracy and Distrust: A Theory of Judicial Review* (Cambridge, Mass.: Harvard University Press, 1980).

83. Brooks, *Critical Procedure*, 28 (quoting Christina Hoff Sommers, *Who Stole Feminism: How Women Have Betrayed Women* [New York: Simon and Schuster, 1994], 74).

84. Ibid. (quoting Sommers, *Who Stole Feminism*, 75). Of course, the knowledge critical race theorists claim outsiders have is experiential. Who knows the outsider experience better than outsiders?

85. See, e.g., the media's portrayal of blacks in the aftermath of Hurricane Katrina discussed in chapter 3, section B1.

86. See figures 82–87 in the appendix.

87. See, e.g., Gwyn Williams, "Gramsci's Concept of 'Egomania,'" *Journal of History of Ideas* 21 (1960): 586, 587; Litowitz, "Gramsci, Hegemony, and the Law," 519.

88. Litowitz, "Gramsci, Hegemony, and the Law," 519.

89. See chapter 4, section D.

90. Homosexuals, for example, lack equal legal status, or formal equal opportunity, under federal law in a number of areas—such as employment and housing—and to that extent are behind blacks in the development of their civil rights. See chapter 1, section A.

EPILOGUE. TOWARD THE "BEST" POST–CIVIL RIGHTS THEORY

1. Tommie Shelby, *We Who Are Dark: The Philosophical Foundations of Black Solidarity* (Cambridge, Mass.: Harvard University Press, 2005), 250.

2. See chapter 4, section D, and chapter 5, section D.

3. Roy L. Brooks, *Integration or Separation? A Strategy for Racial Equality* (Cambridge, Mass.: Harvard University Press, 1996), 104.

4. George M. Frederickson, "The Lincoln-Douglas Debates: The Young Nation Confronts the Issue of Race," *Journal of Blacks in Higher Education* 59 (Spring 2008): 54.

5. Ruben Navarrette Jr., "Race: The Elephant in the Room," *San Diego Union-Tribune*, August 6, 2008, B5.

6. Ibid.

7. Ibid.

8. http://cosmos.bcst.yahoo.com/up/player/popup/index.php?cl=9823541 (accessed September 22, 2008).

9. Glenn C. Loury, *The Anatomy of Racial Inequality* (Cambridge, Mass.: Harvard University Press, 2002), 144.

10. See chapter 3, section D.

11. All quotations are taken from Andres Oppenheimer, "What Finland Could Teach the World," *San Diego Union-Tribune*, September, 5, 2008, B6.

12. Ibid.

13. http://www.kipp.org (accessed December 20, 2008). See generally Christopher Gabriele and Warren Goldstein, *Time to Learn: How a New School Schedule Is Making Smarter Kids, Happier Parents, and Safer Neighborhoods* (San Francisco: Jossey-Bass, 2008).

14. Malcolm Gladwell, *Outliers: The Story of Success* (New York: Little Brown, 2008), 258 (emphasis in original).

15. Ibid., 261.

16. Ibid., 267. See also ibid., 265–66.

17. Mos Def, "The Rape Over," in *The New Danger* (Geffen, 2004).

18. Joy James, "'F**k tha Police [State]': Rap, Welfare, and the Leviathan," in *Hip Hop and Philosophy: Rhyme 2 Reason,* Popular Culture and Philosophy, vol. 16, ed. Derrick Darby and Tommie Shelby (Illinois: Carus, 2005), 71.

19. For a more detailed discussion, see, e.g., Armond White, *Rebel for the Hell of It* (New York: Thunder's Mouth Press, 2002); Michael Eric Dyson, *Holler If You Hear Me: Searching for Tupac Shakur* (New York: Basic Civitas Books, 2001).

20. See, e.g., Title VI of the Civil Rights Act of 1964, 42 U.S.C. §§ 2000d to 2000d-7. See *Alexander v. Sandoval,* 532 U.S. 275 (2001).

21. See, e.g., Roy L. Brooks and Sharon Cheever, "The Federal Loan Guarantee Program: A Unified Approach," *Journal of Corporation Law* 10 (1984): 185.

22. See ibid., 200.

23. http://www.accion.org/NETCOMMUNITY/Page.aspx?pid=501&srcid=253 (accessed September 10, 2008).

24. Ibid.

25. Much of the following discussion about the GI Bill is taken from various sources, including Ira Katznelson, *When Affirmative Action Was White: An Untold History of Racial Inequality in America* (New York: Norton, 2005); Michael J. Bennett, *When Dreams Came True: The GI Bill and the Making of Modern America* (Washington, D.C.: Brassey's, 1996); Congressional Budget Office, *Veterans' Educational Benefits: Issues Concerning the GI Bill* (Washington, D.C.: U.S. Government Printing Office, 1978); *The Problem of Re-employing Servicemen: How to Handle It, an Explanation of the Selective Service Act and GI Bill of Rights* (New York: Prentice-Hall, 1945).

26. The current GI Bill provides $1,101 a month for thirty-six months of school, which covers only about 73% of the tuition cost at public universities.

27. See sources cited in note 25, supra.

28. For a more detailed discussion, see the introduction.

# BIBLIOGRAPHY

Adams, Frank, Jr. "Why *Brown v. Board of Education* and Affirmative Action Can Save Historically Black Colleges and Universities." *Alabama Law Review* 47 (1996): 481.

Alba, Richard, and Victor Nee. *Remaking the American Mainstream: Assimilation and Contemporary Immigration.* Cambridge, Mass.: Harvard University Press, 2003.

Anderson, Eric, and Alfred A. Moss Jr. *Dangerous Donations: Northern Philanthropy and Southern Black Education, 1902–1930.* Columbia: University of Missouri Press, 1999.

Anderson, Jerry L. "Law School Enters the Matrix: Teaching Critical Legal Studies." *Journal of Legal Education* 54 (June 2004): 201.

Appiah, Kwame Anthony. *Cosmopolitanism: Ethics in a World of Strangers.* New York: Norton, 2006.

———. *The Ethics of Identity.* Princeton, N.J.: Princeton University Press, 2005.

———. *Thinking It Through: An Introduction to Contemporary Philosophy.* New York: Oxford University Press, 2003.

Applebone, Peter. "Equal Entry Standards May Hurt Black Students in Mississippi." *San Diego Union-Tribune,* April 24, 1996, A10.

Ards, Angela. "In the Twinkling of an Eye." *Black Issues Book Review,* June/July 2005.

Baldwin, James. "Many Thousands Gone." In *Notes of a Native Son.* Boston: Beacon Press, 1984. Quoted in Watson Branch, "Reparations for Slavery: A Dream Deferred," *San Diego International Law Journal* 3 (2002): 182.

Banks, Taunya Lovell. "Two Life Stories: Reflections of One Black Woman Law Professor." In *Critical Race Theory: The Key Writings That Formed the Movement,* edited by Kimberlé Williams Crenshaw, Neil Gotanda, Gerry Peller, and Kendall Thomas, 329–36. New York: New Press, 1995.

Barone, Michael. *New Americans: How the Melting Pot Can Work Again.* Washington, D.C.: Regnery, 2001.

Barrett, Paul M. *The Good Black: A True Story of Race in America.* New York: Dutton, 1999.

Bates, Timothy. *Banking on Black Enterprise: The Potential of Emerging Firms for Revitalizing Urban Economies.* Washington, D.C.: Joint Center for Political and Economic Studies, 1993.

Baynes, Leonard M. "Racial Justice in the New Millennium; From Brown to Grutter: Methods to Achieve Non-discrimination and Comparable Racial Equality." *Notre Dame Law Review* 80 (November 2004): 243.

Bell, Derrick A., Jr. *And We Are Not Saved: The Elusive Quest for Racial Justice.* New York: Basic Books, 1987.

———. "Brown v. Board of Education and the Interest-Convergence Dilemma." *Harvard Law Review* 93 (1980): 518.

———. "Brown v. Board of Education and the Interest-Convergence Dilemma." In *Critical Race Theory: The Key Writings That Formed the Movement,* edited by Kimberlé Williams Crenshaw, Neil Gotanda, Garry Peller, and Kendall Thomas, 23. New York: New Press, 1995.

———. "Brown v. Board of Education: Forty-five Years after the Fact." *Ohio Northern University Law Review* 26 (2000): 171.

———. *Faces from the Bottom of the Well: The Permanence of Racism.* New York: Basic Books, 1992.

———. "On Grutter and Gratz: Examining 'Diversity' in Education." *Columbia Law Review* 103 (2003): 1622.

———. *Race, Racism, and American Law.* Boston: Little, Brown, 1973.

———. *Race, Racism, and American Law.* 2nd ed. Boston: Little, Brown, 1980.

———. *Race, Racism, and American Law.* 2nd ed., 1984 supplement. Boston: Little, Brown, 1984.

———. *Race, Racism, and American Law.* 3rd ed. Boston: Little Brown, 1992.

———. *Race, Racism, and American Law.* 4th ed. New York: Aspen Law and Business, 2000.

———. *Race, Racism, and American Law.* 5th ed. New York: Aspen, 2004.

———. "Racial Realism." *Connecticut Law Review* 24 (1992): 363.

———. "Racial Realism." In *Critical Race Theory: The Key Writings That Formed the Movement,* edited by Kimberlé Crenshaw, Neil Gotanda, Garry Peller, and Kendall Thomas, 306. New York: New Press, 1995.

———. *Silent Covenants:* Brown v. Board of Education *and the Unfulfilled Hopes for Racial Reform.* New York: Oxford University Press, 2004.

———. *Teacher's Manual—Race, Racism, and American Law.* 5th ed. New York: Aspen, 2004.

———. "Who's Afraid of Critical Race Theory?" *University of Illinois Law Review* 1995 (1995): 893.

Bender, Thomas, ed. *The Antislavery Debate: Capitalism and Abolitionism as a Problem in Historical Interpretation.* Berkeley: University of California Press, 1992.

Benedict, Ruth. *Patterns of Culture.* Boston: Houghton Mifflin, 1989.

Benhabib, Seyla. *The Claims of Culture: Equality and Diversity in the Global Arena.* Princeton, N.J.: Princeton University Press, 2002.

Bennett, William J. *Our Children and Our Country: Improving America's Schools and Affirming the Common Culture.* New York: Simon and Schuster, 1988.

Bickel, Alexander. *The Morality of Consent.* New Haven: Yale University Press, 1975.

Blassingame, John W. *The Slave Community.* New York: Oxford University Press, 1979.

Blumrosen, Alfred W., and Ruth G. Blumrosen. *Slave Nation: How Slavery United the Colonies and Sparked the American Revolution.* Naperville: Sourcebooks, 2005.

Bork, Robert. *Slouching toward Gomorrah: Modern Liberalism and American Decline.* New York: Regan Books, 1996.

Boyd, William Kenneth. *The Story of Durham, City of the New South.* Durham, N.C.: Duke University Press, 1925.

Branch, Watson. "Reparations for Slavery: A Dream Deferred." *San Diego International Law Journal* 3 (2002): 177.

Breitman, George, ed. *Malcolm X Speaks: Selected Speeches and Statements.* New York: Grove Weidenfeld, 1990.

Brezina, Timothy, and Kenisha Winder. "Economic Disadvantage, Status Generalization, and Negative Racial Stereotyping by White Americans." *Social Psychology Quarterly* 66 (2003): 402.

Brooks, Roy L. *Atonement and Forgiveness: A New Model for Black Reparations*. Berkeley: University of California Press, 2004.

———. *Critical Procedure*. Durham, N.C.: Carolina Academic Press, 1998.

———. *Integration or Separation? A Strategy for Racial Equality*. Cambridge, Mass.: Harvard University Press, 1996.

———. "Race as an Under-inclusive and Over-inclusive Concept." *African-American Law and Policy Report* 1 (Fall 1994): 9.

———. *Rethinking the American Race Problem*. Berkeley: University of California Press, 1990.

———. "Use of the Civil Rights Acts of 1866 and 1871 to Redress Employment Discrimination." *Cornell Law Review* 62 (1977): 258.

———. *When Sorry Isn't Enough: The Controversy over Apologies and Reparations for Human Injustice*. New York: New York University Press, 1999.

Brooks, Roy L., Gilbert Paul Carrasco, and Michael Selmi. *Civil Rights Litigation: Cases and Perspectives*. 3rd ed. Durham, N.C.: Carolina Academic Press, 2005.

Brooks, Roy L., and Sharon Cheever. "The Federal Loan Guarantee Program: A Unified Approach." *Journal of Corporation Law* 10 (1984): 185.

Brooks, Roy L., and Mary Jo Newborn. "Critical Race Theory and Classical-Liberal Civil Rights Scholarship: A Distinction without a Difference?" *California Law Review* 82 (1994): 787.

Brophy, Alfred. *Reconstructing the Dreamland: The Tulsa Riot of 1921*. New York: Oxford University Press, 2002.

Brown, Dorothy A. *Critical Race Theory: Cases, Materials and Problems*. St. Paul, Minn.: Thomson/West, 2003.

Brown-Scott, Wendy. "Race Consciousness in Higher Education: Does 'Sound Educational Policy' Support the Continued Existence of Historically Black Colleges?" *Emory Law Journal* 43 (1994): 1.

Browne, J. Zamgba. "Black Bikers Bring Suit." *New York Amsterdam News*, May 29, 2003, 3.

Brubaker, Rogers. *Ethnicity without Groups*. Cambridge, Mass.: Harvard University Press, 2004.

Bumiller, Elisabeth. *Condoleezza Rice: An American Life*. New York: Random House, 2007.

Butler, John Sibley. *Entrepreneurship and Self-Help among Black Americans*. Albany: State University of New York Press, 1991.

Caldwell, Christopher. "Daughter of the Enlightenment." *New York Times Magazine*, April 3, 2005, 26–31.

Caldwell, Paulette M. "A Hair Piece: Perspectives on the Intersection of Race and Gender." *Duke Law Journal* 1991 (1991): 365.

Caplan, Arthur, James J. McCartney, and Dominic Sisti, eds. *The Case of Terri Schiavo: Ethics at the End of Life*. Amherst, N.Y.: Prometheus Books, 2006.

Carbado, Devon W. "Critical Race Studies: Race to the Bottom." *UCLA Law Review* 49 (2002): 1283.

Carbado, Devon W., and Mitu Gulati. "What Exactly Is Racial Diversity?" *California Law Review* 91 (2003): 1149.

Carmichael, Stokely, and Charles Hamilton. *Black Power: The Politics of Liberation in America*. New York: Random House, 1967.

Carnegie Commission on Higher Education. *From Isolation to Mainstream: Problems of the Colleges Founded for Negroes: A Report and Recommendations by the Carnegie Commission on Higher Education.* New York: McGraw-Hill, 1971.

Carter, Robert. "The Warren Court and Desegregation." *Michigan Law Review* 67 (1968): 237.

Cashin, Sheryll. *The Failures of Integration.* New York: Public Affairs, 2004.

Chafe, William H., Raymond Gavins, and Robert Korstad, eds. *Remembering Jim Crow: African Americans Tell about Life in the Segregated South.* New York: New Press, 2001.

Collins, Marva, and Civia Tamarkin. *Marva Collins' Way.* Los Angeles: Tarcher, 1982.

Cone, James H. *Black Theology and Black Power.* Maryknoll, N.Y.: Orbis Books, 1997.

——— Interview with Rev. James H. Cone on National Public Radio, March 31, 2005. http://www.npr.org/templates/story/story.php?storyId=89236116.

Cone, James H., and Gayraud S. Wilmore, eds. *Black Theology: A Documentary History.* 2nd ed., rev. Maryknoll, N.Y.: Orbis Books, 1993.

Conley, Dalton. "The Cost of Slavery." *New York Times,* February 15, 2003.

Connerly, Ward. "Why I'm Still Fighting Preferences in Florida." *Wall Street Journal,* November 18, 1999, A26.

Cose, Ellis. "The Hidden Rage of Successful Blacks." *Newsweek,* November 15, 1993, 52.

——— *The Rage of a Privileged Class: Why Are Middle-Class Blacks Angry? Why Should America Care?* New York: HarperCollins, 1993.

Cowling, Mark, ed. *The Communist Manifesto: New Interpretations.* New York: New York University Press, 1998.

Crenshaw, Kimberlé. "Demarginalizing the Intersection of Race and Sex: A Black Feminist Critique of Antidiscrimination Doctrine, Feminist Theory, and Antiracist Politics." *University of Chicago Legal Forum* 1989 (1989): 139.

———. "Race, Reform, and Retrenchment: Transformation and Legitimation in Antidiscrimination Law." *Harvard Law Review* 101 (1988): 1331.

———. "Race, Reform, and Retrenchment: Transformation and Legitimation in Antidiscrimination Law." In *Critical Race Theory: The Key Writings That Formed the Movement,* edited by Kimberlé Crenshaw, Neil Gotanda, Garry Peller, and Kendall Thomas, 103–26. New York: New Press, 1995.

Crenshaw, Kimberlé, Neil Gotanda, Garry Peller, and Kendall Thomas, eds. *Critical Race Theory: The Key Writings That Formed the Movement.* New York: New Press, 1995.

Cruse, Harold. *The Crisis of the Negro Intellectual.* New York: Morrow, 1967.

Culp, Jerome M., Jr., Angela P. Harris, and Francisco Valdes. "Subject Unrest." *Stanford Law Review* 55 (2003): 2435.

Delgado, Richard. "Alternative Dispute Resolution Conflict as Pathology: An Essay for Trina Grillo." *Minnesota Law Review* 81 (1997): 1391.

———. "Crossroads and Blind Alleys: A Critical Examination of Recent Writing about Race." *Texas Law Review* 82 (2003): 121.

———. "Derrick Bell's Toolkit: Fit to Dismantle That Famous House?" *New York University Law Review* 75 (May 2000): 283.

———. "Locating Latinos in the Field of Civil Rights: Assessing the Neoliberal Case for Racial Exclusion." *Texas Law Review* 83 (2004): 489.

———. "Review Essay: Recasting the American Race Problem." *California Law Review* 79 (1991) 1389.

———. "Rodrigo and Revisionism: Relearning the Lessons of History." *Northwestern University Law Review* 99 (Winter 2005): 805.

———. "When a Story Is Just a Story: Does Voice Really Matter?" *Virginia Law Review* 76 (1990): 95.

Delgado, Richard, and Daniel A. Farber. Krinock Lecture Series: "Is American Law Inherently Racist?" *Thomas M. Cooley Law Review* 15 (1998): 361.

Delgado, Richard, and Jean Stefancic. *Critical Race Theory: An Introduction*. New York: New York University Press, 2001.

———, eds. *Critical Race Theory: The Cutting Edge*. 2nd ed.. Philadelphia: Temple University Press, 2000.

———, eds. *Critical White Studies: Looking behind the Mirror*. Philadelphia: Temple University Press, 1997.

"Departments: Race Relations on Campus." *Journal of Blacks in Higher Education* 47 (Spring 2005): 106.

"Detroit School Board Push for Black Curriculum." *Jet*, March 18, 1991.

Dorn, Edwin. "Truman and the Desegregation of the Military." *Focus*, May 1998, 3.

Dowd, Gregory Evans. "Declarations of Dependence: War and Inequality in Revolutionary New Jersey, 1776–1815." *New Jersey History* 103 (1985): 47.

Draper, Theodore. *The Rediscovery of Black Nationalism*. New York: Viking Press, 1969.

D'Souza, Dinesh. *What's So Great about America*. Washington, D.C.: Regnery, 2002.

DuBois, W.E.B. *Black Reconstruction: An Essay toward a History of the Part Which Black Folk Played in the Attempt to Reconstruct Democracy in America, 1860–1880*. Cleveland: Meridian, 1935.

Dudziak, Mary L. *Cold War Civil Rights: Race and the Image of American Democracy*. Princeton, N.J.: Princeton University Press, 2000.

———. "Desegregation as a Cold War Imperative." *Stanford Law Review* 41 (1988): 61.

Dyson, Michael Eric. *Holler If You Hear Me: Searching for Tupac Shakur*. New York: Basic Civitas Books, 2001.

———. *Is Bill Cosby Right? Or Has the Black Middle Class Lost Its Mind?* New York: Basic Civitas Books, 2005.

Ehrenreich, Barbara. "A Soldier in the Army of the Lord." *New York Times Book Review*, April 17, 2005, 17.

Ellsworth, Scott. *Death in a Promised Land: The Tulsa Race Riot of 1921*. Baton Rouge: Louisiana State University Press, 1982.

Epstein, Richard. "On Property Discrimination and the Limits of State Action." Interviewed by Steve Chapman. http://reason.com/9504/epstein.apr.shtml (accessed June 22, 2005).

Feagin, Joe R. ———. "The Continuing Significance of Race: Antiblack Discrimination in Public Places." *American Sociological Review* 56 (1991): 101.

———. "Documenting the Costs of Slavery, Segregation, and Contemporary Racism: Are Reparations in Order for African Americans?" *Harvard Black Letter Law Journal* 20 (Spring 2004): 49, 73–81.

———. "Heeding Black Voices: The Court, *Brown*, and Challenges in Building a Multiracial Democracy." *University of Pittsburgh Law Review* 66 (Fall 2004): 57.

————. *Racist America: Roots, Current Realities, and Future Reparations.* New York: Routledge, 2000.

————. "White Supremacy and Mexican Americans: Rethinking the Black-White Paradigm." *Rutgers Law Review* 54 (Summer 2002): 959.

Feagin, Joe, and Eileen O'Brien. *White Men on Race: Power, Privilege, and the Shaping of Cultural Consciousness.* Boston: Beacon Press, 2003.

Feagin, Joe R., and Melvin Sikes. *Living with Racism: The Black Middle-Class Experience.* Boston: Beacon Press, 1994.

Feagin, Joe R., and Hernan Vera. *White Racism.* New York: Routledge, 1995.

Federal Bureau of Investigation, U.S. Department of Justice. "Hate Crime Statistics (2003)." http://www.fbi.gov/ucr/03hc.pdf (accessed July 2005).

Fehrenbacher, Don E., ed. *Abraham Lincoln: Speeches and Writings 1859–1865: Speeches, Letters, and Miscellaneous Writings, Presidential Messages and Proclamations.* New York: Literary Classics of the United States, 1989.

————. *The Dred Scott Case: Its Significance in American Law and Politics.* New York: Oxford University Press, 1978.

————. *The Slaveholding Republic: An Account of the United States Government's Relations to Slavery.* Edited by Ward M. McAfee. New York: Oxford University Press, 2001.

Finkelman, Paul. *Slavery and the Founders: Race and Liberty in the Age of Jefferson.* Armonk, N.Y.: M. E. Sharpe, 1996.

Flagg, Barbara. Interview. *Washington University School of Law Magazine,* Spring 2005, 14.

"Florida Black Colleges Receive Settlement from Hotel Bias Case." *Black Issues in Higher Education,* April 11, 2002, 15.

Foner, Eric. *Reconstruction: America's Unfinished Revolution 1863–1877.* New York: Harper and Row, 1988.

"For Financing Higher Education, the Racial Wealth Gap Remains Huge." *Journal of Blacks in Higher Education, Weekly Bulletin,* March 1, 2007.

Ford, Richard T. *Racial Culture: A Critique.* Princeton, N.J.: Princeton University Press, 2005.

Foucault, Michel. *Madness and Civilization: A History of Insanity in the Age of Reason.* Translated by Richard Howard. New York: Vintage Books, 1973.

Franklin, Jimmie Lewis. *The Blacks in Oklahoma.* Norman: University of Oklahoma Press, 1980.

Franklin, John H., and Alfred A. Moss Jr. *From Slavery to Freedom: A History of African Americans.* 6th ed. New York: Knopf, 1998.

Frazier, Thomas, R., ed. *Afro-American History: Primary Sources.* New York: Harcourt Brace and World, 1970.

Freeman, Alan. "Legitimizing Racial Discrimination through Antidiscrimination Laws: A Critical Review of Supreme Court Doctrine." *Minnesota Law Review* 62 (1978): 209.

————. Review of "Race and Class: The Dilemma of Liberal Reform." *Yale Law Journal* 90 (1980): 1880.

Friedman, Leon, ed. *Southern Justice.* New York: Pantheon Books, 1965.

Friedman, Thomas L. "Democracy's Root: Diversity." *New York Times,* November 11, 2007, sec. 4, p. 12.

Fukuyama, Francis. *America at the Crossroads: Democracy, Power, and the Neoconservative Legacy.* New Haven, Conn.: Yale University Press, 2006.

———. *The End of History and the Last Man.* With a new afterword. New York: Free Press, 2006.

Gabrieli, Christopher, and Warren Goldstein., *Time to Learn: How a New School Schedule Is Making Smarter Kids, Happier Parents, and Safer Neighborhoods.* San Francisco: Jossey-Bass, 2008.

Gates, Henry Louis, Jr. *Colored People: A Memoir.* New York: Knopf, 1994.

Gates, Henry Louis, Jr., and Nellie Y. McKay, gen. eds. *The Norton Anthology: African American Literature.* New York: Norton, 1996.

Geertz, Clifford. *The Interpretation of Cultures.* New York: Basic Books, 1973.

George, Charles. *Amish.* Farmington Hills, Mich.: KidHaven Press, 2006.

Gibbs, David, and Bob DeMoss. *Fighting for Dear Life: Inside the Terri Schiavo Story and What It Means for All of Us.* Minneapolis, Minn.: Bethany House, 2006.

Gibson, Truman K., Robert S. Huntley, and Steve Huntley. *Knocking Down Barriers: Fighting for Black America.* Chicago: Northwestern University Press, 2005.

Gite, Lloyd. "The New Agenda of the Black Church: Economic Development for Black America." *Black Enterprise,* December 1993, 54.

Gladwell, Malcolm. *Outliers: The Story of Success.* New York: Little, Brown, 2008.

Glaser, Gabriella. "Study Questions Blacks' Treatment in Emergency Room." *San Diego Union-Tribune,* December 28, 1999, A10.

Gooding-Williams, Robert, ed. *Reading Rodney King/Reading Urban Uprising.* New York: Routledge, 1993.

Greene, Christina. *Our Separate Ways: Women and the Black Freedom Movement in Durham, North Carolina.* Chapel Hill: University of North Carolina Press, 2005.

Gregory, Dick. *Nigger: An Autobiography.* New York: Dutton, 1964.

"The Gun Windmills." *Wall Street Journal,* December 13, 1999, A34.

Gutmann, Amy. *Identity and Democracy.* Princeton, N.J.: Princeton University Press, 2003.

Hacker, Andrew. "Andrew Hacker on George Fredrickson's *Racism.*" *Journal of Blacks in Higher Education* 38 (Winter 2002/2003): 100.

Halliburton, R., Jr. *The Tulsa Race War of 1921.* San Francisco: R and E Research Associates, 1975.

Harris, Angela P. "Race and Essentialism in Feminist Legal Theory." *Stanford Law Review* 42 (1990): 581.

Harris, Cheryl. "Whiteness as Property." *Harvard Law Review* 106 (1993): 1707.

*Harvard Encyclopedia of American Ethnic Groups.* Cambridge, Mass.: Belknap Press of Harvard University, 1980.

Headden, Susan. "Cover Story: How They Do It Better." *U.S. News & World Report,* March 26, 2007, 38.

Hecker, Sean. "Race and Pretextual Traffic Stops: An Expanded Role for Civilian Review Board." *Columbia Human Rights Law Review* 28 (1997): 551.

Hein, Jeremy. "Interpersonal Discrimination against Hmong Americans: Parallels and Variation in Microlevel Racial Inequality." *Sociological Quarterly* 41 (Summer 2000): 413.

Herbert, James. "1 after 1: In Pop Culture, Who or What Is No. 1 Changes in a Flash." *San Diego Union-Tribune,* October, 9, 2006, D1.

Higginbotham, A. Leon, Jr. *In the Matter of Color: The Colonial Period*. New York: Oxford University Press, 1978.

Highsmith, Carol M.. and Ted Landphair. *The Amish*. New York: Crescent Books, 1999.

"Holding a Four-Year College Degree Brings Blacks Close to Economic Parity with Whites." *Journal of Blacks in Higher Education* 47 (Spring 2005): 6.

Hollinger, David A. *Postethnic America: Beyond Multiculturalism*. 10th anniversary edition. New York: Basic Books, 2005.

Hope, Richard O. *Racial Strife in the U.S. Military: Toward the Elimination of Discrimination*. New York: Praeger, 1979.

Horowitz, David. *Hating Whitey*. Dallas, Tex.: Spence, 1999.

Howard-Filler, Saralee R. "Two Different Battles." *Michigan History* 71 (January/February 1987): 30.

Hughes, Michael, and Melvin E. Thomas. "The Continuing Significance of Race Revisited: A Study of Race, Class, and Quality of Life in America, 1972 to 1996." *American Sociological Review* 63 (1998): 785.

Hunt, Alan. "The Big Fear: Law Confronts Postmodernism." *McGill Law Journal* 35 (1990): 507.

Hunt, Kasie. "Ex-House Speaker Newt Gingrich Mocks Requirement That Ballots Be Printed in Multiple Languages." Associated Press, March 31, 2007.

"Images." *Time*, December 28, 1987, 59.

International Helsinki Federation for Human Rights. "Intolerance and Discrimination against Muslims in the EU. Developments since September 11." March 2005. http://www.ihf-hr.org.

Jefferson, Thomas. "Notes on the State of Virginia (1781–82)." In *Writings/Thomas Jefferson*, 18–34. New York: Literary Classics of the U.S., 1984.

Jehn, Karen A., Gregory B. Northcraft, and Margaret A. Neale. "Why Differences Make a Difference: A Field Study of Diversity, Conflict, and Performance in Workgroups." *Administrative Science Quarterly*, December 1, 1999, 741.

Jensen, Merrill. *The Articles of Confederation: An Interpretation of the Social-Constitutional History of the American Revolution*. Madison: University of Wisconsin Press, 1948.

———. *The New Nation: A History of the United States during the Confederation 1781–1789*. New York: Knopf, 1950.

Joffe, Josef. "The Perils of Soft Power: Why America's Cultural Influence Makes Enemies Too." *New York Times Magazine*, May 14, 2006, 15.

Johnson, Alex M., Jr. "Bid Whist, Tank, and United States v. Fordice: Why Integrationism Fails African-Americans Again." *California Law Review* 81 (1993): 1401.

Johnson, Constance. "The Sad Ways Kids Look at Integration." *U.S. News & World Report*, May 23, 1994, 33.

Johnson, Kevin. "Roll Over Beethoven: 'A Critical Examination of Recent Writing about Race.'" *Texas Law Review* 82 (2004): 717.

Kairys, David, ed. *The Politics of Law: A Progressive Critique*. 3rd ed. New York: Pantheon Books, 1998.

Karlan, Pamela S. "John Hart Ely and the Problem of Gerrymandering: The Lion in Winter." *Yale Law Journal* 114 (2005): 1329.

Keeva, Steven. "Not Quite Equal: Minority Partners." *ABA Journal*, February 1993, 50.

Kennedy, Randall. *Nigger: The Strange Career of a Troublesome Word*. New York: Pantheon Books, 2002.

——. *Race, Crime, and the Law.* New York: Pantheon Books, 1997.

Klarman, Michael J. *From Jim Crow to Civil Rights: The Supreme Court and the Struggle for Racial Equality.* New York: Oxford University Press, 2004.

Klinkner, Phillip A., and Roger M. Smith. *The Unsteady March: The Rise and Decline of Racial Equality in America.* Chicago: University of Chicago Press, 1999.

Kristol, Irving. *Neoconservatism: The Autobiography of an Idea.* New York: Free Press, 1995.

Kristol, William. *Neoconservative Imagination: Essays in Honor of Irving Kristol.* Edited by Christopher DeMuth and William Kristol. Washington, D.C.: AEI Press, 1995.

Kryder, Daniel. *Divided Arsenal: Race and the American State during World War II.* Cambridge: Cambridge University Press, 2000.

Kuhn, Thomas S. *The Structure of Scientific Revolutions.* 3rd ed. Chicago: University of Chicago Press, 1996.

Kujovich, Gil. "Equal Opportunity in Higher Education and the Black Public Colleges: The Era of Separate But Equal." *Minnesota Law Review* 72 (1987): 29.

——. "Public Black Colleges: The Long History of Unequal Instruction." *Journal of Blacks in Higher Education,* Spring 1994, 65.

Kunhardt, Philip B., Jr., Philip B. Kunhardt II, and Peter W. Kunhardt. *The American President.* New York: Riverhead Books, 1999.

Kupperman, Joel J. "Relations between the Sexes: Timely and Timeless Principles." *San Diego Law Review* 25 (1988): 1027.

La Ferla, Ruth. "The Changing Face of America." *Upfront,* February 2, 2004, 12.

LaFrance, Marianne. "The Schemas and Schemes in Sex Discrimination." *Brooklyn Law Review* 65 (1999): 1063.

Lamb, Brian, ed. *Booknotes on American Character: People, Politics, and Conflict in American History.* New York: PublicAffairs, 2004.

Lawrence, Charles. "The Id, the Ego, and Equal Protection: Reckoning with Unconscious Racism." *Stanford Law Review* 39 (1987): 317.

Laycock, Douglas. "The Broader Case for Affirmative Action: Desegregation, Academic Excellence, and Future Leadership." *Tulane Law Review* 78 (2004): 1767.

Lemann, Nicholas. *The Promised Land: The Great Black Migration and How It Changed America.* New York: Knopf, 1991.

Levitt, Steven, and Stephen Dubner. *Freakonomics: A Rogue Economist Explores the Hidden Side of Everything.* New York: William Morrow, 2005.

Lie, John. *Modern Peoplehood.* Cambridge, Mass.: Harvard University Press, 2004.

"Limbaugh Returns to Radio after Rehab for Painkillers." *San Diego Union-Tribune,* November 18, 2003, A8.

Litowitz, Douglas. "Gramsci, Hegemony, and the Law." *Brigham Young University Law Review* 2000 (2000): 515.

Liu, Goodwin. "Methods to Achieve Non-discrimination and Comparable Racial Equality: Race, Class, Diversity, Complexity." *Notre Dame Law Review* 80 (November 2004): 289.

López, Ian F. Haney. *White by Law.* New York: New York University Press, 1996.

Lopreato, Joseph. *Italian Americans.* Toronto: Random House, 1970.

Loury, Glenn C. *The Anatomy of Racial Inequality.* Cambridge, Mass.: Harvard University Press, 2002.

——. "Some Truths about the Confederate Flag." *San Diego Union Tribune,* January 18, 2000, B7.

Lueck, Thomas J. "New York's Cabbies Show How Multi-colored Racism Can Be." *New York Times*, November, 7, 1999, sec. 4, p. 5.

Lyotard, Jean François. *Postmodern Condition: A Report on Knowledge*. Translated by Geoff Bennington and Brian Massumi. Minneapolis: University of Minnesota Press, 1984.

Maclin, Tracey. "*Terry v. Ohio*'s Fourth Amendment Legacy: Black Men and Police Discretion." *St. John's Law Review* 72 (1998): 1271.

Magnet, Myron. "What Is Compassionate Conservatism?" *Wall Street Journal*, February 5, 1999, A14.

Malcolm X. "The Ballot or the Bullet" (April 3, 1964). In *Malcolm X Speaks: Selected Speeches and Statements*, edited by George Breitman, 23. New York: Grove Weidenfeld, 1990.

Maltz, Earl. "Slavery, Federalism, and the Structure of the Constitution." *American Journal of Legal History* 36 (1992): 468.

Mangum, Charles S. *The Legal Status of the Negro*. Union, N.J.: Lawbook Exchange, 2000.

Markovitz, Jonathan. *Legacies of Lynching: Racial Violence and Memory*. Minneapolis: University of Minnesota Press, 2004.

Martinez, Elizabeth. "Beyond Black/White: The Racisms of Our Time." *Social Justice* 20 (1993): 22.

Marva Collins Preparatory School. "Frequently Asked Questions. http://www.marva collins preparatory.com/faq.html.

Marxists Internet Archive. http://www.marxists.org/archive/marx/txindex.htm (accessed March 2005).

McCoy, Mary Patillo. *Black Picket Fences*. Chicago: University of Chicago Press, 1999.

McGrath, Charles. "Mapping the Unconscious." *New York Times Book Review*, March 6, 2005, 1.

McGuire, Philip. "Desegregation of the Armed Forces: Black Leadership, Protest and World War II." *Journal of Negro History* 63 (Spring 1983): 147.

McPherson, James M. "Days of Wrath." *New York Review of Books*, May 12, 2005, 13.

———. *For Cause and Comrades: Why Men Fought in the Civil War*. New York: Oxford University Press, 1997.

McWhorter, John. *Losing the Race: Self-Sabotage in Black America*. New York: Free Press, 2000.

———. *Winning the Race: Beyond the Crisis in Black America*. New York: Gotham Books, 2006.

Mershon, Sherie, and Steven L. Schlossman. *Foxholes and Color Lines: Desegregating the U.S. Armed Forces*. Baltimore: Johns Hopkins University Press, 1998.

Michaels, Walter Benn. *The Trouble with Diversity: How We Learned to Love Identity and Ignore Inequality*. New York: Metropolitan Books/Henry Holt, 2006.

Miles, Jack. "Blacks vs. Browns." *Atlantic Monthly*, October 1992, 53.

Mills, Charles W. *Blackness Visible: Essays on Philosophy and Race*. Ithaca, N.Y.: Cornell University Press, 1998.

———. *The Racial Contract*. Ithaca, N.Y.: Cornell University Press, 1997.

Moran, Chris. "Suit to Fight for Bilingual Testing." *San Diego Union-Tribune*, June 1, 2005, B1.

Moskos, Charles C. "Blacks in the Army: Success Story." *Current*, September 1986, 6.

Murray, Charles. *Losing Ground: American Social Policy: 1950–1980*. New York: Basic Books, 1984.

———. *What It Means to Be a Libertarian: A Personal Interpretation*. New York: Broadway Books, 1997.

Myrdal, Gunnar. *An American Dilemma: The Negro Problem and Modern Democracy*. New York: Harper and Brothers, 1944.

National Urban League. "National Urban League's State of Black America 2006." Press release, March 29, 2006.

Navarro, Mireya. "Census Reflects Hispanic Identity That Is Hardly Black and White." *New York Times*, November 9, 2003, sec. 1, p. 1.

Nelson, Rob. "The Word 'Nigga' Is Only for Slaves and Sambos." *Journal of Blacks in Higher Education* 21 (Autumn 1998): 117.

Nussbaum, Martha C. *Cultivating Humanity: A Classical Defense of Reform in Liberal Education*. Cambridge, Mass.: Harvard University Press, 1997.

Oliver, Melvin L., and Thomas Shapiro. *Black Wealth, White Wealth: A New Perspective on Racial Inequality*. 2nd ed. New York: Routledge, 2006.

O'Reilly, Bill. *Culture Warrior*. New York: Broadway Books, 2006.

———. *Who's Looking Out for You?* New York: Broadway Books, 2003.

Packard, Jarrold M. *American Nightmare: The History of Jim Crow*. New York: St. Martin's Press, 2002.

Paglia, Camille. "Ask Camille." In *When Sorry Isn't Enough: The Controversy over Apologies and Reparations for Human Injustice*, edited by Roy L. Brooks, 353–54. New York: New York University Press, 1999.

Patler, Nicolas. *Jim Crow and the Wilson Administration: Protesting Federal Segregation in the Early Twentieth Century*. Boulder: University Press of Colorado, 2004.

Perea, Juan F. "The Black/White Binary Paradigm of Race: The 'Normal Science' of American Racial Thought." *California Law Review* 85 (October 1997): 1213.

Picca, Leslie Houts, and Joe R. Feagin. *Two-Faced Racism: Whites in the Backstage and Frontstage*. New York: Routledge, 2007.

Pickering, Michael. *Stereotyping: The Politics of Representation*. New York: Palgrave, 2001.

Podhoretz, Norman. *My Love Affair with America: The Cautionary Tale of a Cheerful Conservative*. New York: Free Press, 2000.

Rampersad, Arnold. *Ralph Ellison: A Biography*. New York: Knopf, 2007.

Reed, John Shelton. "A Flag's Many Meanings." *Wall Street Journal*, January 20, 2000, A22.

Reich, Charles A. *The Greening of America*. New York: Bantam Books, 1971.

Reynolds, David S. *John Brown, Abolitionist*. New York: Knopf, 2005.

Roberts, Gene, and Hank Klibanoff. *The Race Beat: The Press, the Civil Rights Struggle, and the Awakening of a Nation*. New York: Vintage Books, 2006.

Robinson, Eugene. *Coal to Cream: A Black Man's Journey beyond Color to an Affirmation of Race*. New York: Free Press, 1999.

Rodriguez, Gregory. "A New Way of Joining the Mainstream." *Wall Street Journal*, July 31, 2003, D8.

Roman, Ediberto. "What Exactly Is Living La Vida Loca? The Legal and Political Consequences of Latino-Latina Ethnic and Racial Stereotypes in Film and Other Media." *Gender, Race and Justice* 4 (2000): 37.

Rosales, F. Arturo. ¡Pobre Raza! Violence, Justice, and Mobilization among México Lindo Immigrants, 1900–1936. Austin: University of Texas Press, 1999.

Roszak, Theodore. The Making of a Counter Culture: Reflections on the Technocratic Society and Its Youthful Opposition. Garden City, N.Y.: Anchor Books, 1968.

Rowan, Carl T. "The Hidden Costs of Racial Profiling." San Diego Union-Tribune, June 4, 1999, B13.

Salins, Peter D. Assimilation American Style. New York: Basic Books, 1997.

Salzberger, Ronald P., and Mary C. Turck, eds. Reparations for Slavery: A Reader. Lanham, Md.: Rowman and Littlefield, 2004.

Samuels, Albert L. Is Separate Unequal? Black Colleges and the Challenge to Desegregation. Lawrence: University Press of Kansas, 2004.

Samuels, Suzanne V. "The Fetal Protection Debate Revisited: The Impact of U.A.W. v. Johnson Controls on Federal and State Courts." Women's Rights Law Reporter 17 (1996): 209.

Scarry, Elaine. On Beauty and Being Just. Princeton, N.J.: Princeton University Press, 1999.

Schafer, Daniel. "Freedom Was as Close as the River: The Blacks of Northeast Florida and the Civil War." Escribano 23 (1986): 91–116.

Schlesinger, Arthur M., Jr. "American Multiculturalism." In Booknotes on American Character: People, Politics, and Conflict in American History, edited by Brian Lamb, 186. New York: PublicAffairs, 2004.

———. The Disuniting of America. Rev. ed. New York: Norton, 1998.

Scott, Janny, and David Leonhardt. "Class in America: Shadowy Lines That Still Divide." New York Times, May 15, 2005, sec. 1, p. 16.

Seidman, Michael. "Brown and Miranda." 80 California Law Review (1992): 717.

Selmi, Michael. "Remedying Societal Discrimination through the Spending Power." North Carolina Law Review 80 (2002): 1575.

Shapiro, Thomas M. The Hidden Cost of Being African American: How Wealth Perpetuates Inequality. New York: Oxford University Press, 2004.

———. "The Racial Wealth Gap." www.atsweb.neu.edu/jkenty/j.kenty/The%20Black White%20Wealth%20Gap_Chapter_072803.doc (accessed July 7, 2005).

Shatz, Adam. "About Face." New York Times Magazine, January 20, 2002, 18.

Smith, Maureen M. "Church Combines Activism, Spiritual Guidance." Minnesota Daily, April 15, 1991.

Sniderman, Paul M., and Edward G. Carmines. Reaching beyond Race. Cambridge, Mass.: Harvard University Press, 1997.

Sowell, Thomas. Black Rednecks and White Liberals and Other Cultural and Ethnic Issues. San Francisco: Encounter Books, 2005.

———. Cosmic Justice. New York: Free Press, 1999.

———. "Is Yankee Stadium a 'Level Playing Field'?" Wall Street Journal, October, 27, 1999, A18.

———. Race, Culture, and Equality. Stanford, Calif.: Hoover Institution on War, Revolution and Peace, 1998.

Spann, Girardeau. "Pure Politics." In Critical Race Theory: The Cutting Edge, edited by Richard Delgado and Jean Stefancic, 21–34. 2nd ed. Philadelphia: Temple University Press, 2000.

Staples, Brent. "A Short History of Class Antagonism in the Black Community." New York Times, May, 29, 2005, sec. 4, p. 9.

———. "Why Slave-Era Barriers to Black Literacy Still Matter." *New York Times*, January 1, 2006, sec. 4, p. 7.

"State, ACLU Settlement Affords Little Funding for Shoddy Schools." *San Diego Union-Tribune*, August 11, 2004, A5.

Steele, Shelby. "The Content of His Character." *New Republic*, March 1, 1999, 31.

———. *The Content of Our Character: A New Vision of Race in America*. New York: St. Martin's Press, 1990.

Stokes, David. "Racial Lawsuits Filed against Waffle House." *Atlanta Inquirer*, January 29, 2005, 1.

Su, Julie, and Eric Yamamoto. "Critical Coalitions: Theory and Praxis." In *Crossroads, Directions and a New Critical Race Theory*, edited by Francisco Valdes, Jerome McCristal Culp, and Angela P. Harris, 36–47. Philadelphia: Temple University Press, 2002.

Thernstrom, Stephan. "Diversity and Meritocracy in Legal Education: A Critical Evaluation of Linda F. Wightman's 'The Threat to Diversity in Legal Education.'" *Constitutional Commentary* 15 (1998): 11.

Thernstrom, Stephan, and Abigail Thernstrom. *America in Black and White: One Nation, Indivisible*. New York: Simon and Schuster, 1997.

Thomas, Evan. "Cover Story: Rush Limbaugh's World of Pain." *Newsweek*, October 20, 2003, 45.

Totten, Christopher D. "Constitutional Precommitments to Gender Affirmative Action in the European Union, Germany, Canada and the United States: A Comparative Approach." *Berkeley Journal of International Law* 21 (2003): 27.

U.S. Census Bureau. *Current Population Reports: Income in the United States: 2002*, Series P-60, no. 221. www.census.gov/prod/2003pubs/p60-221.pdf.

——— Historical Poverty Tables—People, table 2. www.census.gov/hhes/www/poverty/histpov/hstpov2.html.

U.S. Department of Justice, Office of Justice Programs, Bureau of Justice Statistics. *Criminal Victimization in the United States, 2002 Statistical Tables*. Table 42: Personal Crimes of Violence, 2002.

Vaca, Nicholas C. *The Presumed Alliance: The Unspoken Conflict between Latinos and Blacks and What It Means for America*. New York: Rayo, 2004.

Valdes, Francisco, Jerome McCristal Culp, and Angela P. Harris, eds. *Crossroads, Directions and a New Critical Race Theory*. Philadelphia: Temple University Press, 2002.

Vélez-Ibáñez, Carlos G. *Border Visions: Mexican Cultures of the Southwest United States*. Tucson: University of Arizona Press, 1996.

Waterhouse, Carlton. "The Full Price of Freedom: African Americans' Shared Responsibility to Repair the Harms of Slavery and Segregation." Ph.D. diss., Emory University, 2006.

West, Cornel. *Race Matters*. Boston: Beacon Press, 1993.

"Whole Lott of Trouble." AbcNews.com, December 11, 2002.

Wideman, John Edgar. *Fatheralong: A Meditation on Fathers and Sons, Race and Society*. New York: Pantheon Books, 1994.

Wildman, Stephanie M. *Privilege Revealed: How Invisible Preference Undermines America*. New York: New York University Press, 1996.

Will, George F. "Why Civil Rights No Longer Are Rights." *San Diego Union-Tribune*, March 10, 2005, B12.

Willhelm, Sidney. Review of "The Supreme Court: A Citadel for White Supremacy." *Michigan Law Review* 79 (1981): 847.

Williams, Gwyn. "Gramsci's Concept of 'Egomania.'" *Journal of History of Ideas* 21 (1960): 586.

Williams, Patricia. *Alchemy of Race and Rights*. Cambridge, Mass.: Harvard University Press, 1991.

Williams, Robert A., Jr. "Documents of Barbarism: The Contemporary Legacy of European Racism and Colonialism in the Narrative Traditions of Federal Indian Law." In *Critical Race Theory: The Cutting Edge*, edited by Richard Delgado, 103. Philadelphia: Temple University Press, 1995.

Williams, Timothy. "N.Y. Cabbies Have a Fare Day." *San Diego Union-Tribune*, November 13, 1999, A2.

Wilson, William Julius. *The Truly Disadvantaged: The Inner City, the Underclass, and Public Policy*. Chicago: University of Chicago Press, 1987.

Wise, Jim. *Durham: A Bull City Story*. Charleston, S.C.: Arcadia, 2002.

Woodward, C. Vann. *The Strange Career of Jim Crow*. 3rd rev. ed. New York: Oxford University Press, 1974.

Yamamoto, Eric. *Interracial Justice: Conflict and Reconciliation in Post–Civil Rights America*. New York: New York University Press, 1999.

Yancey, George. *Who Is White? Latinos, Asian, and the New Black/Nonblack Divide*. Boulder, Colo.: L. Rienner, 2003.

Zellner, William W. *Countercultures: A Sociological Analysis*. New York : St. Martin's Press, 1995.

# INDEX

abolitionism, xix

abortion, 23

ACCION INTERNATIONAL, 120

"activist" policing, 23

ad hoc political nationalism, 83, 84, 86

*Adarand Constructors, Inc. v. Peña,* 184n11, 200n35

Adjusted Compensation Act (1924), 121

"adopt-a-family" programs, 56, 85

affirmative action: antidiscrimination principle, 8; for Asians for education, 208n79; case law, 184n11; class-based, 49–50, 59, 197n113; college enrollment action and, 126; critical race theorists on, xix; effect on education, 18; effect on statistics, 126; Ely on, 13; occupational status and, 126; race-based, 49–50, 59, 114; realists on, 101; reformism on, xvii, 48, 49–50, 57, 59; as reverse discrimination, 13; Sowell on, 30; Steele on, 19, 30; Thomas on, 17–18, 30; traditionalism on, 17–19, 28; West on, 49–50, 59; for whites, 6

African American Academy (Seattle), 72

*The African American Book of Values* (Barboza, ed.), 63

Afro-American, use of term, 9

Age of Obama: nature of race problem in, 10–13; racial landscape in, x–xiii

Airaskorpi, Ossi, 116

*Akeelah and the Bee* (film), 79

Ali, Ayaan Hirsi, 14, 188n1

aliens, civil rights of, 4, 5

Alito, Sam, ix

*An American Dilemma* (Myrdal), xi

Americans with Disabilities Act (ADA), 7

Amish people, 78

angry defiance, 61, 62

anti-objective society, xix

antidiscrimination principle, 8–9

antiessentialism, 106

antiobjectivity of critical race theory, 93

antiracist organizations, coalition of, 56

*Anup Engquist v. Oregon Department of Agriculture,* 184n7

*Ash v. Tyson Foods, Inc.,* 188n55

Ashe, Arthur, 40

Asia, education in, 117

Asians and Pacific Islanders: affirmative action for education, 208n79; business ownership statistics for, 153f; disparate resource statistics for, 12–13, 129f–82f, 184n1, 188n56; education statistics for, 154f–59f; family structure statistics for, 163f–67f; hate crimes statistics for, 176f–78f; home ownership statistical disparity for, 126–27, 152f, 188n56; incarceration rates for, 172f–73f; income statistics for, 129f–36f, 140f–51f; occupational status of, 160f–62f; as "people of color," 106; post–civil rights problem, 109; poverty statistics for, 129f–36f; racial profiling in traffic stops, 175f; unemployment statistics for, 168f–71f; voting statistics for, 179f–82f

asset poverty, 46

authentic blackness, 55

backstage racism, 38, 41–42, 48, 57

*Bakke* case, 126, 184n11

balkanization, 81–82

BALSA, 76, 77

Barboza, Steven, 63

Barrett, Paul, 35, 39–40

*Batson v. Kentucky,* 194n36

Baynes, Leonard, 45–46

Bell, Derrick: on equality, 94; on racial progress, 102; on racial realism, 206n40; on school integration, 68; on white self–interest, 97–98, 99

benign discrimination, 18, 49

BFSQ. *See* bona fide selection qualification

black businesses: black churches for microloans, 75; developing financial capital resources in, 119; financial assistance to, 71, 75; microlending for, xx, 75, 115, 119, 120

black church, 79; Black Liberation Theology, 64–65, 79; as source of financial assistance to black businesses, 75

black communities: black-mainstream communities, 63–64; Brooks on, 114; developing capital resources in black businesses, 119; exodus of middle class to white communities, 75, 77

black experience, x–xiii